Get Up Dress Up Show Up

The Biography of Thera Nicholas Huish

By: Larina Grigg

I

Thera and Larina dedicate this book to:

*All who struggle with finding the strength to continue forward

*All who have experienced the death of a loved one

*Each of Heavenly Father's children

*God, the eternal Father of us all

*Jesus Christ, the Healer of ALL hurts

*Our families for their unwavering love, support, belief and patience throughout this project

It is with humility that we acknowledge those family members whom have journeyed beyond this realm of mortality. This book was written under their heavenly inspiration.

Sincere gratitude is extended to both Thera's family and Larina's family who have supported them through the process of completing this project. Both wish to thank those of Thera's family who have taken the time to add memories and messages found within these pages.

Larina wishes to especially thank her amazing husband, Tom, for his patience and love during the endless hours it took to write this book.

Thank you to Jacob Harmon, President of Harmon Graphic & Web Design for bringing Larina's vision for the cover and angel artwork to life.

Thank you to Betty Richards for all of your work editing.

We wish to thank NASA for their beautiful photography of the earth found on the cover.

Finally, both Thera and Larina want to thank you. Their sincere prayer is that your life will be touched by the messages they share.

About the Author

Larina Grigg is a passionate author. Her talent in writing enables the reader to enter the story of that with which she has written. The composition techniques she uses bring her pages to life with vivid descriptions, as well as emotions. Through her gift, each reader has the opportunity of mentally experiencing what her words share. Married since 1979 to Tom Grigg, her high school sweetheart, Larina is blessed with an ever-growing beautiful family who love and support her.

This book is available for purchase on Amazon. eBook versions are also available on Kindle, iBooks, and Nook. To see all purchasing options, visit http://get-up-dress-up-show-up.webflow.io

I am privileged to share with you the biography of one of the most remarkable women whom I have ever had the privilege of knowing. As her protégé, I have personally witnessed her irrefutable integrity of character. In this book I will share accounts of her life experiences, personally selected by her. Several consist of endured extreme occurrences of tragedy that thankfully few will ever encounter.

- *The loss of a husband from an airplane crash.*

  (Dorian Conrad Toland 7/6/1925 ~3/12/1949)

- *The loss of a son from alcoholism.*

  (Richard Mark Huish - Rick 2/9/1952 ~ 8/3/1989)

- *The loss of a daughter from violent murder.*

  (Trish Huish Willoughby 6/5/1948 ~ 2/23/1991)

- *The loss of her 2nd husband from negligence in a hospital without Monetary recompense.*

  (Sterling Smith Huish 11/27/1924 ~ 6/23/2001)

- *The loss of a six-year-old great-granddaughter from cancer.*

  (Sadie Brynne Huish 1/3/2003 ~ 6/25/2009)

- *The loss of a 2nd son from sleep apnea.*

  (Robin Smith Huish – Bob 4/22/1955 ~ 4/16/2012)

Wonderful insights will be revealed that have the potential to change one's perspective of personal trials, as well as the finality of death. I have not written this book alone. Those of Thera's loved ones who have returned to our heavenly home have been by my side inspiring my heart, mind and writing. I have felt the pure and limitless love for Thera from each of them, as well as the love her family remaining here have for her. Through Thera's life story, valuable teachings as to the vital role our attitudes play in the creation of living life with inner peace amidst the severest circumstances will have the potential to be learned.

I love the giant redwoods! I have contemplated these astonishing trees that adorn our earth for most of my life. As a small girl, I stood next to one of them. My eyes followed it up to what seemed a literal path leading into the heavens. I remember thinking, "If only that tree could speak to me, I would just sit quiet and listen to all the stories it would share." With the average redwood tree being 500 to 700 years old, their stories would most assuredly be incredible. In my life, I have used the redwoods as one of the foundations for my perspective of this mortal existence.

These mighty trees have stood strong through all the confrontations nature has challenged them with. I strive daily to face my life with faith, strength, grace and endurance just as the magnificent redwoods that influenced my world so many years ago. The wonderful example, in which my role model has chosen to live her life, portrays the very essence demonstrated through the existence of the resplendent redwood species. Our world is greatly enriched through the life lived by this elect woman of God. Truly she is the human epitome of faith, strength, grace and endurance. Open your heart, and your soul will be abundantly blessed by the extraordinary life of Thera Nicholas Huish.

Thera wants you to understand and know with certainty that no matter what you may be going through, or what you will yet go through in your life, *you can get through it*! Her hope is to give you added strength to push forward, ever forward.

The quickest way through every storm,
Is straight through the middle of it!

Larina Grigg

Thera's hope is that her posterity will carry the knowledge that they come from an ancestor who journeyed through some unfathomably devastating experiences, **and she made it**. To Thera's posterity: she loves you. She wants the world to know her secret of how she not only survived, but also thrived throughout this life. From this book, may you reap from her strength and be blessed by the life this amazing woman has lived. Thera asked me to write her story in order to make our world a better place. This is her goal. Dear sweet Thera, our world is already a better place just because of you. Thank you.

'I walk slowly, but I never walk backward.'

Abraham Lincoln

Please note that, as the author of this book, I refuse to use the name of the murderer whose hands took Trish's life. He does not deserve to ever have his name uttered. He no longer exists to the beautiful family who has suffered greater than any can imagine from his actions. He does NOT exist to me. With his last breath, God will hold him accountable for his unforgivable acts.

Table of Contents

~Chapter One~

Do What Needs to Be Done!

On the 21ˢᵗ day of September 1930, our world became a brighter place with the birth of a precious baby girl. Thera Nicholas arrived safely from heaven welcomed by her earthly eternal parents, Joseph Gordon Nicholas and Doran Morella Howard Nicholas. Joseph was born the 12ᵗʰ day of December 1907 and Doran was born March 3, 1909. Joseph and Doran were married October 24, 1929. Thera shared many stories with me of her incredible parents whom she loves so much. Joseph and Doran Nicholas laid a solid foundation for their children by arming them with knowledge, not only from example, but also by allowing them the invaluable gift of learning through personal experience.

Once married, Joseph Gordon Nicholas took his new bride and settled in Promontory, Utah, approximately two hundred miles from the family and home Thera's mother knew and loved. Doran left her parents, eleven siblings, extended family, and friends in order to begin her new life as Mrs. Nicholas. Coming from a family of twelve children, there were occasions where Doran missed them terribly. At times she felt intensely lonely for the family she had left behind. Doran was oblivious to the fact that, in the future, her Thera would feel piercing loneliness for the opposite reason caused by family members being torn away from her by death. Doran's little girl watched her mother when she knew Doran was feeling lonely or overwhelmed.

"Through some of those difficult times my mother went through, I would watch her work, work, work! Mother had a garden, which provided for much of our family's food. When my mother was struggling with something, she would go into the garden and engage in working it. I would say to her, 'Mother, we've worked so hard. Please let's go in.' Mother's reply, "Nope, it is better to work when you have problems."'

What a blessing for young Thera to have learned such a powerful lesson from her wonderful mother. With all that Thera would have to endure, this lesson would bless this sweet little girl immensely in the years to come. Through watching her mother work whenever there was a problem, Thera made a very important decision. She decided that during life's difficulties, no matter how challenging, she would always engage in being busy by getting up, getting dressed and showing up!

Together Thera's parents bestowed a wonderful gift upon their daughter. Joseph and Doran blessed Thera with priceless knowledge empowering her to create an incredible life founded upon Christianity. From her first memories as a small child, she recalls rich values being instilled in her through the examples of her loving parents by the life they jointly lived. Since her entrance into this mortal life she was taught a deep reverence for the living God, even our divine Heavenly Father, and His son, Jesus Christ. Thera, a beloved daughter of God, has weaved this perfect wisdom within her very being.

Thera was Joseph and Doran's first child of seven. She was born in Ogden,

Utah, on an autumn day. Many times Joseph shared with his beautiful daughter that she cost him twenty dollars, which was a full months pay for him as a hardworking dirt farmer during the depression. Those young parents are an example of what dedicated parents can accomplish in order to provide for their family. Joseph and Doran's life together gave unarguable proof of the irreplaceable value in parents teaching children proper principals with which to live by.

Both Joseph and Doran educated their seven children well. They did this not only by personal example, but also with patience as they took the time to teach them. Life gets busy for everyone. None of us should ever be too busy to find the time to teach our own children, as well as positively influencing the lives of the children around us. Those who shirk personal duty as parents by not teaching their own children, whom God has entrusted to their care, are definite contributors to many of the problems of our world today. Children learn respect from their parents. Both the teaching and learning of respect is most definitely lacking. Too many parents today don't respect each other, their children, or even themselves. With the numerous distractions at our fingertips, parents absolutely need to stop and evaluate where their children are placed on their personal list of priorities. Thera's parents had their priorities in proper order.

Thera became well-educated with invaluable wisdom in regards to honesty, respect, loyalty to oneself and one's family, kindness, service to fellowmen, gentleness yet strength, independence, as well as vital insight on how to live life in complete self sufficiency. These gifts were imparted to her from goodly parents. Combined together these qualities produce integrity. Thera is the embodiment of true integrity! Yes, her brilliant light illuminates the way for her posterity and for those of us blessed enough to preview portions of her valiant life through the words of this book.

The Nicholas children had manners. They learned from both Joseph and Doran to be polite and respectful. Though their father did not attend one year of high school, he was a gentleman. Joseph would not allow his children to put their elbows on the table, they had to sit up straight, and he made sure that they always said thank you. Joseph looked like John Wayne and was a simple dirt farmer. I must interject that in my interviews with Thera, I dubbed her father as the *gentle giant*. Thera agreed that my opinion just about described him perfectly.

When other men would get bucked off a horse, Thera's father would walk up to the horse doing the bucking. Joseph would softly talk to it settling it right down. He would mount the wild animal and hang on! The horses he broke would buck and buck. Thera would watch as she mentally noted that her father simply *held on*. The horse would eventually stop bucking. Her father would dismount, take the reigns, and gently lead the horse to a post to tie it up. It was over. From that moment on the newly tamed horse loved Joseph. Throughout the tragedies over the years of Thera's life, holding on wasn't always easy. Thankfully, the vital wisdom she gained from her parents while growing up has remained with her. An impressionable child watching her father *hold on* to the reins taught Thera to '*hold on*' during times of acute grief, anguish and devastation she has braved so many times.

"Daddy loved his family! He always did all he could to make our lives wonderful on the farm. He bought us a little black Shetland pony named Jimmy. He was a wild little horse and wasn't very tame. Daddy said to my brother, 'Okay Bud, you gotta get on that horse and break him.' Daddy called us girls, Sis, and my brother, Bud. He would never call us by our names. Daddy put my little brother on that pony and Jimmy threw him. Eventually after being thrown three to four times, my brother got our new pet to the point where we could ride him.

That horse was a terror! He never wanted any other horse to beat him. One day I was on my way to my grandma's house riding on Jimmy. My uncle was on his way home riding my grandmother's big horse and said 'Lets race!' I said, 'No.' But I said no too late. My uncle took off on his horse. Jimmy took off with me! By the time I got to grandma's, Jimmy stopped dead still in his tracks and I flew right over his head. The saddle that was supposed to be on his back had turned and worked itself clear around Jimmy, and was upside down still attached under his stomach. I was on the ground."

One day Thera's mother asked her to go get Jimmy, and to tell her father to come for dinner. In their fields they had wells that continued to flow all the time. These wells would make a big black gooey mess that was filled with pollywogs. Thera tried to get Jimmy to stay away from the wells, but he loved them.

"Jimmy would get right in the middle of the murky pond. He would lie down and roll in the thick substance. I was obeying my mother and had to go in after him. I ended up covered in black muck and pollywogs from the artesian well Jimmy had taken a swim in! He was special to us kids. We thought we were something because we had our pony. Other children would come to the house and say, 'Wow! I wish I had a pony. Wow! I wish my mother cooked like yours.' As Nicholas children, we knew we were blessed."

Joseph Gordon Nicholas wasn't afraid of work; he was thankful for it. Thera's father was a humble man. He was grateful for every blessing given to him and his family. He acknowledged that every blessing he received came from God. His greatest blessings were his wife and his children. Even during the financial stresses of the times back then, Joseph did everything he could to take care of his family. He started a project for his children making them an awesome swing. Thera loved that swing!

4

"There isn't a kid in the world that ever had a swing like we did! My father made our swing with huge tree posts that stood about twelve to fifteen feet high. I remember when he dug the postholes and put the cement in with those giant tree posts. That swing was the greatest gift! It was magnificent! I could sit there swinging, daydreaming, and planning my life."

Times were difficult for families during Thera's childhood and youth; it was the great depression of the United States of America. Though her parents were extremely poor, the unwavering belief of this vibrant dirt farmer's daughter was that the Nicholas family was indeed the richest household on the planet! The mother sets the tone in the home. Thera's mother was absolutely wonderful at making their home a heaven on earth. Giving birth and rearing seven children without the conveniences our modern world offers to us, most assuredly was no simple task. Giving birth and raising seven children is no easy task even today! Running water, electricity and inside plumbing were obsolete. Yet through a combination of an optimistic outlook and intense work, this ideal mother fashioned a warm pleasing home for her energetic family.

On chilled nights, Thera and her siblings went to bed in cold unheated rooms sleeping three to a bed. Before her children would fall asleep, Doran would remind them that when they would wake in the morning to be sure and look for the latest picture Jack Frost would have painted on the window while they slept. Of course sweet Thera believed Mr. Frost really had come in the night painting the exquisite design she would find decorating the ice-covered window the next morning! As this little one gazed at the art-filled window, she was somehow unmindful of just how cold the bedroom was. Becoming aware of the intense chill, it took her only a few seconds to jump from her bed and leap into the kitchen reaping warmth from the crackling morning fire that had heated the entire room.

Skilled with her abilities to cook on her old coal stove, Thera's mother would produce food that was nothing short of perfection. The meals she prepared for her family so many years ago could never be copied today, even with all of our modern conveniences. Every morning before school the children ate a delicious breakfast consisting of an array of warm milk gravy made from bacon grease with homemade biscuits or pancakes, bacon or sausage, eggs or hot cereal. What a gift Doran's meals were to her family. What a gift Doran was to them.

"I think of kids today that have to go to school hungry while their parents are still sleeping. I never remember a morning that mother wasn't already up cooking pancakes, bacon, eggs, etc. for her family."

At the end of the school day the bus driver released a bunch of hungry Nicholas kids saying, "I can smell your mother's food from here!" The minute they got off the bus each child could smell the fragrances of fresh baked bread, homemade butter, honey, cakes, cookies, etc. coming from their mother's kitchen about a city block away! Running down the lane they arrived into the love and security of their home.   Thera never remembers coming into her house from school when her mother did not have something waiting for them to eat. Many times she could smell her mother's vegetable soup brewing for her and her siblings to enjoy. Whenever Thera has fixed a pot of homemade vegetable soup, memories of the divine aroma of her mother's cooking overcome her.   The taste of her mother's homemade bread with home churned butter could not be matched. Then, to top it off honey dripping onto the bread made it taste like heaven!

Today, we have almost everything at our fingertips. Joseph and Doran had to work for all they had in order to provide for their family. Taking just a few minutes each week to plan a healthy, nutritious menu for our families is wise. Utilizing the wonderful recipes of most anything one wants to eat can be found on the Internet. Wholesome, nourishing food is a great blessing for you and those you love not only physically but also mentally. If Doran created the heavenly meals she did for her large family during one of the toughest times in our nation's history, what can possibly be our excuse? Both Joseph and Doran Nicholas took our excuses away of not getting back to the basics and eating to feed our bodies properly!

~Journal Entry March 3, 2008~

I was thinking about Mama yesterday. I always remember that her birthday, her mother's and Grandmother Nicholas's birthdays were all on the same day. My how time flies from those days when I was a tiny girl, when I would listen to my mother read by a lantern on the kitchen table. I was indeed a blessed child. Of course, I had this incredible father who always came into the cozy kitchen from the cold outside. He would be holding a bucket of warm milk for all of us from the cows. Mother strained it through a cloth setting it out on the porch. The cream would rise to the top then she skimmed it off. The milk was poured in the pan for the dogs and cats after we had our fill with what we wanted to drink. We churned what was left in an old wooden churn and made the most wonderful butter in the whole world. At night the same process started again. Memories... and the dear wonderful feelings they bring to my heart."

As a child, Thera would lay under a tree. She would stare up at the sky while making castles from the clouds. The sky was crystal clear. No pollution, no airplanes. Simply a vivid blue canvas with the effortless movements of the clouds as they traveled on a breeze. The air was clean and her lungs filled with life each time she inhaled.   The continual rejuvenation of her body happened daily with the fresh air, sunshine, and the pure food she ate. The importance of health became a part of Thera at a very young age.

Simplify

It was a much simpler time back then compared to the chaotic, confused and stressed circumstances many of us live today. Perhaps living a life cherishing our simple pleasures is not out of reach after all. We have the power to take control of our individual life creating whatever we choose to create. It is up to us to eliminate the negative clutter around us, and thankfully we can. Yes, the world our lovely Thera grew up in was a very different place from now. Yet the fundamentals for both, no matter the differences of time, are very much the same. Living a simplified life based on true and honest principals is something we all can accomplish, if we decide to do so.

Though the times of Thera's youth were simpler, life lessons still had to be learned. The children had a pet fawn that they loved. They played with it in their cornfields. The baby deer had become part of the Nicholas clan. One day the family had been away. Upon their arrival home, the fawn was nowhere to be found. Within a short time, it was discovered that someone had killed it while they were gone. All of the children were terribly sad, but during the depression people were starving. Desperate measures are taken when one's family is hungry with no food.

While Thera was still very young, the family had two dogs that she loved. Everyone went to town one day. When they reached home, blood was on the faces of their dogs. Both had made it into the chicken coop. Thera's father immediately got his gun and shot both dogs and they dropped dead in front of Thera. Joseph explained to his children that once the dogs had killed chickens they would continue to kill chickens. Death is difficult for a child to understand; it is difficult for adults to understand. Thera has dealt with agonizing grief in her world. Her grief caused from losing so many of those most precious to her whom have not escaped death's grasp. Joseph cared for his dogs. Shooting them without hesitation was another example to Thera that when something needs doing, one need not hesitate completing the task at hand.

Procrastination paves the way to misery.

Lessons of courage were taught to the Nicholas children. One night while in bed, Thera felt a snake at her feet under the covers. This normally brave little girl couldn't speak she was so afraid. Her mother came in to say goodnight, and Thera slowly lifted the sheets showing her the snake. Her mom immediately reached down, grabbed the snake and threw it out the window! Doran Nicholas showed her children how to live with self-control, and so did Thera's father. Both took immediate action whenever action was required. Thera never forgot the lessons she learned as a child from both of her parents. All those years ago, that sweet little girl never realized how many times tragedy would necessitate her delving deep inside her memories for the wisdom acquired from her good and loving parents.

"I still have the iron my mother gave me. We washed on Monday, and hung everything on the line. Mother would sprinkle them with water and wrap them tight. On Tuesday we'd iron all day long. She would never let us stop until the job was done. The iron was called a cold iron and it was heavy. We would put the iron on the stove to get it really hot. Then, we'd take the iron by the handle and iron the clothing. From that experience growing up, I learned not to stop until a job is done."

Every Saturday the family would lay the foundation for the following week in order to be prepared to keep the Sabbath day holy. Later in her life Thera was visiting her mother. She woke early ready to help with the work only to find her mother sitting in her chair crocheting. Thera spoke to Doran, "Mother, it's Saturday. We've got to do Saturday work." Her mother continued her crocheting and calmly said, "We don't have to do Saturday morning work, because now I don't have any daughters that need to be trained anymore."

"Train up a child in the way he should go, and when he is old he will not depart from it."

Proverbs 22:6

Thera's father was a choice man who made sure everyone, even strangers, had food to eat when they came to his home. And needless to say, many came during those trying times. In a special blessing, Thera's mother was given the promise that she would have food for her family and for the stranger that came to her door. To Thera it was nothing short of a miracle watching her mother prepare a meal. Within twenty minutes Doran would have the table filled with food that could feed twenty people and still have left overs! This was accomplished through the hard work of both Joseph and Doran. The Lord provided Joseph the animals to hunt in order for his family to not go hungry. Our Lord also provided the Nicholas family with herbs, fruits and vegetables from the earth. Doran tended her garden well in order for this to be. She canned not only fruits and vegetables, but also much of their meat. The promise she was given in her blessing blessed her life, the lives of her husband and children, as well as many others who were welcomed.

Joseph and Doran were obedient in doing their part of showing the Lord that they not only had faith and trusted in Him, but Thera's parents were also willing to engage in the physical work necessary in order to receive the blessings.

"Faith Without Works is Dead."

James 2

Thera explained that it took a lot of work to safeguard provisions enough for their large family to live.

"Work is a good thing!"

Thera has taught each of her children that in order for Heavenly Father and our Savior to provide their sustenance, they must work. All of Thera's children learned the value of work from both her and Sterling just as she learned it from her father and mother. If Thera's parents were able to provide for their family of nine during the Great Depression, surely we can follow suit. Joseph and Doran Nicholas had abundance through harsh winters where little means were to be found. How was this accomplished in those days of so much need? This was achieved with a husband and wife of great faith. Both were first and foremost completely committed and dedicated to God and to each other. Joseph and Doran didn't overthink things, nor did they complicate life. They didn't question when the world threw them a curve ball. These two remarkable people simply did what needed to be done in every circumstance they faced.

We don't know exactly what the future has in store for us, or for those we love. We do, however, have glimpses of what lies ahead through many warnings including those found in the Bible. The spring, summer and fall months allowed Joseph and Doran the necessary preparation time insuring provisions for the survival of their family through the months of winter. Thera shared that they always had plenty. Just as Mr. & Mrs. Nicholas, we have the ability of preparing now to the best of our abilities for events yet to come.

Joseph and Doran were members of The Church of Jesus Christ of Latter-day Saints (nickname - Mormon), as is Thera. For many years the leadership of the Church have given this council:

*Minimize debt, and get completely out of debt as soon as possible
*Be self-sufficient
*Have a one to two year supply of food storage and living essentials
including
Water
Food
First Aid Supplies
Things to start a Fire
Protection from the elements
Clothing
Blankets
Toiletries

9

Tools

Thera's father and mother did what needed to be done without hesitation. Both Joseph and Doran Nicholas worked together. From their actions they deservingly received blessings for their family. Throughout Thera's life she has certainly followed in her parents' footsteps honoring them every step of the way. I know that Joseph and Doran couldn't be prouder of their cherished daughter.

~Journal Entry~

"We had to work through the summer in order to have all we needed for the winter. It was so simple, so wonderful. That was my life. Tough days. Working was how Daddy and Mother survived during the depression."

With each event of overpowering blows to Thera's world, this courageous woman of strength opted to stay in control by getting up, dressing up, showing up and doing whatever needed to be done. Thera has been a recipient of many blessings because of her unfaltering focus and determination to accomplish the task at hand, through each of the devastating circumstances she has faced. Amidst grave trials at the most critical of moments Thera has been given blessings of strength, wisdom, guidance and enlightening inspiration. Are not those gifts also available to us? Indeed they are as we follow the examples of Thera and her parents, by doing what needs to be done in our individual lives.

~Journal Entry May 3, 2009~

It is Mother's birthday today. I remember as a child how interesting it was to me that my mother, her mother, and my father's mother all had their birthdays on the 3rd of May. Mother was born in 1909. She would be 100 now! She was indeed an angel.

The Nicholas children learned how to can meat, vegetables and fruit. They would go to town and get bushel baskets of peaches, pears and other fruits. The only running water was from a hose outside. The children would sit under a tree with their mother preparing the fruit to be canned. The fruit was cold-packed. As soon as the lids would pop, the cans were set and the food was ready to store in the cellar.

The cellar was five-steps underground. The shelves were lined with canned meat, fruits, vegetables, jams and other necessary items like cheese, candles and soap. The family would go into the garden and dig up the potatoes and carrots. They would take them down to the cellar layering them with sand. They also did this with bushels of apples. Shelves and shelves of colorful fruit that Thera's mother canned to feed her family which included lots of apricots, peaches, strawberries, raspberries, apples, and also the jams Doran made from them. In the cellar Thera's mother had sweet pickles in a big pickle jar. She'd pick all the cucumbers when they were small and then make a mixture of water, sugar and vinegar. Thera expressed to me during our interview that her mouth was watering as she remembered her mother's pickles! Doran would make dill and mustard pickles.

Waste Not, Want Not

Doran instilled in Thera not to waste anything. Her mother never let one thing go to waste. If she ever saw anyone throw celery leaves away, she'd get upset. Doran dried the celery leaves using them for seasonings to flavor her yummy homemade soups.

In Thera's opinion the apricot jam the children made with their mother was the best. They would dry the pits and crack them open and eat them. Today, it is said that apricot pits are poisonous. The children would give some of the pits to their mother, and she would grind them to put into food. The family didn't have many nuts. Doran always made due with what they were blessed to have, teaching her children to do the same.

When winter came the snakes liked the cellar. Thera would reach for a can of something and many times there would be a snake there. They were called blow snakes because they hissed. Doran would not allow anyone to kill them. These snakes were important to the family, because they killed the mice and rats. Black widow spiders shared the cellar as well. As the patriarch protecting his family, Joseph knew that his wife and children went down in the cellar to get food. A black widow spider bite could be deadly. Joseph would go down into the cellar with a torch burning all of the spider webs. Thera hated the black widows and was always happy when her father torched the webs killing the spiders.

"We had lots of milk on the farm. Mother would fill a big rectangular boiler with milk letting it sit until the milk soured and curdled, then she would cut it. Afterwards, we put it in a net or cheesecloth. Mother would season it, then put it in a big round tin. She would set it on a table lowering a big piece of wood into the tin. She'd put rocks on the sides of the post causing the wood to push down onto the cheese. Each day she put more rocks on it, as the weight squeezed the juice out. Four to five days later Mother would take the big, round, beautiful, orange cheese down to the cellar. By the end of the year the cheese was flavored. We had delicious cheese everyday on the table!

With the boiler, she would also make lye soap with lard. Mother would cook it on the stove and let it sit in order for it to gel. Once gelled, she would cut it with a knife. When she did laundry, she'd heat the soap and put it in the wash. Our laundry would come out clean. The whites would come out bright white with the pure soap mother made.

Every Sunday we had fresh chicken for dinner. Mother would go out to the chicken coop, get a chicken, put it on the butcher block, and then cut the chicken's head off. She used our ax from the woodpile, where we cut wood every night for the wood stove. After the duty was done, she'd throw the chicken and let it jump around till it died. We'd take it down to the house and mother would put it in hot water. We would pluck the feathers off, cut it up, and cook it. Sunday dinners were always a treat!"

Deer ate the alfalfa on the Nicholas farm. The family would work together driving away the deer to kill it for food. After hanging the carcass, they would take the hindquarters and meat of the deer over to the salt flats. The salt preserved the meat. Thera's mother had a pressure cooker that she used to can meat. Even in the harshest winters, a full meal including meat could always be found in the Nicholas home.

The family had rabbits. Thera recalls that they ate a lot of rabbit meat. She remembers the baby rabbits squeal when the snakes would try to kill them. Many times the children watched their mother grab snakes throwing them far away, but again never killing them. Thera learned of pro-creation from the rabbits. She watched as they would jump on top of each other and yelp and squeal. She was told that it was the male rabbits on the female rabbits. This was the same with the family cows and the bull they had. In her young mind, Thera decided that the male had to jump up on the back of the female and then the babies would come. She associated this as a little child.

Thera's mother had a favorite rooster, or so Thera thought. The rooster was terribly mean. When Thera went outside with bread and jam, he'd attack her and take her bread. One day Thera thought, 'I'm gonna get even with him!' Thera had finished putting the cows away in order for them to be milked. The rooster was sitting on the fence. The yard had big, tall, beautiful sunflowers growing in it. She pulled one of the sunflowers out from the ground. Then, this free-spirited little girl began swinging the sunflower hitting that mean old rooster in the head. It fell dead. She meant to hit it. She was really mad for all the times he had attacked her. Her intention was to hit him, but not to kill him. It wasn't until she was in her twenties that Thera confessed the truth to her mother about how that rooster had died. Doran wasn't fazed a bit with the news.

One man's junk is another man's treasure.

People would give the family used clothing to help them. Dressing seven children during the depression would have been quite a job! With her old pedal sewing machine, Doran would cut up the donated clothes making *new* clothes for her family out of the material. She made Thera a skirt and a vest out of a man's old brown suit. Thera felt so dressed up and thought she was the most well dressed gal in the whole world! Of course, no member of the

Nicholas family had many clothes. The children had one pair of oxford shoes each year. The girls had but one dress each.

Once a week the children would bathe in an old round tin tub. Thera's mother would use the hot water from the reservoir in the stove so the bath water was warm. The younger kids went first. The older ones would spoon out the dirty water and add more hot water. Eventually, a pump was installed in their kitchen. It was so wonderful for the family to finally have running water in the house! Of course the pump had to be primed by adding water each morning. Once primed though, they all enjoyed having running water. After baths on Saturday each family member would shine their oxford shoes with Shinola, so they would be polished and shiny for church the next day.

From the deer her husband had killed, Doran would make moccasins for her children out of deer hide for the summer months. If the shoes wore out, Thera's father would put on a lasp. He would cut the heavy leather, measuring what was needed for the sole. Thera remembers her father tacking the leather onto the soles of his family's worn moccasins.

~Journal Entry~

I reflect on days gone by as a little girl. It was a joyous time whenever we went to Ogden over Memorial Day. We would visit the graves of loved ones, watch the parade, and visit cousins. We had some fun times! We always got to go to the carnival and ride the Ferris wheel and the merry-go-round. We usually got to buy an ice cream cone. Life was pretty wonderful with ALL those gifts! Times were very different for children, and we were happy and appreciated every little thing. I remember when Daddy went to the store and bought a couch for mother. He put it on a trailer, and we took it home to Promontory. My mother had very little in her life. She had never had a couch. All she had was the back seat of an old car that was placed in the front room. She had so little, yet she never complained. What an angel she was to everyone! As children, we learned gratitude for each blessing we had from our parents no matter how small the blessing. Today children have so much.

Of course there was no indoor plumbing for using the bathroom. And, there was no toilet paper. The family used old Sears Catalogues for toilet paper. Thera would sit in the outhouse and go through the pages. She would see the women with their hats and nice clothes. A dream was born in that precious young girl's heart because of those Sears Catalogues. From viewing those pictures, Thera determined that she was going to be a successful businesswoman someday. Thera certainly made her dream come true.

"We didn't have any electricity. Sterling Huish, who I later married, was five years older than me. Sterling actually helped lay the lines that brought electricity to Promontory after I was in the 8th grade. I can

remember Daddy and Mother had a Delco engine that had wet cell batteries. We had two shelves of these batteries. The engine would run charging the batteries up. We had one line that went from the Delco building to the kitchen in order to turn on the one electric light in the house. We could only turn it on, not off. When the light started to dim it was time for bed. We used a coal oil lamp before that. I still have that lamp."

Starting high school was a traumatic experience for Thera. She had very little self-confidence and didn't think she was pretty, because her teeth weren't straight. She worked at a store in town after school for twenty-five cents an hour, with which she always paid her tithing.

"We thought we were rich. I never knew we weren't rich until we moved to town when I was in high school. At the end of every season I learned tithing by my daddy sitting down with his money as he said, 'Nine for me; one for the lord.' When we would gather the wheat and put them in bags, we'd put them in the granary and daddy would say 'Nine for me; one for the Lord'. Daddy usually paid his tithing in silver dollars, as well as ten percent of whatever the farm produced."

Thera spoke about how everything is the Lord's, yet He gives us all that we have and asks only for 10% of what is already His. It is a privilege to pay tithing, and the blessings for paying it are abundant! Those blessings may not always be financial, but blessings come none-the-less.

Many people living in our society and time, place little value and have a lack of appreciation for what they have. Nor are they content with the priceless gift of *right now*. Merely existing with the mentality of always wanting more inhibits the joy of truly living. Being happy and having gratitude for what one has will bring feelings of security and gladness. Peace is created by living in the moment, while enjoying that moment to the fullest. Remember, you never know how many moments you have.

~Journal Entry~

I was so blessed to have such good parents who taught me so many important things about life.

~Chapter Two~

Life

Thera worked at Liberty Theater, the only movie theater in Tremonton, Utah. The owners were Alfred and Pearl Toland. Thera had been told by one of the Toland girls that her wonderful big brother was coming home. He was in the military returning because his father had suffered from a stroke. The stroke left Mr. Toland severely handicapped. He could talk, but he couldn't walk from the effects of the stroke. He needed assistance with everything. This young man's parents needed help. As the oldest, he was willing to sacrifice and leave his military career in order to come home for his family. His family consisted of him, his parents, one brother and three sisters. Dorian Conrad Toland was their oldest child who had been born on the 6th of July 1925.

Shortly after Thera found out that this young man was returning home, she went in to work. She was working as an usher at the Toland's theatre and went to the Toland residence to pick up the change bag for selling tickets. Dorian Conrad Toland was at the house looking very handsome in his uniform. At sixteen years old, Thera thought it would be so fun to go on a date with him! While working together, Dorian and Thera got to know each other. Dorian had taken over running the theatre for his father. The two soon started dating. They had been dating for about four months when Thera found out she was pregnant.

"I was so young and naïve."

Thera shared with me that Dorian married her, because in those days, that was the proper thing to do.

"If a boy got a girl pregnant, he married her. We drove to Wyoming, got a marriage license, and got married on January 27, 1947. After we were married, we had a little reception."

Once married, Thera didn't work at the theatre anymore. For about two months Dorian and Thera lived with his family.

"Mrs. Toland was a very proper lady. She was most unhappy about her son marrying me."

Thera's new mother-in-law had resentment towards Thera. She always had to be addressed as Mrs. Toland by her son's wife. At Dorian's parents' home, Thera was continuously nervous. She never knew what Dorian's mother would say to her. Thera never felt accepted by the Toland family, including her own husband much of the time. Thera remembered one time she was in the basement of the Toland home using Mrs. Toland's sewing machine. She didn't have one of her own. Thera was making a green dress with little baskets of flowers on the material and struggled to get the sleeve sewn in right, so she asked Mrs. Toland if she could please help her. Dorian's mother grabbed the dress from Thera's hands. Then looking at Thera she stated, "You are a stupid farmer's daughter, and will never amount to anything! You are not worthy of marrying my son!"

"I will never forget those words."

I recognized pain in Thera's voice hidden behind those six words that she had quietly repeated to me. It was a pain that had been triggered from the resurfaced echo of Mrs. Toland's voice in Thera's mind. She was experiencing that very same hurt from those harsh words that had pierced her young heart almost seven decades earlier. Thera paused speaking with much thought.

"Words are so important whether they are said to a child, or to an adult. Most everyone is very sensitive when it comes to cruel words. My mother never allowed any of us children to say mean or cruel things. She would tell us, 'Keep your words soft and sweet, because you'll never know what you'll have to eat.'"

Be careful what comes from your mouth. Once words are spoken, they can never be taken back.

"Mrs. Toland chastised both Dorian and I much of the time. She would list all the things we didn't have. I remember her being upset because of us not having a place to live. Yet, Dorian was there to help his father after the stroke. He lifted him, bathed him, and did what his mother was not capable of doing. He left the Army for that very reason. Dorian did everything his mother couldn't do for her husband. That is one of the main reasons we were living in their home, but Mrs. Toland was very critical of us."

Dorian continued running the theatre for his father. He and Thera lived in the Toland home for about eight weeks. Mrs. Toland was always telling them what to do, and how to live their lives. It was during this time that Dorian decided to use the GI Bill he had in order to go to Brigham Young University.

"I am sure Mrs. Toland was having a severely difficult time dealing with her husband suddenly being completely disabled, and four of their children still needing to be raised. One of their daughters was not well and died when she was only about twenty years old."

Mrs. Toland must have been quite overwhelmed at that time in her life with the condition of her husband. Not only that, but Dorian being her firstborn son, was more than likely his mother's pride and joy. With all the ordeals she was personally facing, for Dorian to marry so suddenly had to have caused her great disappointment. As his mother, I am sure Pearl had great aspirations for her boy who had already sacrificed so much in order to step in as provider for her family. Feeling as though I have gained some enlightenment on Mrs. Toland, I have the impression that she felt that her son's union would inhibit his accomplishments.

I am not condoning the way Thera was treated, because it is NEVER okay to be unkind or cruel. But, there is always a story behind each and every one of us. Mrs. Toland's story at that time in her life consisted of grief, disappointment, and an enormous amount of stress. Perhaps she was being prepared for the loss of her husband, son and daughter that she would be facing shortly thereafter. I am sure that in heaven someday Thera and Pearl will have much in common to visit about.

Thera did not want me to have Mrs. Toland painted as a bad person. Both Thera and I have compassion for this woman, and all she endured. I expressed to Thera that I felt it was important for each of you reading this book, that I include experiences she had with Dorian's mother. Each occurrence became a part of forming Thera into the woman she has lived to be. As you learn more about Thera, our hope is that you will gain insight for specific things you may be dealing with in your life.

I visualized sweet Thera at only sixteen years old thrown into a world where those around her didn't accept her, or care about her feelings. I imagined her loneliness existing without much joy at all after coming from such a full, happy life with her parents and siblings. But through those times of isolation, Thera could feel her unborn child stir within her. This little one journeying from heaven to earth gave her strength despite the unkindness surrounding her.

"Dorian wasn't an affectionate person. He came from a family that wasn't affectionate. I knew that he would finish college, and do his thing."

The time came for Dorian and Thera to move to Provo. They lived in a small apartment in student housing. Thera fully understood that it would be her job to care for her brand new precious child that would soon be arriving from heaven. There were no classes to help her with the delivery on how to breathe, or what to do to make the process of giving birth easier. She had never had any education on having a baby. Thera went into labor and Dorian dropped her off at the hospital. He left her to attend one of his BYU classes. Thera was completely alone.

"I was in a room all by myself. The nurses would come in the room to check me. I had gotten up out of bed to go to the bathroom. The nurse came in and found me on the toilet and had a fit saying, 'Don't you know that you can have that baby in the toilet?'

Eventually they came and hauled me away to the delivery room. I was still completely alone. I had no one there to help me breathe through the contractions. The pain and pressure were extreme for me and at seventeen I was uneducated on having a baby. In the delivery room after I delivered, I don't even recall them holding Val up to show him to me. They immediately took my baby away from me to put him into the nursery. That was how it was done in those days. Then, they took me to a room and put me in a bed.

By the time Dorian came back, it was about an hour to an hour and a half after our baby was born. It wasn't until then that they finally brought my baby boy back to me to meet his parents in person."

On the 8th of July 1947, a perfect little son was born to Dorian and Thera.

"We named our new son Val Conrad Toland. Val was the most beautiful baby boy!"

As a child Thera had rubber dolls with beautiful faces. Thera remembers the wonder she had as she gazed at her baby. She would study his little face, hands and feet. Thera said her Val was the most perfect thing she had ever seen in her life. Thera had no family close by. She was in the hospital about four to five days after having Val. With the birth of their first grandchild, Joseph and Doran made arrangements to go to Provo, Utah to meet the newest addition to their family.

"Dad owned a plane, and he and mother flew from Tremonton to Provo. Mama stayed with me for about three to four days. She brought with her lots of baby clothes for Val. I put a bellyband on Val's naval so he wouldn't have an outy belly button. Mother brought me about 24 flannel diapers, t-shirts, some tiny little shirts to keep him warm, and flannel baby gowns all of which she had made. In those days babies wore cloth diapers and rubber pants. Mother had also crocheted little booties for him."

Thera expressed her deep appreciation for her mother teaching her to care for her newborn son when Doran visited her daughter after Val was born. When Thera came home from the hospital with her baby boy her mother taught her daughter what to look for when her grandson would cry, how important it was for Thera to burp him over her shoulder, how to bathe him, how to feed him and so much more! Joseph and Doran cherished their first grandchild, and also their daughter very much. As they had always been there for Thera throughout her life, Thera's parents continued to be attentive to her needs. How very grateful Thera was to know that they were now also there for her son. Joseph and Doran flew back to Promontory, Utah.

"I wasn't able to nurse my baby boy, though I tried desperately to for six weeks. Val was hungry. Mother told me to simply start him on formula and I did just that. Val was a happy, healthy baby after I did."

As her parents, Joseph and Doran's love and support for Thera never changed. I know that Joseph and Doran continue from heaven to love and support their family here. These two devoted parents, grandparents, great grandparents, great-great grandparents, and so on have provided innumerable blessings for their daughter, her family, and all of their posterity. Such remarkable people!

"I had no washer or dryer, so everyday it was quite a job to hand wash all the baby diapers and baby clothes."

Doing her best to adjust to being both a wife and a mother at such a tender age was challenging for Thera to say the least. Dorian, still a very young man himself, had also been thrown into his own unknown territory. Having to leave his military career in order to run his father's business for his parents was a lot of responsibility for him. In addition to that, he had become a new husband and also a new father. While they lived in Provo Thera became pregnant again.

"I was shocked when I found out I was pregnant with Trish. I had barely healed from having Val."

As Thera's mind went back in time, she explained that when it came to Dorian, it was his way or no way. Once she disclosed that to me, her mood seemed to change. I could sense that the memories flooding her mind, of the circumstances she had found herself in during that time in her life, were mostly unpleasant ones. She had never had anyone be so stern with her. Val was only six weeks old when she got pregnant again. One day Thera was quite sick, lying on the couch, while expecting Trish.

"Dorian came home and told me, 'I want you to fix me a sandwich.' I explained to my husband that I didn't feel very good. Dorian came over to me and proceeded to pull me off of the couch. He put me up against the cupboard telling me that I had to stand there until I fixed him a sandwich."

Thera stood against that cupboard, ill and pregnant, for over an hour. Thera did not make him a sandwich. She again stated that Dorian had been raised in a home that was a complete contrast to the loving family environment Thera had been provided with by her caring parents. In the home Dorian and Thera had, he ran everything strict and disciplined.

"That was how he was raised, that was what he knew. Dorian was a visionary in many ways and very smart. He loved science and airplanes. I remember that he would draw airplanes talking about them breaking the sound barrier. Dorian was quite a stubborn man, most definitely an extremely determined man."

While they were in Provo, Dorian decided that he wanted to build an outdoor drive-in movie theatre up in Spokane, Washington. Once that decision had been made, Dorian stopped attending BYU to pursue his dream. He and Thera purchased a dumpy, little trailer. Thera's father hooked it up to his truck, pulled it up to Spokane, and parked it for them. Dorian's parents gave their son an old car to help him. Dorian and Thera moved to Spokane. They lived in that trailer for about five months during which time they were blessed with Trish.

"I was always so tired. I would buy one pound of hamburger, and make that last as long as possible by dividing it into three separate meals. I had no money, and I didn't eat well."

Of course Thera was tired. She had barely given birth to her boy, when Trish was on her way. Just ten months and twenty-eight days after Val was born, Thera gave birth to a beautiful baby girl, Patricia Toland, on June 5, 1948.

"A special couple in the ward took Val when I went into the hospital to have Trish. Dorian took me to the hospital and dropped me off just like he had done when I had Val. He didn't stay with me. I was alone again as I went through labor. Dorian came back to the hospital just before I delivered Trish.
I remember them putting this little girl in my arms. I was so trilled to hold her! She was a tiny baby, only five pounds. My mother really loved her daughters, and as I met my baby girl I instantly wanted a close relationship with my daughter the way my mother's relationship was with me. Being a mother to Trish, the way my mother was for me, was very important to me."

There was a very special bond between Thera and her only daughter that happened the moment their eyes met for the first time in this life. That bond has not been severed by death.

"When I was wheeled out of the delivery room, Dorian was standing in the hall by the door. Our baby daughter was in my arms. He stood and looked at Trish. It is hard for me to remember his reaction, because his family just didn't show a lot of emotion or love. He didn't look at her little hands, or her little feet. Dorian wasn't like that. His mind was always on other things. He was distant most of the time."

Thera expressed with some sadness that Dorian had never really been taught how to love, so he had never learned how to love her. Dorian had been instilled with discipline, which was magnified by both his military mentality and family background. Thera experienced these traits from her husband firsthand.

"My name has always been important to me. I wanted to name my new daughter Thera, because nobody I ever knew had my name other than me. I told Dorian that her name was going to be Thera, but he refused to let me name her. He said her name would be Patricia. I had no choice what my baby girl's name would be. I had no choice in a lot of things.

I was able to spend five days in the hospital with Trish at the beginning of her life. Those days will always be precious to me! I would stare at her perfect little face while holding her tiny hand in mine. I spoke softly to her as I held her in my arms. I shared with her how much I loved her, and expressed that our lives would be intertwined with many adventures that we would share as mother and daughter. I nursed her for probably two to three months, which I believe enhanced our bond together."

After Trish was born, Thera's father pulled his daughter's meager home back to Tremonton. Moving to Spokane had been premature. Joseph parked it in his and Doran's backyard. That is where she lived with her two beautiful babies, and husband. Being near her parents again allowed her to finally feel somewhat calm, safe and secure for the first time in a long time. Since finding out she was expecting her first baby, she had been thrown into a family where she was shown little or no respect or love. Thera could not have helped but to lose sight of some of her identity at this time in her life.

Though very happy to be back with her family, Thera had only a little running water in their trailer. She had no plumbing for bathroom use, laundry, or showers as she cared for her eleven-month old baby boy and newborn baby girl. Following the examples of her mother and father, Thera always made due with what she had by counting the blessings she was given.

Dorian continued pursuing his goal of building a drive-in theater in Spokane. He made the decision to take a trip up there in order to finalize all the details of purchasing the property for the theater, and work everything out for him and his family to once again move there.

"Dorian was focused on what he wanted, how he was going to get it, and how he wanted things done."

Dorian took flying lessons at the airport in Tremonton. He used his GI Bill from serving in the Army to achieve becoming a pilot. For his trip to Spokane, Dorian used a plane from the Tremonton airport. His father wanted to go with him. Mr. Toland's parents lived in Star Valley, Wyoming, where Dorian landed. He left his father for a visit there as he continued on alone to Spokane. Once his business was finished, Dorian flew himself back to Star Valley and picked up his father. His plan was to be back in Tremonton in time to open his parent's theatre for the three o'clock matinees on Saturday.

"I called the airport a little after noon to check to see if he had landed. They told me he should have been back by twelve, and I asked the person on the phone if anyone had heard anything from Dorian. The person responded that they had heard nothing since the report came in that the plane was lost. That was the first I had even heard about it."

At nineteen years old, this mother of two little babies hung up the phone and immediately turned on the radio. The news was on. Thera heard the announcer inform listeners that a plane being flown by Dorian Toland had been reported missing. His father, Alfred Toland, was a passenger. Thera walked out of the house. She was alone. She didn't say anything to anybody. She walked up and down the sidewalk. When she walked back in the house, her father was there to meet her.

"It was a LONG Saturday with no word. On Sunday morning, the town decided to send out search planes to fly over Dorian's flight plan in order to see if they could find the missing plane and the missing father and son. On Sunday morning, the pilots took off in planes to retrace where Dorian had flown. Daddy was one of them."

Joseph owned a small plane of his own that he used for flying his older children to Tremonton for high school. They would stay at their house in Tremonton during the week, and on the weekends they would fly back to their farm in Promontory.

"It was about five in the afternoon when Daddy walked in the door. I was sitting on the couch. He was always kind of a joker, but not this time. His look said, 'I want to make it better for you, but I can't. Dad's so sorry. I don't know how to help you.' It was the first time I had ever seen that look, and I knew Dorian was dead.
My daddy's look was one of helplessness as he sadly shook his head and said, 'They found the plane.' I know that look well, for I have seen it in the faces of each person who has let me know when I have lost a loved one."

On the 12th day of March 1949, Thera became a widow after being married just twenty-five and a half months, at the age of eighteen with a twenty-month-old toddler son, and a nine-month-old baby daughter. Somewhere within the one hundred and sixty-four miles between Star Valley and Tremonton, the plane Dorian was flying crashed into the top of a mountain. Both Alfred and Dorian Toland died that day leaving their families behind. Thera's mother said, "Thera we have to go see Mrs. Toland."

"I didn't want to go. But, dad and mom took me around the corner to the Toland home. They knocked on the door, someone opened the door

and we went in."

Shock and grief had overcome Mrs. Toland with the terrifying news of losing both her husband and her son. Those were emotions Thera would become all too familiar with in her future. Pearl Toland, feeling her loss intensely, was wailing. When she saw Thera she cried out to her, "What are we going to do?" Mrs. Toland threw her arms around Thera.

"I just stood there, and didn't say a word. My mind was going so fast I could hardly keep up with it. I didn't know what I was going to do. I had my two children and no money."

Two caskets, both closed, were in the Toland home. Thera innocently asked the mortician why Mr. Toland and Dorian couldn't have open caskets. He answered that when the crash happened the entire front of the plane had come in on both Dorian and his father, killing them instantly. He went on to explain that battery acid from the engine had charred their faces, and affected their bodies. He then proceeded to tell her that Mr. Toland had been through the LDS Temple, and the only place on his body that had not been burned by the acid was where his garments were. Those of the LDS religion wear temple garments as a protection.

"Dorian, on the other hand, had not been through the temple. His body was burned terribly. I pondered upon the mortician's words, and knew that going through the Temple was what I had to do."

At Dorian's service, Thera recalls that she didn't have feelings of great sorrow.

"I was just in shock that they were both gone."

Because Mr. Toland was the one who owned the theater and was a prominent businessman in Tremonton, the focus was mostly on his death. Thera felt as though she was just along for the ride with her two children.

"Everybody in the whole valley came, and businessmen lined up while we walked out. The next day I went downtown and pushed my two babies in their buggy up one side of the street and down the other side. Not one person on the street, or in the stores came up to me and even noticed me. I knew then and there that I was on my own."

Val shared with me that his mother had told him later in life, that she had feelings of utter despair as she pushed that buggy. After Dorian and Mr. Toland were buried, Joseph sold his plane. Thera said her father never flew again. Mrs. Toland had lost her husband and her son. Within a few years, she also lost her daughter, Diane, who had a hump on her back and had difficulty breathing. She died as a young woman around twenty-years old. Pearl Toland buried her husband and two of her children leaving her with three of her five children. Her family of seven went down to four. She eventually re-married the mortician in Tremonton.

"Mrs. Toland ended up in a nursing home with dementia. My sister Janet went to the nursing home often. One time while passing Mrs. Toland's room, Mrs. Toland walked into the hall and grabbed Janet's wrist in a death grip. Then with tears running down her cheeks she said, 'Thera, please forgive me.' That happened shortly before she died."

Even through the dementia, the way she had treated Thera was still on Mrs. Toland's mind. Thera had already forgiven her long before Janet spoke to Thera about her experience with Dorian's mother. Though only babies, Val and Trish unknowingly gave their mother strength. Her deep love for both of her children blessed her with determination and fortitude, not only during the time she was married to Dorian, but also as a teenage widow following his sudden death.

During one of my sessions with Thera, as we went through this specific time in her life, she confided that she knew she would never have been able to accomplish all she has achieved in her life, had she stayed married to Dorian. Though Thera's time with Dorian was difficult, the experiences she lived opened her mind to the life she wanted for her and her cherished children in the future. She made the choice to move forward leaving the past where it belongs, in the past.

~Chapter Three~

Sterling - Chivalry

Sterling Smith Huish, Thera's second husband, was born November 27, 1924. At the Brigham City, Utah, courthouse on the 5th day of June 1943, he was inducted into the military Army. During World War II, Sterling served as a Sergeant in the 275th Infantry Regiment. In January of 1945, in the European Theater of Operations, Sterling S. Smith earned an award for **Exemplary Conduct in the Ground Combat Against the Armed Enemy**. At an ROTC camp in Riverside, California, in August of 1948, Sterling also received the **Bronze Star for Valor**

Words from Sterling

"As I remember, my military service ended and I was separated from the military at Fort Douglas in Utah on the 19th of April, 1946. Met by my family, I was home and alive! It seems that everyone else who was going to meet me was too busy, but I did not care. I was back in Zion."

When Thera worked in the theater with Dorian, Sterling used to come in and sit and talk to her. He was dating Dorian's sister Pamela. Dorian would open the theater, and Sterling would go into the box office and visit with Thera while he waited to take Pam on a date.

Sterling was six years older than Thera. He was part of a barbershop quartet, and his group would come sing for the high school when Thera went to school there. She knew him from watching him perform. Sterling did not go on a mission for his church, instead he served our country in the army. He worked at a service station in town. When he got his GI bill, he went to college at Utah State University studying history and psychology while in the ROTC. Sterling and Thera were friends from when he went to the theater. Other than that, there was no association between them when Dorian was killed.

After Dorian's death, Thera was still living with her two babies in the small trailer parked in her parents' yard. It was such a sweet blessing for her to be home with her family, and not in Spokane alone. The Relief Society President from church would bring her food. There was a $3,000.00 insurance policy from the plane Dorian was killed in, which greatly helped Thera and her children.

Joseph and Doran knew their daughter needed to realize that she still had her whole life ahead of her. Thankfully, each of us has the ability to learn from prior choices and personal experiences. One can wallow in self-pity when their chosen path becomes grueling and seemingly impossible to continue on, or one can simply open their mind to the possibilities of change.

When one door closes, another door opens.

"Every fall our community had a harvest ball to celebrate the end of the harvest season, because all the crops were in for the year. The

farmers would come to the dance and it was a fun party. The ball was a big event. An orchestra was brought in to play for it. Mother and Dad LOVED to dance! Mother kept saying, 'Thera, you need to get out and do some things not just always be with your kids.' Of course my parents were going to the Harvest Ball and wanted me to go with them."

Thera didn't graduate from high school. After Dorian's death, she was trying to figure out what to do with her life. When someone could watch the kids, she would work at the theater. The bishop told her that the church would give her the food she and the children needed. He counseled her to not pay rent, to keep her insurance money, and let the church provide.

"Daddy said he always paid tithing and helped people, so it was okay for me and the babies to get help and have the church provide our food."

Though a very serious time in Thera's life, the wisdom from her mother influenced Thera. She decided to go with her parents to the National Guard Amory in Garland, Utah, where the dance was held. All the big events happened there. Tremonton was about fifteen minutes away. Garland was a tiny town with about five stores. It was where Sterling called home.

Thera went into the dance with her parents. She sewed all her own clothes including the dress she was wearing. Thera went and sat down. Joseph and Doran were on the dance floor having a splendid time dancing!

"Sterling came up and sat by me. He started talking to me. He was aware that Dorian was gone, and was well aware of my current situation with two little ones. He asked me if I wanted to dance. Of course I said, 'Yes!' He was a really nice dancer. It was wonderful to dance with him!"

With Dorian growing up in a home lacking in physical love, having Sterling's arms around Thera felt wonderful to her.

"Sterling danced with me all around the dance floor. We danced the jitterbug, and many others. It was like a whole new world opened up for me that night. As we danced, Sterling started singing. He sang a lot of the songs we danced to."

Thera was reliving those treasured moments, and it was amazing for me to be a part of that memory with her. She remembered that when Sterling came to perform at the high school, she would just sit there looking at those four guys singing. She said she just fell in love with them!

"Mother and dad said that it was time to head home. Sterling asked them, 'Would you care if I take her home?' Sterling did take me home that night. We already had become friends from our visits at the theater. He

genuinely cared about me and after he kissed me, I knew it. I had someone who wanted to kiss me, and hold me in his arms. Dorian had never shown me tenderness and love. Instead, he controlled me. I was never permitted to make choices of my own."

Thera had experienced something completely new for her. Thera went home and was absolutely on cloud nine! She was so excited that she had met a man who had feelings for her, had held her, danced with her, and kissed her when he took her home. She fell in love with Sterling while they danced at the Harvest Ball.

"That night was filled with magic. Sterling called me a couple of days later, and he asked if I would go with him to a wedding and a dance. Mother said, 'Go ahead and go! I'll watch the kids.' So, I went."

I am sure that Doran was more than a little thrilled for her daughter! Sterling had been asked to sing at the wedding. Thera recalled that the bride was a little Japanese gal. He sang *I'm in the mood for love*. From then on, that was he and Thera's song. Thera watched and listened as he sang.

"Many, many years after when we were living in Arizona, Sterling went to have some dental work done. A Japanese girl came in and was working on his teeth. She said to him, 'My grandmother told me about a man named Sterling Huish who sang at her wedding. Would that happen to be you? Have you ever lived in Garland, Utah?' After all those years..."

From November to December, Sterling and Thera started dating two or three times a week. Thera, Val and Trish would go with Sterling to deliver gas. The farmers would order their gas tanks and Sterling would deliver the gas. He wasn't going to college yet. The first time Sterling went to Promontory, where Thera's parents' farm was, Thera watched him write a bill to a farmer. She noted that he had the most beautiful penmanship. She thought, "He can dance, sing and write beautiful!"

"Sterling took me to his house and introduced me to his mother. She went into the other room with Sterling, and said, 'Sterling you are not serious about this little Toland widow are you?' Sterling answered with a no. We had dated for about six weeks. We had been on a date and I was in the car. Sterling asked me, 'What would you think about getting married?' The first thing I said after he asked was 'Why would you want to marry me? You know that in March it will be a year since Dorian died. I was going to have the children sealed to him.' Sterling responded, 'I understand. I will just take my chances, and we can take it a day at a time. If you feel that is what you need to do, then that is okay."

29

Both Sterling and Thera knew that they would have to make some decisions. He was going to be going to college in Logan about forty-five minutes away. He came home to Tremonton after he had been to Logan and said to Thera, "Guess what I found?" She responded, "What?" He continued, "I found a little one bedroom apartment, and that is where the four of us are going to live."

"Sterling had his GI bill. We decided that we would get married. We set the wedding date. I told mother and dad. They were happy! My mother asked us when we were going to getting married. I told her January 27th. Mother looked at me and said, 'Thera, you may want to change that date. You married Dorian on the 27th of January.' So, I set it back one day to the 26th."

Sterling and Thera's wedding wasn't anything big or fancy. They wanted to have dinner at a place in Tremonton called The Oak Café. They asked how much it would cost. When they found out, Doran asked how much it would be if they provided the meat. Thera's mother killed a bunch of chickens providing all the meat. Sterling wore a gray suit. Thera bought a new light gray skirt and jacket that fit her perfectly.

That beautiful suit played a part in Thera keeping herself thin. She was able to get back into that suit, staying trimmed and as nice as she could after each of her children. Thera has self-respect, and takes pride in her appearance.

"My mother would slave everyday. But, before daddy got home she would always wash her face, pull her hair back, and put a clean apron on. Mother always would look nice for Daddy."

Sterling was a lucky man. Thera followed her mother's example by taking care of herself and looking her best for her husband. Fitting into her tailored suit she was married in, after having each baby, helped her achieve that.

Thera didn't have flowers, bridesmaids or a reception when she and Sterling got married January 26, 1950. Later, they had a small reception and dance at the church so people could congratulate them. They were given gifts by some of the guests. Thera remembers one of the gifts they received. It was a red dish given to them from Oren Heaton. Thera made red Jell-O in that dish for over fifty years!

"One day my youngest son Nick asked me, 'Mom, do you still have that red dish?' I answered him, 'Yes.' He told me he wanted it and he came and took it. Nick still has that red dish."

The owner of the café cooked the food, including Joseph and Doran's chickens, and everyone ate a nice meal.

"Sterling's mother took Val and Trish, so we could stay in a nice motel in Salt Lake City for three days. We went to a wonderful place to go dancing. Sterling sang 'I'm in the mood for love' to me at the Rainbow Rendezvous where Nat King Cole was performing that night. I remember thinking that nobody could be as happy as I was that night. I thought, 'I have two perfect children, and I am marred to the man of my dreams'."

When the honeymoon was over, Sterling and Thera went back to Tremonton. They got rid of the little trailer, and with it Thera's not so happy past. Then, the four of them: Sterling, Thera, Val and Trish went to Logan to begin their life together as a family.

"I found myself wondering if it were fair to have Val and Trish sealed to Dorian, when Sterling was going to raise them. I went to the Bishop with my concerns. He wisely counseled me to wait until March before I made a decision. I wrote a letter to the prophet expressing to him that I didn't know what I should do. The prophet wrote me back and said, 'You need to fast and pray about what to do.'

I received the prophet's letter after Sterling and I were married, and I did fast and pray. I kept thinking, 'If I am sealed to Dorian, I won't be able to be sealed to Sterling. And, if we have more children they won't be sealed to me and Sterling.' Night after night, I would dream the same dream. Dorian would appear in a suit. I would turn and run from him, and he would chase me. I would run and run. Then Sterling would appear in a white suit, and I would collapse in his arms. When that happened, Dorian would disappear.

For a month or two I kept dreaming this dream. Then one day I said to Sterling, 'Well if you want to go to the Temple and you are sure this is what you still want to do, I want to be sealed to you.'"

Sterling loved Thera, Val and Trish. He knew without any doubt that he wanted them not just for this life, but he wanted them for all time and eternity. The four of them were sealed as a family forever in the holy temple of our Lord Jesus Christ in Logan, Utah. They were sealed together as an eternal family by one holding the Priesthood of God, having the proper authority to perform their sealing. The sacred promises and blessings bestowed upon them extended to any children Thera and Sterling would be blessed with in the future.

Sterling and Thera knelt, holding hands across a holy alter. Once they were sealed as eternal companions, Val and Trish were brought into the room. Sterling, Thera, Val and Trish were all dressed in pure white. Thera and Sterling's smiles lit the entire room as they held their two cherished children in their arms. Val and Trish were sealed to both Thera and Sterling with an eternal bond that can never be broken. The walls on either side of this happy little family were enormous mirrors causing their reflections to go on forever. They gazed at the image of the four of them together. They were like angels going on forever, endless and never ending. Such a joyous day!

~Chapter Four~

Love of Country

"Sterling decided to go through the ROTC program. That way he could go back into the military and be a lieutenant. Sterling was very delighted about this opportunity. His GI bill from the Army allowed him benefits to use however he wanted. He chose to go to college for history and psychology. By doing this, he would receive a monthly check for about two hundred and twenty dollars."

The Huish family consisted of Sterling, Thera, Val, and Trish. They lived in a military barrack that had been converted into apartments in Logan, Utah. Rent was about sixty dollars a month. The government paid for Sterling's college, because he was in the military. Thera was working as an usher in a theater. Every Saturday night Sterling would perform with a dance band in order to make money for his family. Thera proudly told me that he would earn more, singing during that one night, than she made all week while working in the theater. This little family didn't have much money. One time while going to Garland, Sterling and Thera had to round up what little change they had between them in order to feed their children.

Sterling, Thera and the children eventually were able to move into student housing. Joseph and Doran continued being amazing parents and grandparents.

"They were so kind to us. Whenever we visited home, Daddy would always fill up our car with gas. Mother would give us eggs and food from the garden. Sterling's parents were very good to us as well."

Sterling's parents received Thera into their family. She had never experienced acceptance from the Toland's. Mr. and Mrs. Huish also loved and acknowledged Val and Trish as their grandchildren.

"His mother was especially kind; she was sweet. She worked for years as a switchboard operator. Our kids used to love to go to work with her. They would watch her take the cord and stick it into the right connection joining the two parties through the phone. Sterling's father, though, was actually quite critical and negative."

Val, Thera's oldest son, once expressed to me that growing up with a strict military father wasn't always easy for him. Perhaps Sterling's way of parenting Val somewhat stemmed from the way his father was. When one becomes a parent for the first time, it is a brand new experience. We all know that children don't arrive with step-by-step manuals on how to raise them. (Which by the way would sure come in handy!) Goodness, every child is so unique how could there possibly be an instruction guide?

As a brand new father to not just one but two ready-made children, Sterling had the knowledge of how to be a dad from how his own father had raised him. As first time parents, we all mess up. I have six children, and I certainly haven't been a perfect mom for any of them, but my husband and I have done our best as their parents. I call the first child in a family the guinea pig. It is through experience with the firstborn that most parents learn how to be a parent. Unfortunately for many of those who are born first, parenting knowledge comes from making mistakes much of the time.

Sterling had made his own decision to become a husband to Thera. And, at the same time the father of two little ones before he even proposed to Thera. He understood the circumstances and also the responsibility he was taking on. The fact of the matter was he loved the three of them, and couldn't imagine his life without them. From the moment he married Thera, Sterling loved Val and Trish unconditionally as his own children. He became their dad.

I was blessed to know Sterling, and would like to interject that his love for his family and country meant everything to him. I will forever love both Thera and Sterling. I am so fortunate to have their influence as a part of who I am today. Through writing this book, I have also grown to love all of their remarkable family.

"Sterling went through the Air Force ROTC program at Utah State. After graduation, he was commissioned in the Air Force as a Second Lieutenant. He was called back into service receiving the assignment of being stationed in Victorville, California, at George Air Force Base. Sterling and I had been married about two years at that time."

Years of military life led them to Washington D.C. where Sterling attended Georgetown, University. He studied Psychological Warfare Training. While he was at school in Washington D.C., Thera stayed in Utah. Richard Mark Huish (Rick) was born February 9, 1952.

"I was alone yet again when my third baby was born. Richard Mark Huish was born at Hill Air Force Base. After Rick was born, my parents then drove me, Val, Trish, and Rick to Washington D.C. Sterling and I were able to show the children all the sights in our nation's capital. It was a special time for all of us to be together."

After Washington the family was off to Bloomington, Indiana. Sterling studied the Hungarian language there. He was being prepared to go to Hungary when that area was opened. After his courses, Sterling and his family moved to Wiesbaden, Germany. Thera drove from Garland, Utah, to Chicago with her mother. She then continued on from Chicago to New York, so their car could be shipped to Germany. Thera and her three little ones had to stay in New York at a military apartment until their flight came up. The Huish family lived in Germany for four years. Thera explained that during that time Sterling's work required extra security.

"I knew very little about what he did. We visited England crossing the channel on the ship. I saw the White Cliffs of Dover. As a child, I remember my mother singing the song, Bluebirds Over the White Cliffs of Dover. What a thrill it was for me to see the place my mother had sung to me about when I was growing up! We had some wonderful trips. We were able to take the children to Holland, Paris, and all over the battlefields where Sterling had fought in World War II. One of our most amazing trips was the one where he took us back to the areas where he dug foxholes to fight from. He showed us some of the German homes they had used as barracks while fighting."

Sterling and Thera were able to attend the dedication of the temple in Switzerland. It was an incredible experience for Thera. The films shown in the LDS Temples teach those members, who live their lives worthy, amazing eternal principals that are very sacred. Because of the sacredness of the contents, those worthy to enter the temple are the only ones able to view the films. Most members of the church reverence their temples and Jesus Christ. They choose to live their lives as Disciples of Christ. In order for one to enter the temple, their membership in the church is to be in good standing. There are specific guidelines of living a Christ-like life by being honest, living morally clean, honoring one's self and family, showing respect to others, paying a ten percent tithing (where the money goes to bless the lives of both members and non-members alike), and blessing those in need.

"This was the first time they brought films into a foreign country to show at the temple. The brethren were afraid they would be viewed, because the films had to be left at the airport. They were told they could pick them up the next morning after the viewing. When those who were to pick up the films went back, the films were returned at which time those picking up the films were told that there had been no need to view them. Living so far from home, the church became our family."

It was a unique experience when they would meet on Sundays with the German Saints. Part of the meeting would be in German, some in English. Thera explained that they had glorious times with the missionaries. Sterling was serving as a part-time missionary. The mission home was located in Frankfurt Germany. There was a continual stream of missionaries going in and out of the Huish home, which was wonderful for the family.

"They were years of fun, fun, fun! Lots of servicemen knew Sterling from both Garland and Tremonton. Also, friends we had known from previous assignments would end up in Germany. There were so many of them who came to our home to visit us. Due to severe headaches at that time in my life, I was seeing many doctors seeking for help. To this day, I

still suffer from headaches. Perhaps it was the epidural they put into my spine to help me with Bob's delivery."

When Thera was young, her brother would tease poor Thera because her teeth protruded and weren't straight.

"Mother would get so mad at him and make him stop. But, the mental damage was done. I was extremely self-conscious of my teeth. I remember how excited I was when at twenty-five years old, married to sterling, living in Germany, I was finally able to get braces through the military! I had them for about two years wearing those braces through my pregnancy with Bob. I shall never forget the day they removed my braces. I came home and looked in the mirror. Looking at my reflection I cried. As the tears rolled down my cheeks, I finally realized something. I said out loud for the first time in my life, "I am beautiful." And, I meant it. I went around Smiling! Smiling! Smiling! I had covered my mouth with my hand for so many years uncomfortable and embarrassed because of my teeth. After my braces came off, I realized the great value of a simple smile."

Thera has never stopped smiling! Long after they had moved back to the states, she was waitressing. She served a man the wrong food. He looked up at her and said, "You could serve the wrong food to many people, but you'll never be in trouble as long as you keep smiling like you do!"

While they still lived in Germany, Sterling and Thera's fourth child, Robin Smith Huish (Bob) was born April 22nd, 1955. Returning home to Utah from Germany, the Huish family settled in Orem, Utah, where Thera gave birth to Todd Nicholas Huish (Nick), their fifth and last child on March 12th, 1959. Sterling was an Instructor at BYU in the college ROTC program. Because Sterling was an instructor there, Thera was able to go to BYU. She studied courses in order to be a secretary learning to type, and write in shorthand.

"I thought that being a secretary would be fantastic. I soon found out that shorthand, typing and sitting in an office was not for me, even though I had some of my first valuable sales experiences at that time. Through these experiences, I found out that I was capable of becoming quite a saleslady. Sterling served on the high council at church and was in charge of the genealogy in the stake. He spent hours and days in Salt Lake gathering his genealogy. We made many trips to the Salt Lake Temple, blessing those who had passed on before they had received the wonderful blessings from Heavenly Father for themselves and their families. Through our standing in as living proxy for them, we were able to do for them what they could no longer do for themselves because of death."

From Orem, the family moved to Reno, Nevada. Sterling was stationed at Stead Air Force Base. The children were a bit older, so Thera started to do some part time waitress work along with some sales work. After Reno, the military transferred the family to Okinawa, Japan. Thera had no idea where it was, but soon found that living there would be quite an experience. The family flew over to Okinawa. While living there, they helped build a church along with many other things that positively impacted the lives of those around them. The life of a military family means going where the next assignment is given whenever the assignment is given. Val was ready to graduate from Kuvusakie High School, when Sterling had to report back to the states with his family just before Val's graduation. The family returned to America, where Sterling was stationed at Hill Air Force Base for his last duty.

During the three years before her husband's military retirement, Thera knew she was going to need to do something to create more financial security for their future. Up until that point, she had mostly stayed at home in order to raise the children working as a waitress along with a few other jobs in order to help her family get by on a military budget. Thera became very active in Multi-Level Marketing with the Figurette bra business and, boy oh boy, did the lifestyle of this amazing family change! Sterling retired from the Air Force as a Major on the thirtieth of June 1968. He had dedicated twenty-three years, two months and nine days of his life serving his country he deeply loved. He served honorably, proudly and loyally in the military for The United States of America. His name is on a memorial in Tremonton, Utah, as one of the veterans having served in both World War II and Viet Nam. Sterling's entire life consisted of him giving of himself to his family, his country and to serving all those around him.

~Journal Entry~

July 4, 2008

Interesting how life has so many ups and down. Now we mourn over a nation that is facing one of the biggest challenges it has ever faced. I pray daily for our protection.

October 29, 2008

What a month this has been, filled with so many events and wonderful gifts along with many changes. This has been one of the most fearful months in my life as we near the end of this time to elect a president. I have seen the economy crash, and recall the time my father said the day would come when a wheelbarrow full of money would not buy a loaf of bread. Our money has lost its value and food and gas are out of the range for many people. It is so scary. Yet, I feel a sense of peace knowing that this is a blessed land and it is a nation under God.

November 5, 2008

I believe with all my heart that the time is close at hand when every knee shall bend and every tongue will confess that God has control of this, His land. I am so grateful to know that I have a prophet of Jesus Christ to follow and that he will be my guide through dark days ahead. I know that paying my tithing and doing the best I can is, and will be, my salvation. I pray that each of my children also get this message, but I cannot force it upon them.

~Chapter Five~

Val - Integrity

"Our son, Val, was pretty much the perfect young man growing up. He worked hard, got good grades and was always dependable for anything I needed done. Val graduated from Kuvusakie High School, the first American school in Okinawa. We lived there for three years while Sterling continued serving in the military. Val was eager to make his own way and be independent. He consistently earned his own money for anything he needed. Throughout his life, he has always shared what he has with others. He inherited Dorian's quality of determination, which has served my son well in his life.

Today Val is an amazing man. He is a very successful man in so many ways. He is married to a wonderful woman named Cathe and the two of them are happy and so good for each other. I am extremely thankful for Cathe and the daughter she is to me. Val is a family man. He is a great dad. And, is dad to Trish's children also. That is how his sister wanted it to be. Cathe calls me mom, and treats me so well."

Being close to Cathe was very important to Thera. She appreciates and loves Cathe and the relationship they share together.

"Val is an absolutely wonderful father! He has raised not only his children, but also Trish's children who he raised as his own after she was taken from us. When he married Cathe, he became father to Danielle as well. Danielle is one of us!"

With Val and Trish being so close in age, Thera said that Trish would call her big brother on his birthday saying, "How old are you? We're the same age!"

Val would call Trish on her birthday reminding his little sister that he was a year older than her. It was a fun game between two siblings who, together as infants, had endured tragedy before they understood it. One day Trish asked Val if he would take care of her children if anything ever happened to her. Of course Val said yes, and Trish put it in her will. I am sure the connection between Val and Trish extends beyond any earthly comprehension.

With the death of his father, Dorian Toland, Val chose never to change his name from Toland. Thera felt that this was in part because of his grandmother, who, of course, had a very special place in her heart for him after the death of her eldest son. Thera explained that when Val and Trish were little, Mrs. Toland would bring large gifts for Val, and a small trinket of some sort for Trish. Dorian's mother's feelings for her grandson were obvious.

When Thera was sealed to Sterling, Dorian's mother was very hurt. As previously explained, Val and Trish were sealed to Sterling and Thera. Mrs. Toland said that Thera took her son's children away from her. Pearl Toland had already suffered so much loss that she didn't want the children to be sealed to Sterling. But, Sterling loved both Val and Trish as his own from the day he and Thera were married. Sterling was very attentive to all of the children. Each were disciplined the same, and he loved them the same. He was stern, and he did discipline. All the kids got spankings.

"My daddy had a razor strap that hung on the kitchen door. When one of us kids would get a little out of hand, daddy would look at the one acting out and say, 'Don't make me use this on you.' That was usually all it took for us to be good. Sterling and I believed in spankings."

Thera was content with giving the kids a swat on the bum. There was some clashing between Sterling and Val, because both had strong personalities. Val admitted that growing up he liked things done his way. When Sterling wasn't there he would push the limits to show his mom that he could do what he wanted.

"During my oldest son's years of growing up, he may have felt Sterling was tough on him. That doesn't change the fact that Val had a military father who loved him."

In 1965, Val stayed in California and worked with Joe Toland, Dorian's younger brother. Val learned the swimming pool business from his Uncle Joe. After which, he returned to Utah attending the University of Utah until 1966. He then left for his LDS mission to serve the people in California.

"Mrs. Toland never really got over Val and Trish being sealed to Sterling and Thera until Val got ready to go on his mission. At that time, she told both Sterling and me that she was happy Val and Trish had both of us as their parents. She said she was proud of us for the way we raised them, and knew that her husband and son were also proud of the way we had raised them."

Following his mission Val was married to a woman named Diane for twenty-five years. Life's circumstances and difficulties caused that marriage to end in divorce. Diane and Val remain friends, which is always a blessing for the children. Thera appreciates all that Diane did while she was married to her son, and all that she does as the mother of her grandchildren.

Val met an amazing woman named Cathe. Val and Cathe married and are *happily* married. Cathe loves all of the children and grandchildren. She is a very special member of the family.

Throughout my session with Thera on Val, she could not hide the abundant love and pride she has for her firstborn! She spoke of his military service with extreme pride.

Val's Military History from Val

"I went through the ROTC at BYU from 1968 to1972. Graduating early in 1972, I entered the USAF mid-year. I went to Denver for Supply School during which time Diana, my wife at that time, stayed with my dad and mom. While there, Diana gave birth to our daughter Lisa. Once out of school, I was assigned to the 9th Reconnaissance Technical Squadron at Beale Air Force Base in Marysville, California. My mission there was to support America's premier spy plane and the operation. The plane was officially called the Lockheed SR-71, but was known by all as the *Blackbird*. It flew higher than 80,000 feet, traveled at Mach3+ in speed, and carried a wide variety of cameras and sensors in order to look out from all angles with different resolutions. We flew it anywhere we needed to go. Since nothing could catch it, there were no missiles that could shoot it down. While there in 1974, the plane's existence was announced to the world when it flew from New York to London in one hour and fifty-four minutes! That was even with a refuel over the Atlantic. Forty years later, that speed record still stands for the fastest jet ever!

I worked with the intelligence gathering side of the operations. I was there the day we found a new high performing Russian jet landing in North Viet Nam. When that information was sent to Washington, it was only a few weeks later that ending the war was negotiated.

The time I spent stationed at Beale Air Force Base was a great growing time for the family. I was receiving my first regular pay check each month. I had made my way through school at BYU by selling food plans and freezers. I was promoted to 1st Lieutenant. I had the military put fifty dollars per month into a savings account because the five hundred dollars they were paying me was more than we needed to live on, and more than I had ever had. I tried to become a pilot, but my eyes were not good enough. It was suggested that I get a rating, which sets one up later in their career for being a commander of an operational wing of weapons. In order to do that, I had to become a Missile Launch Officer.

I went to school at Vandenberg Air Force Base in California, eventually being assigned to the 321 Missile Launch Squadron at the Frances E. Warren Air Force Base in Cheyenne, Wyoming. My family moved there and eventually found an older house to buy in town. My job was very stressful. I was in a concrete bunker that was built like a thermos bottle lying on its side. The bunker was buried ninety feet in the ground behind two blast doors that weighed eighteen tons. While down in the capsule my junior officer and I had to be on alert at all times. We answered and decoded messages. We monitored the status, maintenance and security of ten to fifty ICBMs (Inter Continental Ballistic Missiles), each with three warheads. Our job was to retarget the missile warheads, and be ready to turn the keys that would launch massive destruction on locations all over the world. Having the potential of inflicting destruction at my simply turning a key was a sobering thought for me. Everything I did was recorded. My entire career would be ended if I made one mistake. That was a hard job that inevitably led to more divorces in that field than any other job in any service.

While we were down below, whenever we had slack time, the Air Force had an agreement for allowing us to take study courses from the University of Wyoming. With that opportunity I was able to get my MBA in business during my two and a half years working the job. I was promoted to Captain while there. My son, Lee, was born on a very snowy night, while I was out in the field a hundred miles away. Luckily Diana had help getting to the hospital and his birth went well.

After my two and a half years with missiles, I was assigned to Offutt AFB in Omaha, Nebraska. I joined the 55th Strategic Reconnaissance Wing. We took care of the President's three flying Command Posts. Each one a 747 filled with people and equipment for the president to jump into. Everything was there for the President of the United States to run the country from up in the sky. One plane is always within fifteen minutes from wherever he is. There is always another plane on standby should the first plane be in maintenance. Talk about a very high priority job!

I also ran the flying command post for the Air Force. The flying command post is a plane loaded with several generals and equipment in order to run the Air Force if our land command and control system is out. I believe that system has had a plane in the air, switched out three times a day, flying a figure eight over the middle of the country twenty-four hours a day since 1955. It was a great job with exposure to many high-ranking officers at Strategic Air Command headquarters. I was awarded a regular commission instead of the reserve commission most officers operate under.

If I had kept progressing the way I was, I would have more than likely made it to a Colonel rank possibly achieving General. I would have been able retire after twenty to thirty years of military dedication. My next assignment would have more than likely been in Germany for four years. I would have been placed in a position rated for a higher rank. That would have allowed me to be promoted to a Major in approximately ten years, instead of having to serve twelve to fourteen years to accomplish Major.

I was stationed in Omaha when we bought our first big house along with a rental property. Things were going well. At the end of 1978, we had been visiting the family in Arizona for Christmas. We had only been home a few hours when a call came in for us. My wife's mother had passed away unexpectedly in Seattle, Washington. Diana took our baby son, Shane, who had been born during our time in Omaha, and flew out to Seattle. I loaded our other three kids and drove across the northern states. That proved to be one of the worst drives of my life, because of the weather. We decided to take a longer route home in hopes of not hitting such bad weather. We ended up stopping in Pleasanton, California, to visit my uncle, Joe Toland. He had just started a pool construction company.

We spent a day or two there, and I walked around with him looking at pools in my short sleeves. Uncle Joe offered me a job being my own boss building pools. When we got back to Omaha, I had to dig through three feet of snow to get into my garage. Needless to say, Uncle Joe's offer sounded pretty good at that point! By the middle of 1979, after a series of events, I decided to make the change. Resigning my commission I moved my family to California in order to start my pool business. We opened my office on December 15, 1979.

My seven and a half years in the Air Force were wonderful times. We grew as a family, and met many new people. I lived with a great sense of pride while serving my country. Feelings tug at my heart for those who did stay in the military, for all who have served, and for those who now serve. There is no job that compares with being a part of something so vital to our nation. And, having the knowledge that I agreed to die for the freedom of our great country."

No wonder Thera is such a proud mother of her son! She informed me that Val makes the most delicious sugar cookies. From her description, I certainly hope I get to enjoy one someday! Thera felt that including the story about the sugar cookies in Val's chapter was important, because his sugar cookies bring smiles and happiness to others. Both he and Nick are good at bringing happiness to others.

"Val's ward loves his sugar cookies, and so does everyone in our entire family! Val is a strong member of The Church of Jesus Christ of Latter-day Saints, and always has been. Through his service in the church, he has taught many a young boy how to treat and respect women. Sometimes Val has parties in his home for the young men. He is focused on teaching them how to respect their elders, how to have good manners and how to be gentlemen. Teaching those valuable qualities to boys is way too often overlooked today, but not by my son. If the Stake President visits their ward, all the young men Val teaches stand up and shake his hand showing him great respect. The boys he teaches wait outside before church on Sunday watching for anyone who is handicapped or older that needs help. They open the doors for their mothers and sisters."

I love the word chivalry. I must interject here that Val and Nick certainly exemplify this word, as did their father.

"Val once told me of an experience that he had. 'Mom, I went to the wedding of one of the young men I taught in church. The young man shook my hand and said to his wife, 'This is the man who taught me to be the man I am.' His new wife hugged me and said, 'I married him because of the respect he shows me, and how wonderful he treats me.'

45

The parents of those boys my son has taught in the Young Men's program of our church have such high regard for my son. That is just who Val is. He honors his Priesthood, loves his wife, all of his children, he loves our entire family and is a fine businessman."

Both Thera and Sterling taught their children that they needed to be responsible. As parents they gave them the basic knowledge of how to earn their own money.

"It doesn't matter what you do in life. If you know how to talk to people, and how to sell, you will always have a job. Even when those who have degrees don't have work, you will always have work. All of my children learned that. Val excelled with the talent of selling and being a people person. None of my children were lazy. They never came home from school and watched television. They went outside and were busy!"

Val sent Thera flowers all the time. But, fruit flies would come and she could only keep them for a couple of days. As much as Thera enjoyed fresh flowers, she finally told her boys not to waste money on them. Val has given his mother lovely jewelry. For family reunions or trips, in whatever home Val would stay in, he would tuck hundred dollar bills in different places for his brothers and sister to find.

"Val was such a wonderful big brother growing up. When something happened and nobody fessed up, Val would step up and take the blame. It didn't matter whether he was the one who caused it or not. He did this to protect his younger siblings.
Mother's Day, 2014, I was sitting in my house alone. I heard the garage door come up. I thought, 'Who is coming in my garage?' I stood up and started walking through my kitchen and heard Val's voice. 'Hey, I've come to hang some pictures that Nick said you needed hanging.' He drove all the way from Concord, California, twelve hours of driving. Thera asked him why he was there. He answered, 'I came to take you to dinner.' And he did. We went to dinner with everyone! He got up about 4:00 a.m. and headed home."

After Trish was murdered on the 23rd of February 1991, the man who took her life went after Thera for her money.

"Val met with him and said, 'I don't know what the outcome of this will be. But, don't you dare come after my mother. I just want to tell you that I have a bigger bank account than you, and I will take you down.' My boys are my protectors."

Val paid for so many attorney fees in order to bring justice to the man who murdered his little sister. He and Nick have both always been there for their mother. Bob also was always there for his mother, and I am sure he still is from heaven.

"Val has been an absolute savior in my life! He has never been anything but kind and loving. He served an honorable mission in California. He is an incredible son. If anyone has ever needed help, Val has always been the first one to step forward. Val has had the means to help me through so many tough times. His work ethics are the foundation for his thriving business that he started many years ago."

With Sterling's death, Thera lost her home. Fighting the nightmare battle with their daughter's murderer took all of Sterling and Thera's money, and more. Thera didn't have any money coming in, and had no money to purchase another home. Val put a down payment on a beautiful, brand new home for his mother. Thera has since paid her son back and pays for her home with her income from her business.

"I knew that no matter what, I could depend on Val and Nick. They would do anything for me! My knowing that has been a great comfort. Val spent two days with me after I got out of the hospital one time. He fixed the meals and took care of me. Nick has played that role for a long time. Nick is always near, and my first responder. Caring for me was a new role for Val. Those two days are very special to me.

Val once said to me, 'Mom, when I die and go to heaven and see Trish again, I wonder if she will approve of the way I raised her children?' That is one of the most important things to Val. I know how proud I am as his mother, and I know how very proud Trish is of her big brother. What a sweet reunion it will be for the two of them when they are together again! Val is a giver. He would say to me, 'Mom, I am just thankful I can give. The Lord always blesses me for giving.' I am so proud of my son."

Thera's Letter for Val

Dear Val,

Here I am at age eighty-six, and you are a senior age sixty-nine. Life is quickly passing for me. Before I go, I wanted to share with you some of the wonderful traits I have watched you exemplify that I have seen touch so many lives.

I was such a young mother when you were born, being only seventeen years old. As you know, Trish was born just ten months and twenty-eight days later. Oh, how the two of you were buddies! You always took care of her. Maybe that is where you developed the gift of giving to everyone around you.

You did not know your father as he was killed in a plane crash the 12th of March 1959. Life dramatically changed for you, Trish, and me on that day. In spite of not knowing him, you have many qualities from him. Sterling and I were so lucky to be your parents, and to be able to watch your determination to do things your way. You always won at whatever you attempted! How we were blessed when Sterling Huish wanted to have a family, our family. Your dad wanted the three of us to be his eternally. I shall never forget the day we were married in January of 1950.

We watched you and your determination! Early in life, we all had to keep playing games until you would win. As a young man, when others were content with playing or watching television, you were always finding ways to earn money. When you went on your mission for the church, you had more baptisms than any missionary in the California mission. How proud we were of you then; how proud we are of you now. When most missionaries came home with no money, you somehow saved some every month and came home with a bank account. I remember you saying that you never carried more than one dollar, so you were never tempted to spend it.

When we lived in Okinawa there were no jobs for teenagers. But, you soon learned that you could earn tips by being the first one to the commissary to pack groceries for the customers. It became a race every day! As soon as the school bus stopped, you were the first one out the door racing to the commissary. This pattern has continued throughout your life. It has been a very positive thing, as you integrated your work habits into your very successful pool business in Concord, California.

For me to try and share what you have done for others, because of your success, would be impossible. I remember every time you came to visit us when we were having some financial challenges. After you would leave, we would find hundred dollar bills tucked away in different places that you had placed in our home. You have given freely to others who were in need, Val. It matters not where you go, people still find hundred dollar bills placed in different places: at their homes, in their suitcases, etc. The list of places goes on and on!

I know how you loved working with Bob, with your making him a partner in the pool business. If business was not great, you always made sure that Bob was paid before you took money for yourself. There is so much I could write about your giving nature! I want you to understand how grateful your dad and I are to you. We both appreciated so much the help you gave to us during those desperate times, when we had no one to turn to after Trish's death. Her murderer was determined to take me to court in order to take half of the income Trish and I had earned in our business. You informed him that he was not to ever threaten me. You told him he'd better not sue me, because you would be there for me all the way. You were, and have always been there for me. How could I thank you for being the son you have been to your mother? You paid for an attorney. You were more than willing to give whatever was needed every month in order to help us attain justice for Trish's murder. Those were very hard days for all of us. Little did we know everything that was in store for our family in the future.

I watched the day Trish was talking with you in our family room. That specific day she asked you, "Val, if anything happens to me will you raise my children?" I listened to your reply to her request, "I would be happy to do that." About only twenty- four months later, we were faced with that very situation. Trish had her will written after you agreed to her wishes, and I had a copy. When the court finally gave us guardianship of Marsha, Thera, and Hayden, I realized how very wise you were. You expressed to me that I needed to be their grandmother. And, that you would raise Trish's children, as she desired. You were already raising your children, but you selflessly did what your sister had requested of you.

I know that some of those times weren't easy for you having so many lives you were responsible for. It was so hard for me to walk away and leave those children I loved! Both Thera and Hayden had been in my home pretty much every day since their birth. I was Marsha, Thera, and Hayden's grandmother. They were a part of Trish; they were a part of me.

Val, your influence has been vital in their lives. Hayden has served our country in Iraq, Afghanistan, and South Korea. He now attends college. He respects you as his dad. Thera loves you dearly as her father, and was married in the Temple. Marsha knows that she is loved, not only by you, but also loved by all of us. She has had so many challenges growing up living in so many different homes. What an amazing young woman she has grown into. Trish was her mom, and once she was taken, you have provided the foundation Marsha has needed. Those were the very things Trish wanted.
I often think about the time you shared with me that you hope Trish is pleased with what you have done. My son, I know that your sister will throw her arms around you when you arrive in Heaven! Trish will thank you for your love and for being her children's dad. How can I ever thank you for your wisdom when you counseled me, 'You be the grandmother and I will raise these children.'

49

I think of all we have been blessed with. I think of all that we have lost. I know that our losses are only temporary and that our family, who has left this life, await for our return to them in our heavenly home. I am so grateful for the absolute knowledge that I know we are an eternal family. I know that we all will dwell in God's kingdom together as a forever family.

I recall the terrible times we witnessed Rick struggle with his addiction to alcohol. We held onto the constant hope that he would be free of this terrible disease and live a full life. Your dad and I did all in our power to help your brother, and yet the sad truth was we could not change his life. We were all grateful when Rick married Millie! She was an angel to him during his last days. Though their marriage was only three months, as he lay in that hospital bed, she was by his side every day. You already know that Trish and Nick were with him, and held his hands as he passed away from this life continuing on to the next. Nick was so good to make sure that both you and Bob were able to say goodbye to Rick via phone just before he left us. I thought at that time that nothing could be harder than losing your brother the way we lost him. With those thoughts, I was naively unaware that a mere eighteen months later we would be required to face the tragically shocking loss of your sister.

There are many things that happen in our lives that we can remember every detail of. Even things we wish we could not remember. I am sure you will never forget what you felt, or where you stood when I called to tell you Trish was murdered. The details of those days were more painful for all of us than mere words could ever describe. You were always there for me whenever I needed to talk, or to cry over every devastating situation.

I remember well how you told Nick to take care of whatever had to be done in order to get Trish's murderer arrested. You emphasized that you would handle every legal problem. When Bob asked what he could do, I asked him and Arlene to feed the Mormon missionaries serving away from their homes. He said they would do just that. I knew that with all Nick was doing on his end, you providing the support legally, and Bob feeding the Elders and Sisters in their area we would be blessed. Our family's united continual prayers of faith at that time to bring about justice for Trish, all that the three of you brothers were doing, all Rick and Trish were doing from the other side of the veil, and all your father and I were engaged in for Trish's cause, allowed justice to be served in this life. Justice will also be served in the next.

Miracles happened that proved whose hands ripped Trish's life from all of us. Sometimes when I am watching TV the story of her murder is airing. It causes me to reflect upon everything we endured as a family. I find myself

50

remembering the war that we knew we had to win for Trish's children. Trish's murderer had given guardianship of the children to some of the neighbors. We had to go to training in order for the courts to determine if we were fit parents and or grandparents for her children. Those were scary times. You were always there telling me it would be okay.

Standing by Trish's casket the night of her viewing, each one of us knew exactly who had committed the heinous crime that ended her life. We all knew that somehow, someway we would get through all we faced and prove it. We not only made it through the grueling court case once, but we made it through the second time. He was able to get off death row when he was given life sentences. I love the picture taken of you Nick, Bob and I when the jury ruled him guilty the second time around. We felt so relieved! We knew that from a family of seven we were blessed to still have your father, you, Bob, Nick and me left.

Oh how my heart was broken when the day came that Arlene had to accept that Bob could no longer live on this earth with us. The day she knew she had to let him go home. I know how much you love your brother and all the good times you enjoyed together. I understood how much you missed him in every way. Remember our talks when you would call me and tell me of some small things you both did? The tears would flow as you felt how precious those times past were. I wonder if I would ever have as many people attend my funeral as came to Bob's?

I could write an entire book just on all the fun things we did as a family! Bob always had a joke to tell us, or some funny story to share. I know how much you continue to miss him, even though he has been gone five years. Bob was such a peacemaker. He wanted everyone to be happy. You know that those who knew Bob loved Bob. We all miss him. You, and I both understand that Bob now dwells with dad, Trish, Rick and his sweet granddaughter Sadie.

Bob stayed true to his word, and fed the Mormon Missionaries right up to his death. Arlene asked me how I was able to get through all the deaths of our loved ones and keep going. I shared a thought with her that is a true example of you in every way.

When the flowers die, the people go home. You are then left alone with your thoughts after a loved one is gone. There is only one thing to do... GET UP, DRESS UP AND SHOW UP!

Val, how can I end a letter to you without telling you what a great dad you have been? I see your children come to you for advice, and you always help them in everyway you can. I see the respect and love each of them *has for you. I see their successes in their chosen occupations, yet I see them all come back to you for your guidance. I am most grateful to Diana and Cathe for sharing their lives and love with you. I appreciate their kindness to me through all the tough times we have had.*

I am so proud you! I am proud of your success. I am proud of you for your endless hours of service with the young men in our church. They will remember throughout their lives, as will your children, the fine things you have taught them:

> **How to be kind to others*
> **How to respect their moms and honor them at all times*
> **How to respect young women*

The days ahead will be filled with much joy, and we shall live them to the fullest! I thank God each day for you and Nick. I found it strange as the three of us sat in your family room after Bob's death. Looking at each other, we realized that we three were all that was left here on earth of our once family of seven. We are blessed daily!

I love you, son.
Mom

~Chapter Six~

Memories from Val

"When we lived in Indiana, we had a little red stool. Trish was shorter than me, and we used that stool all the time. Written on the stool was this:

This little stool is mine.
I use it all the time,
To reach the things I couldn't
And lots of things I shouldn't.

Rick was just a baby then. One day Mom was lying down for a nap, while Rick was taking his nap. Both were sleeping. Trish and I had taken all the clothes off the clothesline. We took the wet clothes and wrapped them and put them in the basket. We were just little kids, and not thinking we put the basket on the heater. After doing the laundry, we were doing the dishes.

We used to tell mom we wanted a dishwasher. She would say, "I have a dishwasher. It is model V & T." Trish and I were busy when the heater went on. Smoke was pouring from that laundry basket! Mom woke up, grabbed Trish and me before we knew what was going on, and pushed us out on the grass. Then, she grabbed the basket of clothes throwing it on the grass. Before it hit the ground, she was gone back into the house getting Rick.

Mom has an incredible strength and ability to look into the future, and know that everything we go through is temporary.

"This too shall pass."

Being a farm girl, and the oldest child, my mom could run a house at age sixteen! I have learned so much from her. I have sayings that my mom taught me that I always teach the young men at church.

"When you pick up one end of the stick,
You're going to get the other"'

She taught me that ALL choices have either good or bad consequences. With making good choices, one is going to get the blessings that come from making good choices. With making a poor or bad choice, one will live the unpleasant consequences of their personal choice. Either way, good or bad, we live the consequences from the choices we make.

"When you almost keep a commandment,
You almost get the blessing."

Mom used to always tell me those sayings. I have never forgotten them, nor will I ever forget them. I have done my best to live my life by them.

From my perspective it was quite dynamic watching the younger boys. There were no two siblings closer than Trish and I. When we were in charge of taking care of our younger brothers, somehow Trish always made it so that

I had to step in and take control of them when they were out of control. She always had to be the nice one!

Mom always taught us how to earn money. We'd come home from elementary school, and she would have a big box of donuts waiting for us, not to eat! We took those donuts door to door after school and sold them. Mom had a knitting machine she used to make booties to earn money. She'd say,

"Round and round we'd like to paint this town.
Back and forth, back and forth."

Once the booties were made, we'd go door to door and sell them for Christmas.

During that same time when we were living in Orem, Utah, I was being difficult and obstinate. Believe it or not, I could be both of those sometimes. Mom grabbed the broom and started chasing me! I was running and laughing at the same time. I slowed down not being able to run fast, because I was laughing so hard! Mom swung that broom! It broke in half from her hitting me in the back one time with it. She felt terrible, and beat herself up over it saying she wasn't a good mother. I was laughing, and I am still laughing over it!"

I must say that story of Val's sounds a lot like the story of a little girl, a sunflower, and a rooster! I admit I laughed the entire time he shared it with me. My six children tease me about how I spanked them with a wooden spoon, breaking a few on their bottoms! I must explain that I am a whopping 115 pounds, and my boys were taller than me in middle school. I told Val that my youngest boy, found a T-shirt for sale online. Cassidy said he was going to get all his siblings one for Christmas. It has a picture of a wooden spoon and the writing on the shirt reads, *Wooden Spoon Survivor*. I have no idea where my boy found it, but he did. He showed it to me, and I just cracked up! I told Val the next time he sees his mom he needs to be wearing a T-shirt that has a picture of a broken broom on it that reads, *Broom Survivor*. We laughed and laughed!

"On Christmas Eve, dad and mom would tie our doors together. This was to prevent us kids from getting out to invade the presents once mom and dad went to bed. We needed a plan! The boys were no help, but Trish and I thought things through. I had taken a butcher knife so I could cut the rope. I used the old pillow trick. Strategically placing the pillows to look like me under the blankets, then making my escape! Mom and dad looked to see if all of us kids were in bed around 1:00 a.m. after they had a Christmas party at the house. My pillow placing didn't fool them, and of course, I wasn't there.

I had snuck into their bedroom and fallen asleep under their bed. They panicked and called neighbors. Both went out in the neighborhood looking for me. They finally found me and put me safely back in my own bed.

The next morning, Christmas morning, mom and dad were still sleeping. Trish and I got up without waking them. We snuck to our toys. I found my BB gun and she found her dolls! Once our mission was accomplished, we went and woke up the boys. They woke up mom and dad. Trish and I already knew what Santa had brought us!

Every Saturday morning we all got up and got ready for Sunday. My job was to polish everyone's shoes. Food was prepared, cars washed, clothes ready. Once chores were finished, mom used to let me take my BB gun and be with my friends for the rest of the day. Once in a while, mom would give us fifteen cents. Trish and I would walk the eight or nine blocks down State Street to go to the A & W, where root beers were five cents each. I could drink three by myself! Times were very different then. We were still living in Orem, when Trish and I were in grade school. I was in about the fourth grade, about nine or ten. We would walk to school together. Sometimes someone would say something to her that I didn't approve of. I got in lots of fights!

Our years in Germany were fun years spent as a family. We went all over Europe and Holland. We were able to see so many things. I will never forget one of the most memorable experiences I had while we were there. This experience greatly impacted my heart and my life. Hitler's concentration camps had barely been opened for public viewing in Germany. We went to one of the camps. It was shocking to me. They were not yet sanitized. The barbed wire was there.

We went into the rooms where Hitler's army filtered in the unaware Jewish people, telling them they were going to have a shower. Then the cyanide bomb would be dropped in. Some of those poor souls were still alive as the bodies were shoveled out. Those who were still alive were thrown into the furnaces to be burned with the rest of the bodies. I saw the pile of bones with my own eyes.

There was another incident that happened in my youth that influenced me and played a part in me becoming the man I am today. Dad was teaching at Brigham Young University. I knew that dad and mom were struggling financially to care for our family. We all went out one night to get hamburgers. I remember all of my younger siblings saying, 'I want this! I want this! I want this!' I was thinking to myself, 'This isn't right. Dad and Mom can't afford this.' When it came to my turn to put my order in, I said I just wanted fries. Mom came to me later and asked why I had only ordered fries. I explained to her that I thought the other kids were being greedy and that I didn't want to burden her or dad. She wasn't happy with me. She proceeded to tell me that she never wanted me to feel that way again.

When I was eighteen or nineteen, I came home late from a date one night. My mom was sitting there waiting for me. I asked her what she was doing. Her response was that she wanted to make sure I was safe. I fully admit I could be stubborn and defiant at times, and when dad was mad at me he would let me know. In no uncertain terms, he would let me know. I vividly remember the day I was standing on the train leaving for my mission. Dad came up to me and said, "You know, Val, I would really be honored if you would change your name to Huish." I told him that I had been going by Toland for so long that I was going to continue with the Toland name.

Trish was the one that held us all together. I'd call her up and say, 'Trish you've got three brothers, so you have to take care of all the holidays.' Trish's daughter, Thera, is just like her mother. She was about eleven years old when she came to live with me. I would go up behind her and swear it was Trish! Trish always stood on one leg in the kitchen, figure eight. Thera is totally oblivious to things, just like her mom. We'd tell her a joke, and ten minutes later she would start laughing, because she finally got it. When Trish was about sixteen or seventeen, she was the best organizer. Mom was the motivator, and Trish kept track of everything. It was all done by hand back then. There wasn't the electronics we have today. Mom and Trish always complimented each other. Little Thera is the success secret to the company she works for. They crashed in '08 or '09. The company let go of pretty much everyone else, but not her. She has a lot of both her mother and grandmother in her.

Rick was flat out talent and definitely the funniest of all of us kids. He'd ask for something and impersonate Sammy the Snake to get mom to laugh. "Can I borrow the car?" Yep, he knew how to work her that's for sure. He had a beautiful voice! He was so talented. He was in the play *The King and I*. Every time mom and dad would hear the music from it, they would just tear up.

Rick would call the radio show and he would be Bullwinkle. He'd have everyone laughing, even the radio announcer! Rick could walk into a place, get a job, and in two weeks he was in positions of leadership. He had so much going for him. But, addictions took over Rick and eventually took his life.

Diana and I were staying at dad and mom's house, because they were traveling. The police came to the door. They asked if Rick was there. I answered, "Yes, he's upstairs." The police proceeded upstairs, cuffed him, and arrested him. When mom and dad got home they made right all the bad checks Rick had written. (It wasn't a small amount.) It was a lot of money back then. Around 1973, Rick was causing lots of stress with our folks. I wrote him a letter telling him that if he didn't stop, he was going to have to face me! Rick took the letter to dad and mom and they called me and scolded me. Things continued to spiral downward with Rick.

Bob is the peacemaker, lover. Out of all of us boys, the most caring and understanding one has always been Bob. We worked together for twenty-eight years. I started my business in 1979, and he joined me three to four years later. He showed up at my door and had a girl with him. He said, "This is Arleen." I put them up in a condo. He ended up going to build the business in Napa, California. We got together once or twice a week, and we would have a hotdog. We spent so many hours together. We would have a hotdog at Sam's Club, or go to Arby's.

I am the type of person who has no problem getting into a fight. If we were having a confrontation with customers, I would write letters to the customers. Bob would proofread them. He would tell me that I had written a very challenging letter. He let me know that when he wrote letters, he would always think of how he would feel if he were the customer reading the letter. He kept me in check. I miss him terribly. I miss our time together. Sometimes, I'll go sit down and eat a hotdog and just talk to him. I know he can hear me."

Messages from Val's Children:

Cy

Father is a wonderful title. Throughout my life, my father has meant many things to me. When I was a child he was safety and fun in a new great big world. As I grew, he added direction and motivation to my life. When I was a teenager my father was a source of security, prosperity and success. Eventually becoming a father myself my father became a source of inspiration, comfort, reassurance, strength, affirmation. He is a wise counselor. Today I understand the challenges he faced as a husband and father, which helps me to appreciate him even more. My father is a hero, a coach and a captain who I know is always on my side. He believes in me. I am grateful for the man he is and for the man he continues to help me to become.
Cy Toland

Lisa

There is no man more generous than my father. This used to make me angry and protective. I felt so many took advantage and never returned what was due back to him. As I grew older I learned the sheer joy in giving, because of his example. My Dad is strong, determined, disciplined (except when it comes to sugar, of course), beyond hard working, loving, and tenderhearted (even though he pretends not to be).

I remember him reading stories where he would laugh so hard he couldn't finish them. Dad would come home late at night and whisper loving things to us when he didn't think we could hear. I loved stealing candy out of his briefcase during church. He loved the Ranchero. He loves spam, cooked spinach, tapioca, beef jerky, all things lemon flavored, and German chocolate cake.

Now that I'm older, he is my *go-to* for sound wisdom and advice. I am deeply grateful for his love that he has for all of us, especially his love for Jax. I admire my Dad. I'm so grateful he is who he is, and that I am blessed to be his daughter. I am who I am because of my Dad.
Lisa

Shane

I never really felt that I understood my father while I was young. He was always doing everything he knew how to do, in order to provide the best life he could for his family. But, that is something that takes age to understand. Now that I am an adult I recognize all he did. I can also recognize that Dad was always showing us who to be. He is a man who truly practices things like:

* Giving without acknowledgement.
* Helping those in need.
* Loving those in your life in whatever ways you can.

I am proud of my father. I am proud of the man he is. I hope that someday I can make a positive difference in as many lives as he has.
Shane Toland

Lee

Val Toland has been the Atlas of his world, in a good way, for as long as I can remember. He is always willing to take on more burdens if it means he can help those people that he loves and cares about. My father gives to a fault, is willing to serve, and enjoys teaching values as well as life lessons and skills that he feels are important. My father has lived excellent examples of what it means to be both a provider and a protector. My life is better because of his presence. I can only hope to one day be as much of a positive part of the lives of those I care for, as he has been to all of us.
Lee

Daniel

I read something by an unknown author that has had true meaning for me because of my dad.
A stepparent is so much more than just a parent.
They made the choice to love when they didn't have to.

Because of my past track record of families, I had my concerns and doubts coming into the family. Dad didn't give me an opportunity to dwell on anything negative. He has shown and given me more love and respect than I could have ever asked for. I am so grateful that I have this man in my life. I could not be more proud than I am to call him my Dad. I love him more than words can express.
Thank you Val for being my Dad. I love you!!!
Danielle

Thera (Trish's daughter)

Val is a very special man who became my father after my mother, Trish, was murdered. He is the provider for all of us, and the hardest working person I know. My dad taught me the importance of hard work. He is very generous, kind and caring under his sometimes-tough exterior. Dad opens his home, and all that he has, to anyone in need. He is insightful and intelligent. He excels at anything he puts his mind to. He is reliable, responsible and is always there for all of us whenever we need him.

Thanks Dad for everything.
Love you,
Thera

Hayden (Trish's son)

I have only ever needed one word to sum up my father: honor. I didn't appreciate that when I was younger. But, after going out into the world I have realized what a rare thing having a father with honor has truly become. Be it his family, his business, or in his personal dealings, doing the right thing has always been his way. No matter where I go, or what I do in this life, I will always be able to say, "I come from good stock!"
Hayden

~Chapter Seven~

Trish - Spirited

"I will never forget the thrill I felt when my little girl was born!"

The relationship between a loving mother and a cherished daughter is a very special one indeed. The two, more often than not, become best friends. It is both Thera's and my personal belief, that in the pre-existing life we were all a marvelous family! It completely makes sense that those we are the closest to here on the earth, are the ones we were the closest to in our heavenly home before we were born. How wonderful it is that those heavenly connections continue here carrying on into our forevers. What a gift! On the fifth day of June 1948, Thera's one and only daughter was born.

Trish's resemblance to her mother could have had them be twins to most people were it not for their difference in age. I am an only daughter, as was Trish, and I share such a sweet bond with my father and my mother. In the hours and hours of research for this book and in my writing of this book, I have felt Trish's profound love for her mother and her entire family. Thera's love for her daughter has always been, and continues to be, evident.

Thera would always put Trish to bed on her tummy, in a tiny cradle, with a pillow. At that time in history, the knowledge of how dangerous suffocation (SIDS) is for babies while lying on their stomachs was not yet known.

"One day Sister May came over for a visit. She picked up my baby girl. Trish was limp. She almost died. I was very afraid when I nearly lost her as a little baby. Looking back on that incident, I am so humble for the time that I had with Trish those years before she was taken from me."

Trish didn't like having a different last name from her dad and mom, so she made the decision to become a Huish when school started for her. Val, Rick, Bob and Nick would express that they could tell who their mother's favorite was.

"I must admit Trish was the little princess, loved immensely by her father and all of her brothers. She was my only girl, and she was my best friend. It wasn't that Trish was my favorite, it was just that we had a special spiritual connection between us."

Trish had inherited many of Dorian's traits, just like Val.

"My daughter's attitude was, 'I'm going to do it my way, and nobody is going to tell me what to do.'"

When the Huish family got home from Okinawa, Trish felt as though she didn't belong. The girls at both school and church were established with certain friends. Trish wasn't part of their groups and she was left out. At the first opportunity presented to her, she decided she wanted to go to college. She hadn't graduated high school yet, but was very close to graduating. She got into Brigham Young University. Sterling and Thera thought that she would find the right way by going to college there. After she had left for school in Provo, they called to get in touch with their daughter. Her roommate told them that Trish had met a man and a woman, and after meeting, had left for California where they were from. Val was on his mission in California at the time. Because of how close Val and Trish had always been and were, Sterling and Thera didn't want to worry him by letting him know what was going on with his sister.

Trish had left her family, the friends she had made, and the life she knew. No one had a clue where in California she was, or if she was even in California at all. At that time, Thera and Sterling were ready to take Nick to New York on a business and pleasure trip. The police were involved. After about three days, three very long days for her parents, enough information had been gathered to know where Trish was. Facts were gathered about the couple she had left with. They had been around the BYU campus persuading college kids to go with them. Trish had found her way into a hippie colony in California.

Once found, Trish made it clear she was going to stay there. She was sewing dresses for the women in the hippie colony. Sterling and Thera sent the police to get their daughter, but Trish was eighteen. She was considered an adult, so the police said there was nothing they could do. Sterling and Thera knew where their daughter was, but both were helpless in getting Trish to leave her newfound community. They decided not to cancel their already planned trip, and to go to New York with Nick. At least they knew she was alive and okay living somewhere in the Los Angeles area.

After they returned from New York, their immediate focus was on ways they could get their daughter back to BYU. Trish was determined that she wanted to stay in California. Once Trish's mind was made up, it was almost impossible to change it. Thera's brother, Denny, said Trish could live with him in San Francisco.

"Sterling and I explained to Trish that we needed to know she would be safe. She did listen and moved to the San Francisco area where she found a job working for a bank. Trish ended up working for an ice cream company as the company's head accountant. She would go to seven or eight stores and take care of the books. She quickly became a valuable asset to the company. My granddaughter, Thera, is the same way, a genius with figures!"

Trish had been in San Francisco for around eight months. During which time, Thera was slowly trying to weave her way back into her daughter's life. Trish's parents convinced her to come for a little vacation. She agreed and they flew her home. When she arrived, she announced that she was married. Both Sterling and Thera were shocked! Trish said how wonderful he was adding that she could only be home for a few days.

She had moved from Thera's brother's place into an apartment. She had a nice job at the ice cream company. And, her husband was footloose and fancy-free. Trish had bought a little car. She was a hard worker just like her grandparents, parents, and big brother.

"All my kids are hard workers. I flew out there and said, 'Trish is this how you want you live?' Her husband had bought a motorcycle, and was doing his own thing on the money Trish earned from her amazing work ethic. As fast as Trish made money, he spent it. Trish assured me it would be okay."

Shortly after Thera's visit to California, Trish realized that she in fact couldn't live that way. More importantly, she realized through her mother's counsel that she didn't have to. She let her parents know that she had divorced him. Both Sterling and Thera were thankful that Trish hadn't had any children with her first husband. Trish was about twenty at that time, and was married to him for probably less that a year. She then moved in with a girl named Jeanie who had a guy friend who swept Trish off her feet. He sent her flowers and poetry. She fell madly in love with him telling Thera how great he was. After the nightmare they had just been through with Trish, this young man seemed quite stable to Sterling and Thera. He had a job, and appeared to really love their daughter.

He and Trish decided to get married. Sterling and Thera went to San Francisco for the wedding of their only daughter. Thera bought Trish a pink dress, and a hat to match. A woman played the harp and Sterling sang an amazing song. The two were married at a little church. Not many people came. The church was in Cameron Bay. The view from the church looked out to the ocean. Trish was thrilled to have her parents there. Finally Thera and Sterling had Trish back in their lives, and Trish had let them back into hers. She loved her dad, mom and brothers!

Trish decided to go back to church. Once she had made her personal commitment to herself that she was going to have the gospel in her life, The Church of Jesus Christ of Latter-day Saints, she found the church in her area called a ward. She spoke to her Bishop and shared with him her story. Through sincere prayer, she asked for Heavenly Father to forgive her of the unwise choices she had made in the past that she felt were not in accordance to what she felt Heavenly Father had wanted her to do. She realized that by living certain guidelines she could truly live with inner peace. Trish understood that this life is not a perfect place. However, viewing this life in an eternal perspective brought her not only a sweet inner peace, but also a deep-rooted joy. Trish knew that through her own humble efforts, combined with the infinite atonement of our Redeemer Jesus Christ, she was forgiven of all in her past that she felt she needed forgiveness for. It was important to Trish that she started her life over fresh from that point on, with a completely clean slate. Never again was Trish without the joy the Gospel brought to her heart!

The man she married soon joined her and was baptized a member of the Church. He wanted Sterling to give him the priesthood. The priesthood is a gift from God, our Father. The priesthood is the power of God on the earth. Those that worthily hold it have the authority, through Jesus Christ, to bless those who are ill or in need of strength and comfort. They are also able to do wonderful things to serve their families and those around them. Sterling, being the father he was, drove to San Francisco to ordain his new son-in-law with the Priesthood of God. Trish was so happy!

It was at that time that Thera had been hired to be the national sales manager for the Figurette Bra Company. In August of 1976, while Sterling was in San Francisco for Trish, Nick and Thera loaded the moving truck and moved everything to Arizona. Nick was going into his senior year of high school. After Sterling finished in California, he joined his wife and son in Arizona where they settled. Thera's husband had retired from the military after honorably serving the United States of America for twenty years. Sterling retired as a Major.

Sterling and Thera's third child, Rick, was working job after job. None lasted long. His life was one of succumbing to the devastating affects of substance addictions causing him to live in and out of jail. His choices created a life of despair and anguish not just for himself, but also for his family. Thera and Sterling, as Rick's parents, felt heartache from their son's choices.

Trish and Thera went to the mountains to attend a seminar for the bra company. The connection between mother and daughter became rekindled on that trip, never again to be strained. Trish joined the Figurette Company with her mom. Trish was selling bras up in San Francisco. Before the move to Arizona, Thera would go to San Francisco from Salt Lake City to spend time with Trish. Once Thera got to Arizona, Trish had created quite a business for herself selling bras, girdles and nightwear. The Figurette Company Thera was working for sold out. Thera then decided to go to work for Snelling and Snelling Employment. She called businesses and found jobs for people fitting their specific qualifications, while getting paid for it. She really learned how to use the phone and she was good at it! Thera was a headhunter for large companies.

Trish and her husband found out that the Profit By Air Company he worked for had an opening in Phoenix. They decided he would take the position, transferring to Phoenix, in order to live closer to family. Val was married and had his pool business in Clayton, California. Rick continued to struggle with his disease, while married with three amazing sons. The marriage didn't last and ended in divorce. He also lived in Arizona. Bob had moved with his family to Arizona starting to work in the airfreight business where Trish's husband worked. Nick was still in high school living at home.

Thera was making lots of money for the employment company she was working for. After Trish came down to Arizona to settle, Thera and Trish made the decision to open their own employment agency together. They became business partners and were very successful! Their clients would pay them once Thera and Trish found a job for them. They had nice offices and worked extremely well together. Thera and Trish complimented each other, not only as mother and daughter, but also as business partners and best friends.

Trish and the man she was married to were sealed in the temple. Beautiful Trish continues with her precious three children, to have the phenomenal blessings that are bestowed upon families when they are sealed eternally in the holy temple. Thera, Hayden and Martha are all sealed to their angel mother, and to each other forever. The one who took Trish's life forfeited every one of his temple blessings, and his right to ever dwell in the glorious heavenly home awaiting those who live good lives upon this earth.

At the time they were sealed, they had no children as of yet. Trish went through a lot of fertility options. She was finally successfully artificially inseminated. Trish was ecstatic when she found out that she was expecting! The doctor's office called her while she and Thera were working together at their employment agency.

"Trish got the call and screamed! She cried and cried and said, 'Oh, my gosh, I am going to have a baby!' She called everyone to share her happy news! She called all her siblings, her grandmother Doran, and others. Trish would just cry for days, because she was so happy. My daughter had a good pregnancy giving birth to her own beautiful healthy daughter."

Thera was there for her daughter through the pregnancy.

"When Trish's baby was born, I was standing outside the waiting room. When I saw my daughter, Trish was holding her beautiful little baby and said, "Mom I want you to meet your new granddaughter, Thera Catherine."

Thera's heart was overjoyed for her daughter who was now a mother! How very special for her that Trish, who Thera wanted to name Thera at her birth, gave her own daughter her mother's name to carry on. As Val shared earlier, Thera Catherine has so much of both her mother and grandmother in her. What a blessing for young Thera to be the perfect mixture of two such amazing women.

"Trish was inseparable from her baby. Trish took her everywhere! Little Thera went anywhere her mother went. She had a cradle at work for her. Trish was taking voice lessons; she was always singing. Thera would sing and sing with her mother, and was an adorable baby! Trish had singing parts in Les Miserable and The Sound of Music for the Gilbert

66

Community Theater. Thera has a beautiful voice just like her mother. I hope someday my granddaughter will take voice lessons and do something with her voice. Thera Catherine became the center of her mother's world!"

After Thera was born, the decision to adopt was made. Going to an attorney friend, the call came a couple of months later informing Trish she had a little boy! This adorable little guy was named Hayden Sterling. The year was 1984. Trish was thrilled! Once the call came in, mother and grandmother had only one day to go out and get everything for Trish's new baby boy.

"We always had children around. By the time Trish got Hayden, we were working out of Trish's home. Trish got Hayden when he was just two days old. What a cute kid he was! He still is. He had a very sensitive stomach, and would throw up just about everything. _He has fought through wars, and has a wonderful sense of humor. He is an incredible young man. Serving our Country in the Army, Hayden has served in Afghanistan, Iraq and Korea. Trish adored her son! I am proud of Hayden and the good man he is today."

On television, they used to have a segment called Wednesday's child. It was a preview of a child in need of a home, and a family. During the segment, the narrator would introduce the child to the public in order to see if they could find a home for the child. Marsha was a Wednesday's child. Marsha wanted a family who were members of the church. She had been in fourteen families over the course of her young life.

Trish shared with her mother that her goal was to provide Marsha with a family, a secure home, and with a mother who would love her always. Thera agreed. She would do all in her power to create that for Marsha as well. Trish wanted to have a special relationship with both of her daughters. Marsha was a teenager when she entered Trish's world. Trish had a beautiful room ready for her new daughter. Marsha had everything she needed. Most importantly Marsha had Trish, Thera Catherine, Hayden, Sterling, and Thera They all loved her, along with the rest of the Huish clan.

Marsha was a typical teenager. She made lots of friends. She had gained a lot of knowledge from her experiences of living in her prior homes, some positive some negative. She was a good student. Trish watched her carefully, and was there for her children. She was a wonderful mother to Marsha not because she had to be, but because she genuinely loved her daughter. Trish adopted Marsha after the required time in order to do so. Once Marsha was legally adopted, Hayden and Marsha were sealed to their family eternally. Trish is the mother of these three choice souls forever, and they are Trish's cherished children for eternity. Marsha had only been with Trish a couple of years before her mother was cruelly taken from her. Trish was an amazing mother to all three of her children. They were her world!

"I knew Trish's thoughts; she knew mine. I always knew when my daughter needed me from the time she was my little girl. Trish loved to go to her father's performances and we would all enjoy those times so much! Had she not went on that fateful trip, on the night her father performed in the barbershop choir, my Trish would have been sitting with me. As I sat there, I thought of her and said a prayer that she was safe."

Memories of Trish from Nick

"As a young adult Trish chose to take a path to California, and that path greatly concerned Mom. California Dreamin' had all the allure a young woman needed who wanted to let her hair further down. Trish wanted to be in the middle of the 1960's movement. I'm sure no one thought that what happened in the '60s would have the generational impact that it had. The Mama's and the Papa's, Simon and Garfunkel, Iron Butterfly, the Beatles are just a few on the list of incredible music from that era and the list goes on and on. One can only imagine what the time vessels buried during that decade held in them! Trish was lured, hooked and landed in California leaving everything and everyone behind to search for whatever it was she was searching for. It seems to me while in California she was where she needed to be, because she was where she wanted to be.

Trish wanted to be in that moment of time in history. She wanted to be a part of something she felt was bigger than her. She was in it for the long-term and not a quick ride. Trish was like that though. She was fully committed in her decisions and defiant to any who opposed her. I found that out about her later in life. If my sister had set her mind to doing something, there was no derailing her. Trish was determined to see whatever it was through to the end, period. As it turned out, Trish eventually discovered the way of life she thought she needed was still back at home waiting for her, and had been all along.

Mom never gave up on her. She and Dad would take trips, as often as Trish would allow, to California to check on their only daughter making sure she was good. Good, however, was a matter of opinion. What was Trish's good might not reflect the same definition in Mom or Dad's mind. Still she was alive, healthy, employed, and making things happen for herself. It was a tough time for my sis in the beginning. I don't know all the details, but I do remember overhearing calls where there must have been tears involved, because Mom didn't come away from the calls whistlin' Dixie!

I had the good fortune of being the youngest. With that came the requirement of traveling with Mom and Dad on their trips to California to visit Trish. Bob and Rick stayed at home. They were big enough to stay home.

Back then I was a little miffed that I had to go, but now I'm so glad I went. It was great to see the Bay area with all its appeal. Trish, as I recall, was always in good spirits no matter what. It was far beyond her to admit defeat back then, and have to pack her bags and move home. She was making things happen in her life! Come hell or high water, Dad and Mom were going to be firsthand witnesses of her success. You'd think this is the story of Mom in her younger years, in a different decade!

Trish had a soft heart, with a determined mind. I recall being comforted by her more than once as a child. I watched her stand toe to toe with my older brothers. They would all back down from her, running for cover. My Dad used to tell a story about her when she was not more than five years old. He confirmed that her obstinacy wasn't something Trish learned. She was born with it! He told us about the times he used to pick up Mom, Val and Trish to go out for the evening. Trish was defiant and had to be in the middle of the front seat. Val would get in the backseat. Trish would stand, not sit, between Dad and Mom in that front seat. Back then bench seats were the standard front seats in all cars. A guy's girl could snuggle up to him while he drove down the road in his un-air conditioned car, with his arm hanging out the window. Trish would yell out, "Faster! Faster!" Dad would gun the car, and swerve just to try and knock her over. No matter what he did, within reason of course, she'd stand her ground laughing at Dad.

At the time Rick passed away in 1989, Mom and Trish had a very successful business. They were known as TNT - Thera and Trish. Both the ladies in my life were like two peas in a pod, Frick and Frack if you will! Mom and Trish walked, talked and laughed alike. They completed each other. It is great to look back and reflect on those times. I can still feel mom's happiness with life while she shared the grand adventures of a successful business with her daughter.

Trish was an individualistic woman. To be frank, my big sister had a mind of her own! Just like Mom, she knew what in life was important. She also knew what her personal limits were in order to attain her goals. Trish was so smart. Today I fully believe that the *dumb blond* exterior she portrayed at times was only a front. She was crazy like a fox. I believe to some extent that the men in her life were intrigued by her independence, but at the same time very intimidated by her strengths. Both of her husbands were superficially strong on the exterior. Neither were any competition for her internal drive, authenticity, determination and any other positive adjective one could come up with! These men had no idea what they were in for. In the end both never had the stamina to survive her. They did what they could to build themselves up by abusing Trish in the forms of verbal and physical anger towards her.

Trish finally left her first husband after he had physically abused her. She left him and proudly never looked back. In the end, no matter how you look at it, she unfortunately met her second husband. He was a man full of so many stories lacking facts to back them up. He was a flamboyant coveter of the BIG life. Trish tragically trusted him, and married him beginning a new chapter in her life as his wife. My sister's husband was an uncanny perpetrator of the worst kind. His life was too full of sick demented actions to go into here. Needless to say the day my amazing big sister met him, her days were numbered.

Trish and I lived in the same town that Mom and Dad lived in, so many of the holidays and family events took place with all of us gathering at her home. We had plentiful dinners and get-togethers filled with, what seemed like, genuine joy and happiness. Trish and I had great times teasing each other. These times always seemed to come about just as we were cleaning up after enjoying a large meal. The sink was the place that most of the family avoided not because of the work, but because of the activity that always inevitably broke out.

Now mind you, this is my side of the story. It's the side that I know to be true. Well in my mind anyhow! Trish would find the opportunity to splash water from the faucet aiming it at me. I would *always* reciprocate the splash. Soon, those two splashes turned into a full-blown water fight right in the middle of the kitchen! In many cases the water turned into food, and an all out war followed. Usually the war's weapons were whipping cream and pie! What started out as a simple little flick of water ended up turning into an all out assault on, not only each other, but on the entire kitchen! I can't say that there was ever an individual winner. What was the end result? Trish and I had an immense amount of fun, made a huge mess and the entire family enjoyed the show. I can tell you as I write this for my mother's book I truly and deeply miss those times. Trish, I miss you. I miss your courageous smile, and indelible light."

Messages from Trish's Children

Trish's daughter Marsha

Trish was a beautiful woman who thought of everyone else before herself. She was always in the service of others; the one person anyone and everyone could count on. I did not grow up with her, but I wish that I had. She adopted me. I was fourteen years old when I was placed in her home and I thought that I had died and gone to heaven. I finally had a mother who I loved very much, a mother who loved me back just as much. I had a little brother and sister as well.

I could not have asked for a better mother. She and I got along for the most part. What do you expect from a teenager? Of course we were going to have our differences. But in spite of them, I knew I was loved in every way possible. I learned so much from her in the very short time that I had with her. I learned that I too could be a strong, loving and understanding woman.

70

She was such an example to everyone she came in contact with whether in business, personal or spiritual.

My mom was dedicated to her family in every aspect of her life. I saw the way she loved Thera and Hayden. They knew that she loved them without a doubt. We were not spoiled, but we did not go without. She made sure that we worked for what we had. She traveled a lot for work. We got to go with her sometimes on her business trips. I got to enjoy some pretty cool places and I have wonderful memories of those trips. Even on vacations Mom made sure we were learning. I remember one year we went to Hawaii. While we were there she was teaching us about the different plants that were there. All I could think about was when were we going back to the beach?

The day before she was killed we were planning a trip, just for the two of us. I was so excited for that! I had never had a mother, let alone one that would want to take a trip with just me. I could not think of anything else for the rest of the evening while we were in town at the street market area. I was trying to think of a place that would be fun for us to go to. I had dreams about it that night.

Her voice, oh that voice! She sounded so beautiful when she sang. I did not care for the voice practicing while the windows were down in the car. Everyone around could hear her voice exercises! The way that Mom was with Thera and Hayden was so awesome and loving. She was the perfect example of how a mother could love all of her children the same. I say that because Hayden was adopted too. But the way that she interacted with them, no one would have ever known. After she was murdered my little sister and brother went to go live with Val, my uncle. I have some amazing aunts and uncles! They have been such great examples for each of us. They have loved us all so much.

I am so grateful for her being my mother and for her adopting me into this family. The outcome was not one anyone would want, but nonetheless I have become a better woman because of it all. There is not a day that goes by that I don't think of my mom and miss her. I see things and think of how she would be so happy if she was still here with us. I know she would be happy with Hayden and Thera. I would have loved to have her there with me at my wedding. That is a dream that most every girl has, to have her mother next to her on her wedding day. I was no different, and dreamed of my mother helping me on my wedding day. I wish that she could still be here for so many things for the three of us. The one thing that hurts so much is that the children in our family will not grow up knowing their Grandma Trish in person.
Marsha

Trish's daughter Thera

The thing I remember most about my mother was her contagious, warm and sincere smile. She had a smile that cheered everyone up and made

71

people want to always be around her. Mom had a great positive spirit. She loved deeply. Everyone who knew her loved her. My mother's memory lives on with those she made an impact upon. She instilled within me a great sense of wonder and achievement. My mom taught me discipline and the value of hard work from a young age. I am so grateful she was my mom, even if it was just for a short time here. I look forward to the day when I will see my mother again.
Thera

From Val's daughter Lisa:

Aunt Trish always made my dad laugh. She was Grandma's best friend. She was pretty, fun, and kind. She was unique, loving, a good mom and someone we all enjoyed being around. I always felt a kinship with her, because I too had all brothers. And, although they torment me, I know they would do anything for me. I wish I could have had more time with My Aunt Trish... We all wish that.
Lisa

~Chapter Eight~

Rick - Potential

The family's years of Military life led them to Washington D.C., where Sterling attended Georgetown University studying Psychological Warfare Training. While he was attending college in Washington, Thera was pregnant with their third child. She stayed in Utah with Val and Trish during the pregnancy. Thera had been alone delivering her first two babies. With Sterling gone Thera was once again alone. She delivered Richard Mark Huish (Rick) at Hill Air Force Base on February 9th, 1952. Rick was perfect! Thera and Sterling were both elated to add this precious new little guy to their growing family, so was Val and Trish.

"As Rick's mother, I knew how wonderful Rick was! He had incredible gifts, talents and potential. Rick was extremely smart and funny growing up. School came easy for him. He was a good student involved in many activities. He was a natural actor and landed many parts in the school plays. Rick was liked by everyone because of his charismatic personality."

Memories of Rick from Nick

"My earliest memories of Rick are when I was about six or seven. I'm not really sure of exactly when, but they seem to be in my mind from the time I was a very young boy. We were living in Bountiful, Utah in a yellow brick home on 3500 South. Rick, Bob and I all slept in the same room in the basement of the house.

Rick was very much involved in his high school. He seemed to have many, many friends as he was always out doing things with them. He had the lead roles in most of the plays. I remember him performing *The King and I*, and *My Fair Lady*. To me, at my young age, watching my big brother on stage singing while playing different characters made him a star!

During the times he spent at home, Rick was diligent in trying to make everybody in the family laugh. He had a list of jokes that were never ending! He used to come home at night later than the designated time dad and mom had set for him. Whenever Rick got home after his curfew, he would stand at the foot of mom and dad's bed telling them jokes or doing acts from different TV shows. He knew if he could get mom to laugh he wouldn't get in trouble for being late. He would start off with his array of acts and even though mom tried not to, she always gave in and laughed so hard. The harder she'd laugh, the madder dad got! Rick didn't stop his act until dad finally couldn't hold it in any longer, and also gave in with laughter. They would send Rick to bed without any punishment for his late arrival.

Rick would do things that just seemed to catch the attention of every family member. The yard was multi-tiered with three levels. Two large apple trees grew on either side of the top level, the middle level was grass, and the lower level was the level of our home. Dad was over in Vietnam at the time. I think Val was on his mission, and Trish was already living in California when

Rick and I were in the backyard playing catch. I had gotten a new baseball glove. I remember very vividly this backyard game of catch.

The sun had set. Rick was trying to teach me how to catch a ball, because I was just starting a Little League team. At one point he decided to teach me how to catch a fastball. He'd been throwing me pop-ups. I moved my glove just a smidgen to see him wind up. I had moved it just enough, so that when the fastball came in it hit me square in my uncovered left eye instead of my new glove! The pain was excruciating. The pain, along with the look on Rick's face, told me the whole story. From the combination of the two, I knew the story wasn't good. I never blamed my big brother for the unfortunate event, but I admit it took me awhile to get back to playing catch.

There are so many events that took place during that time in my life. The most memorable ones seem to come with pain. One day, mom sat me down to tell me that Rick was in the hospital. My big brother had fallen out of the back of a pick up truck suffering a severe injury to his head. It happened when Rick and his friends were leaving the community swimming pool. He and a couple of his buddies jumped in the back of the pick-up truck sitting on the lowered tailgate. While leaving the parking lot, Rick and his friends sitting in the back of the truck were dragging their feet off of the back end of the tailgate. The truck hit a bump that Rick's feet caught on. Unable to maintain his balance, he fell off the tailgate rolling over striking his head against the pavement in front of the swimming pool parking lot.

Mom told me what happened, and that dad was on his way home from Vietnam. She said that we were going to be able to go down and see Rick in the hospital. Because of my age, I wasn't able to spend much time with him. His condition was critical. When I was able to see him, he was laying in the hospital bed with his eyes shut. I didn't understand the magnitude of what had just happened.

Mom and dad would go to the hospital daily. Mom spent many, many hours at Rick's bedside. She would come home with incredible stories about Rick waking up and doing all kinds of different things. As a matter fact, he would wake up speaking Spanish so rapidly, that dad and mom ended up bringing Rick's Spanish teacher into the hospital to translate what Rick was saying. Interestingly enough, my brother was only in his first year of Spanish!

Through the process of the brain concussion, Rick lost his sense of smell and taste. Because of this, it was great fun to pull pranks on him! We knew that he couldn't taste some of the things we were feeding him, although I think sometimes he knew exactly what he was eating. Regardless, he was a good sport going along with what we were doing just so he could watch us laugh. Rick had an incredible sense of humor.

Like dad, Rick was a great lover of music. I recall that we had just moved to a home on the top of the hill, and we three boys all got our own rooms. I think it was an adjustment for each one of us, like one having separation anxiety. We loved having our own space, but as much as we loved it we all missed being together. Rick had a record player in his bedroom and he seemed to always have music playing. I think my love for smooth jazz, along with various sorts of other genres of music, came from listening to the music he would play. He listened to such a variety of music it was difficult to keep up with his favorites. I know he enjoyed the music of Blood Sweat and Tears, Herbie Hancock, Iron Butterfly, The Beatles, The Doors, Jimi Hendrix, Led Zeppelin and so many others. I used to watch Rick turn on the music and sing so passionately, that I could see the blood vessels in his neck bulging!

Rick definitely was the brain of our family. He knew so many of the answers to the questions that were asked on the TV game shows. It seemed like he had the answer to just about every question that was ever asked. As Rick got older, he started to work at a car dealership. Rick got me my first job at that dealership. My brother, the comedian, would call into the radio station. He became a regular on the show, talking like Bullwinkle and making everyone laugh. I remember watching him call into the radio station one day. He was engaging with the disc jockey in his Bullwinkle voice. Rick started off with a joke by asking the DJ, "Do you know why all Johnny Carson's pencils are red?" The DJ laughed and responded with a no. Ricks reply was; "They're all embarrassed!" His jokes were endless. Everyone at the dealership where we worked laughed so hard as they listened to Rick's Bullwinkle voice come over the radio.

Rick's life changed because of the brain injury he suffered, or at least that's what we'd like to think. My big brother seemed to go to a different place after the concussion. It almost felt like he was struggling to deal with normality. He became seemingly bored with life submitting to temptations, which took over him. There was never enough for Rick. He wanted to live life to the fullest!

I carry within me so many different memories of him. He changed as we grew. We all grow in different ways, but Rick's growth became complicated and very compounded. It was as if he had an additional weight he carried on his shoulders. A weight that was much greater to him than those the rest of us had.

His three boys are the good that came amid all the bad. We were fortunate that Rick met Sonja while he worked at her father's car dealership. Sonja was pregnant at the time, and Rick loved her and the baby she carried unconditionally. At one point, those three boys were the center of Rick's life. Casey, Corey and Cobey have all grown into good men despite the travesties in their lives. I love them deeply and am thankful that they are a part of our family.
Nick"

"As Rick's mother, I had such high hopes for my son's future. Then Rick became friends with a couple of young men who were going to college. They drank and were not a good influence. He decided he wanted to go to college and asked Sterling and I if he could go. I wanted him to finish high school."

With Rick's choice of friends drinking alcohol, Rick began to drink. Addictions took over his life very quickly, as Rick succumbed to the disease of alcoholism.

"I didn't see the signs. If someone would have told me the devastation alcohol could cause, I'm sure I would have been more aware and recognized the severity of my son's situation. I had never experienced alcohol, or it's effects. I honestly had no clue what was happening to my son."

He fell in love marrying a girl named Sonja. Rick did love his family. Rick and Sonja were eventually sealed in the temple. Casey and Corey were sealed to them also. Thera is humble that the sealing blessings extend to Cobey, even though sadly he never knew his father. None of the boys really knew their father. Thera knows that all things will work out as they should in the eternities, and that Heavenly Father knows what He is doing. This I know, she loves those three boys!

While married, Rick was an expert at living two completely separate existences, one with alcohol and one without. After Rick was married, he started not showing up for work. Money started missing from his place of employment. There was one time that Sonja called Thera terribly upset. She let Thera know that Rick had come home that night, but was hanging out of his car. The disease was taking over his life where once upon a time, for a short time, Rick was able to hide his addiction from those closest to him. But, it had come to the point where the dominance of his dependence upon destructive substances became evident to all those who loved him and cared about him. During Sonja's pregnancy with Cobey, their third son, she separated from Rick.

His disease possessed him, and he no longer functioned normally. Rick would lose one job, and move to another fully investing himself in his new job, for a time. Because of his personality and who Rick genuinely was, he would quickly move up in the company he worked for. Shortly after, he would once again surrender to his addictions, which knocked him right out of the position he had worked so hard to achieve. Rick's disease of alcoholism caused him to self-sabotage.

"To those suspicious of their child or a child close to them succumbing to the disease of alcohol or drug addiction, I would counsel that you absolutely have to be smarter than the alcoholic. The entire home environment changes dramatically for a family with a member that is an addict. The deceit is awful. It is a horrible and helpless way to live as a parent. Our energy and focus turned to literally saving our child's life. Doing this can easily become consuming for parents who have an alcoholic child. This must not happen when other children are involved,

for they too have needs. Having a son or daughter who becomes an addict is a living hell."

Rick's life spiraled out of control. His wife divorced him taking with her their children. He started working for a waterbed company where he was given a manager position. He stole from the company to feed his disease. With any job he had he would achieve a level of being trusted, then he would then take money, and disappear.

"At that time, I didn't want to hear from him. I know many can relate to the sleepless nights waiting to hear the doorbell, or the phone ring with the news that their loved one had been hurt, or had hurt someone else."

Rick knew that he had a family who loved him, and he loved them. He loved his children, but both physically and mentally he had lost the ability to function with love. Thera's treasured son was fixated on how, where and when he could feel the effects of the poison that would rapidly ravage his once healthy body, the poison that would eventually rob him of his very life.

Deception is a way of life for one habitually addicted. Rick would profess to his parents that if they would give him the money to move away from the people he drank with, that he would be okay. He wasn't okay. Where he lived made no difference. His lack of turning to God for strength left him powerless against the disease. Shortly after Sterling, Thera, and Nick moved from Utah to Arizona Rick moved there also. Rick's associations were with people who drank. He wrecked his parents' car. Things would go missing in their home. The end result of all their son's promises of positive change, who they loved so much, proved to be of not.

"We would notice little marks on the car after Rick would drive it. Then, dents appeared and the little dents became bigger and bigger. The car began to look like my son's life. It was a wreck. Rick was working one job after another. His life was a nightmare of being in and out of jail. He did so many good things, but his choices created a life of insecurities and heartaches."

Rick no longer lived at home. He was a wanted man by the police. One day Thera got a call from him and he told her he was working in Reno, Nevada. Thera stated that she admires the courage of any mother who could turn their child in to the authorities to help them.

"Sterling and I got a letter, and it was wonderful about how he had met a beautiful gal. The joy we felt was short-lived. Soon after, Rick went into a gun store robbing the store at gunpoint. The levels of alcohol in his blood were so high that a normal person would have died from alcohol poisoning. He was arrested, and taken to jail."

Being the father and mother that Sterling and Thera were, they hired an attorney to defend their son. The only way the attorney could get him out of jail was if Rick would go directly into a rehabilitation center. There were good times of joy when Thera and the family visited him, because he wasn't drinking. Rick was his happy self, and Thera caught a glimpse of her boy's potential once again. When he was released from the center, he had a girlfriend who was also an alcoholic. They got an apartment together, but the relationship was doomed from the beginning.

"I received a book that a friend gave to me titled 'The Way Back'. Quoting from the book, one mother said, 'I don't know what to do, I am going through hell.' 'Keep walking,' the other mother simply said"

The advice Thera reaped from that book became the foundation with which she used to continually move forward through each of the tragedies she had to bear. Rick went back to his self-destructive behaviors doing all the things he was doing before he went into rehab. A therapist explained to Sterling and Thera that as long as they allowed Rick to come home, swim in the pool, feed him, do his laundry and so many other things they were being nothing but enablers to their sons disease.

"We made the difficult decision that we would not allow Rick to come back into our home. We were no longer going to allow him to control our world depriving our lives of peace. We had bought another car for him and night after night we were in turmoil wondering if he would wreck the car. That counselor taught Sterling and I that we had to use tough love for our son, as well as for our own sanity."

Thera had become consumed with changing Rick. As a mother, she wanted him to do all the things that she thought were perfect for him. Through all the despair she and her family went through from Rick's actions, Thera concluded that the only thing she could do for her child was to turn him over to the Lord. She had reached the point where she knew she had to take a leap of faith by demonstrating tough love for her son. Thera missed living her life with peace. She knew that she had to take her own life back. She could no longer allow her son to rob her of her life, her peace.

"I waited up for him the night Sterling and I had made our decision. I had all his things together when he got home. From about two a.m. until around seven a.m. I had to stand my ground, though doing so was one of the hardest things I had ever done thus far in my life. I told Rick he had to leave our home. He responded that he had nowhere to go. My response was, 'I'm sorry about that. If you have money to drink, you have money to find a place to live.' We sent him on his way. I often find myself looking

back thinking about what we should have done differently. I honestly don't know if I could have done anything different. My son was very sick and he was the only one capable of making himself better."

Thera has struggled within herself for the inevitable choice she had to make those many years ago. At the time she had Rick leave, she thought she should feel shame for standing her ground. But, she didn't feel those feelings. Thera and Sterling's marriage was suffering. They had more children who needed them, and grandchildren who needed their grandparents. Rick was all consuming. The disease blinded him of the recurrent tsunami waves his actions buried his family in. He never returned home again.

"I prayed, and prayed, and prayed. I asked for all of those things that would take away free agency, the very thing those of us who followed Jesus Christ in the pre-existence fought for. I found myself making commitments to the Lord, commitments that I would live by if only He would change my son. In church, members are counseled to have:

1)   *Family prayer morning and evening*
2)   *Daily scripture study*
3)   *Family home evening one evening a week together, as a family, for activities or a spiritual lesson*

In doing these things heavenly blessings were promised to the obedient families. I strived to do all those things, but the blessings didn't come in the way I expected that they should. In heaven I fought, as did all who have received a mortal body, for free agency. Our right to choose good or evil was the plan of Jesus Christ and we followed Him in the pre-existing life. The desperation of my prayers as Rick's mother, were not in accordance to Heavenly Father's flawless design for us, His beloved children. Our loving Father heard every plea from me. Blessings came."

Rick met an amazing woman. He and Millie were married. He had been sober for about two years before their marriage. Sterling and Thera paid for their honeymoon, sending them on a cruise. They bought Rick a suit. Millie was a nurse and called to let them know that Rick was bleeding internally.

"I expressed to Millie that I didn't know how long Rick would live, but she didn't care. They really loved each other, and made each other happy. It had been years since Rick had been truly happy."

Message from one of Rick's Children

Rick's son Corey

80

Writing this has been in the forefront of my mind for the last few days. I have put a lot of thought into what to say. I must admit that thinking of writing about my father started to make me a little angry at first, because of the selfishness that he exhibited through his drinking. Once a man becomes a father, his child becomes his life, his priority. Negative attitudes and habits all must change for the good of the child. When a life is brought into this world, it is the job of the parents to make sure that the life they have created has the best chance of survival. We are no different than most any other animal with regards to parenting and protecting.

It does anger me that my father chose to make decisions that focused on him rather than us, his three sons. It also angers me when I think of my own boys and how much they mean to me, how much they have changed my life, how much they would have enjoyed meeting their grandfather and getting to know him, and how he would have benefited from knowing them as well. But then, I stop being angry. A sense of peace comes over me.

Yes, the choices he made affected me as I grew up. They shaped how I was raised. But, my father's choices have played a part in me being the man I am today. The things my father chose have led me down the path I am on. Had he not chosen the life he did, I don't know that my life would be the life I have now. If he had made the decision not to drink and to have a healthy marriage with my mother, things would be different. Maybe my life would have been better, maybe it wouldn't. Maybe I would be on the same path I now travel, maybe I wouldn't.

The point is, I don't blame my father for anything he did. His decisions keep me working to be the best father I can be for my sons. I don't want them to grow up in the same manner as I did. As they grow older, I want to be there for them. I want to be there for my grandchildren the way my Grandma Thera and Grandpa Sterling were there for me, and my brothers.

Perhaps the choices my father made are in some way an odd twist of fate. Perhaps somehow, he was meant to make the choices he did in order to shape me into the man I am. I'm not perfect by any means. I know I have my struggles. But, who knows whom or where I would be had he not lived the way he did.

I spent two years of my life with him. Those two years were some of the best years that I can remember. Maybe that short time was all I needed to make up for what I missed out on.
Corey

~Chapter Nine~

Bob - Peacemaker

Robin Smith Huish (Bob) was born in 1955 on April 22nd, in Wiesbaden, Germany where Sterling was stationed at that time.

"When Bob was born I went through yet another delivery on my own. I delivered him in a military hospital, and they wouldn't let Sterling in with me! My husband was waiting to see his wife and baby as soon as Bob was born, and that was special. Bob was a pleasant, happy baby. His personality from day one portrayed that life was wonderful! When he got his Patriarchal Blessing, which is a personal blessing through a worthy Priesthood holder in the Church, the Patriarch paused and didn't say anything for a time. Then he came up with a wonderful statement that truly epitomized my son; he called him a peacemaker. Bob never wanted anyone to be unhappy, that was one of the many things that were outstanding about him."

At the age of eight, Bob was baptized in the East China Sea in Okinawa, Japan. Bob always went the extra mile. Before he would leave a job, the job had to be completed, as well as meet his approval. As a youngster whenever he was given the chore of pulling weeds, he would wait until his father went to inspect the task before Bob would leave. His work met Sterling's approval.

"As a child, if there was any conflict in the house, Bob would walk with his hands in his pockets and sing 'Love at Home'. He never wanted to have any type of contention. Bob always said that he learned from his father to pick his fights carefully, and to always think first."

Bob struggled with a stuttering problem and he hated it. He had a good friend in high school that convinced him to get on the debate team. This friend took the time to teach Bob how to stop and think about what he was saying before he spoke. Bob worked hard to overcome his speech impediment. He ended up on the state team and did very well in his debate competitions. Thera's son had standing jobs at two to three different places that he worked after school. He was a dedicated worker. He could go into a bakery anytime he wanted and punch in his time clock. He also worked for a gas station. Those were the days where the friendly attendant checked the oil, washed the windows and put gas in the car. Bob was an amazing completely dependable worker.

Bob lived his life centering all his plans around going on a mission. Thera kept reminding the Bishop that she felt if the proper papers weren't sent in her son wouldn't go. The paperwork was sent in, but the Bishop fell through on part of what he was supposed to do. Bishops are human just like the rest of us. Thera's mother's intuition was right.

Bob didn't go on a mission after he graduated, instead he fell in love with Lynette Nielson, marrying this young seventeen-year old girl in the temple. About a year or two after they were married, they had a little girl they named Mackenzie. Not long after, Bob and Lynette had a little boy that they named

Zachory. Bob loved his wife and children. Lynette was her mother's only daughter. They were very close, which perhaps contributed to Lynette coming to Thera telling her, "I just want you to know that I am divorcing Bob and taking Mackenzie and Zachory. I am going home to Salt Lake with my mother."

"Bob was totally devastated. He was a devoted husband and father. He loved his little children. When Lynette took his daughter and son and moved away, it broke Bob's heart. He didn't want to fight with Lynette; he wanted to protect his children from problems between their parents. So Lynette, for reasons of her own, left Bob taking Mackenzie and Zachory with her. When Christmas came around, he was never able to have his children because he didn't want contention with Lynette. My son never missed one payment for his children he loved so much."

Bob would work all day for Air Freight. Sometimes after he finished, he would drive twelve hours to spend some time with his children. He made huge sacrifices to see his children, even if it was just to take them to a movie. Thera always taught Bob that no matter what he needed to be a good father. Bob did his very best at being dad to Mackenzie and Zachory so his children would always know that he loved them.

"The divorce was so heartbreaking and stressful on Bob. His faith was shaken and he was lost without his family. He didn't fight Lynette, because Bob would never do anything to hurt his children. He knew that conflict of any kind between him and Lynette would not be good for either child."

Bob became a long distance father overnight and his life was turned upside down. Bob married another woman on the rebound. Her name was Teri. They were only married for about a year. She wanted children, but because of the heartbreak Bob had been through by not being able to have his two children with him most of the time, Bob said no more children. Their difference in opinion led them to divorce. Bob was inactive in the church at that time. Lynette stayed active, and raised both their children in the church, which Thera is eternally grateful for. Mackenzie and Zachory's grandmother Thera loves them and their families very much.

Bob worked for a shipping company where each evening he would call to report on the high value shipments of the day. For about a year and a half, through his calls to the company's Alabama office, he talked on phone to Ms. Arlene Ann Mac. He finally went to Atlanta for a sales meeting, which was the first time the two met in person. When he came back a second time for another sales meeting, Bob asked Arlene out. She accepted! After their first date, he invited her to visit him in Denver for a weekend. The two spent a total of only nine days together before they knew that they both wanted to spend their lives together. Arlene packed up her things, had a job waiting for her, and the two drove to Denver. The week Bob was moving her to Denver, Val offered him a job in California. Bob asked Arlene what she thought. Her response was simple. California was warmer. They ended up in California where bob started working with Val. Bob was the perfect man for Arlene. And, Arlene was the perfect woman for Bob. They were married on November 15, 1986.

Memories from Arlene

"Bob had an awesome relationship with his kids. They would visit in the summer and talk with their dad on the phone when they weren't with him. When they grew up and got married, both Mackenzie and Zachory would call their dad for advice all the time. They were very close to their father. Bob's love for his children was unconditional. The kids would talk to their father about anything! He would never judge them, not ever. Bob would do anything for them as their father. His world centered on his children and grandchildren.

Bob was not only my husband, but he was also my very best friend and soul mate. If we would disagree about something, my husband would start singing or cracking jokes. So, of course our disagreements never lasted long. He was the best husband any girl could have, even though he couldn't cook or boil water. We worked together, played together, laughed together, and always had good conversations together. He got perks with his work, which allowed us to be able to travel. Our whole life was fun! Our life together was wonderful. The only thing that keeps me going is my knowing that I will see him again one day."

Arlene and Bob always had big dogs because Arlene was a dog person. She had been fostering pit bulls until a new home could be found for them. She would drive an hour to go pick up the homeless dogs, and another hour to return back home to Bob with the dog in tow. She had become very sick on a day she was scheduled to go pick up an orphaned dog. Bob told her that she was not driving an hour one way alone, because of how bad she was feeling. Arlene had fostered four to five pit bulls, so that is what they expected to take home with them.

The woman who worked at the facility brought out a little dog named Sid. She explained that she knew Bob and Arlene were big dog people, but the little dog she held needed to get out fast before it was too late. Upon hearing that, Arlene immediately said, "We'll take whatever dogs need to go!" Arlene told me that she could feel Bob's eyes burning a hole through her! He didn't want a *little* dog. The entire way home Bob complained telling Arlene that if the little dog was a yapper he would drive the hour to take him back the next day. Finally, Arlene looked at Bob and said, "Who is the yapper? I haven't heard one yap out of this little guy yet. All you've done is yap, yap, yap for the last hour!"

By the time they got home it was late at night. The next morning Arlene told Bob it would be great if he would go get rawhide for the little dog to chew on, a toy for him and some dog food. Three hundred dollars later Bob returned home with a bed, a new wardrobe for the dog, a ton of toys, rawhide and dog food! Arlene looked at Bob's collection and asked, "All this for a foster dog?" Our big-hearted Bob put his hands over Sid's ears and whispered, "I think we might keep him. We're going take him to Utah. If he makes Sadie laugh, we're going keep him." Little miss Sadie was their oldest granddaughter. Sadie wasn't a dog person, but it was love at first sight between her and Sid. That special little dog would just lie on Sadie and lick her with his kisses, while Sadie just giggled! Sid had become a permanent resident with Sadie's first giggle when she met him!

Sterling took his little dog Barney everywhere. Bob used to make fun of his dad for it. By the time Bob and Arlene got home from their visit with Sadie, he looked at Arlene and said, "I get it." Sid turned Bob's heart to mush just like Barney did to Sterling! Bob took Sid everywhere! He used to ask Sid if he wanted to go to the bank, and see the girls that worked there. Sid would jump up and down getting so excited! Arlene still has Sid today. Bob and Arlene rescued that little dog. Now that Bob is gone, Arlene shared with me that Sid has rescued her.

Zachory and Mackenzie's mother Lynette remarried a man named Brad. The relationship between Bob, Arlene, Lynette and Brad became a good one. The relationship was based upon respect for one another as the parents of two very special children. Bob would always thank Brad for being such a wonderful father to his and Lynette's children. I know that both Zachory and Mackenzie are grateful for each of their *four* parents.

Bob loved all of his family deeply. He loved his wife, his children, his grandchildren, his dad and mom, his brothers and their wives, his sister, his nieces and his nephews. His love continues for his entire family still today, and will continue forever. Both Mackenzie and Zachory served honorable missions for the LDS church, and Jesus Christ is the foundation of their lives.

The morning that Mackenzie was getting sealed to her husband, Bob had tears in his eyes when they drove up to the Temple.

"Bob looked at Sterling through his tear-filled eyes and said, 'Represent me well Dad.'"

It broke his heart to not be able to go into the temple with Mackenzie. Mackenzie and Zachory both love their father, and unquestionably their father loves them. Bob and Sterling both share the same kind of love between them as father and son. If Sterling went to California, Bob would always take work off to go golfing with his dad. The two shared a very close bond.

"Bob's life was all about his family, and giving his best in whatever he was involved in. My son was a private person. Grandma used to say to all of us, 'Dead fish and family start to stink after a couple of days.' He would let people come for a couple days, but made sure that he told them ahead of time that's all they could stay for."

Arlene was so thrilled to be a grandmother to Mackenzie and Zachory's children. When sweet, beautiful Sadie became gravely ill with a brain tumor, Bob and Arlene would constantly go to Utah every chance they could in order to spend time with their cherished grandchildren.

When people were having problems with their pools, Bob would simply fix the problem. One family couldn't get their pool to work no matter what they tried. They had party guests coming, so Bob went over to fix the pool. When he finished, the pool was working perfectly. The homeowners asked what in the world Bob had done while explaining to him that they had tried everything. Bob responded by letting them know that he always had his angels with him. Those angels Bob spoke of were Rick and Trish. Whenever he left, he would let his clients know that his brother and sister traveled with him wherever he would go. He would say, "They are my angels. You won't have the problem I fixed today with your pool again." People would call and say that they never did have the problem again!

Thera went to visit Bob and Arlene after the battle had been fought with Trish's murderer. Bob said, "Mom, I know Val and Nick have helped you so much through all of this. I feel that I haven't helped." Thera turned to him and said, "Feed the missionaries. If you do that one thing, we can ask Heavenly Father for anything, because our Father in Heaven loves his missionaries." Bob and Arlene had six missionaries in their ward. From that point on, Bob and Arlene honored Thera's counsel and just kept feeding the missionaries. Their Bishop noted what was happening.

That good Bishop extended a call to Arlene to keep the calendar to feed the missionaries. She did a wonderful job at it! Once when Thera was visiting them, Arlene had a calendar all spread out on the table. Thera asked what it was and Arlene explained what the Bishop had called her to do. She then explained to Thera, "When I talk to the people in the ward about feeding the missionaries, some people aren't very responsive to the needs of the missionaries." The next day just happened to be fast and testimony meeting.

"I looked across the chapel and it was filled with so many people! Sterling, Bob and Arlene were there with me. I walked up to the front, and bore my testimony."

On the first Sunday of each month many members of the LDS church do not eat for two of their meals, usually over a twenty-four hour period. During which time they pray sincerely for specific needs of their own, or for the needs of others. On that first Sunday, the Sacrament meeting is turned over to those members who choose to go to the pulpit and express their feelings for the Savior. Beautiful personal experiences of growth are expressed. We can all grow from many of the experiences of others. Hearing the stories of others is a wonderful way for us to learn.

"I introduced myself as Bob's mom. They knew him from the times he performed. I told everyone how surprised I was that the ward was so big. I continued that I was quite shocked to find out that many times their responses weren't always positive when Arlene would call members asking them to feed the missionaries. I asked them, 'If your son or daughter was on a mission, wouldn't you want them to be fed?' I then asked Arlene to please stand up. I said, 'If all of you committed to feed the missionaries once a month, Arlene would have no trouble at all making sure your ward missionaries are fed."

Shortly after, Thera got a letter from Bob and Arlene's Stake President and Bishop. "It is wonderful to have a mother call a ward to repentance!" Thera went back later, and someone said, "Sister Huish, come here. I want to show you something." She was guided to a missionary meal calendar in the foyer, and of course it was completely full! A woman shared with Thera that she had gotten sick, and called to cancel making dinner for the missionaries that day. She said she laid back down when all of the sudden she saw Thera on television. Thera's face was filling the whole TV screen. This woman jumped up, and put her hands in the air saying, "I'll feed the missionaries! I'll feed the missionaries!"

"Bob never really celebrated Christmas with any enthusiasm, because he was not ever able to spend Christmas with his children. It always made him sad to not be with them at such a special time of year."

The Christmas before Bob passed away Mackenzie surprised her father with a visit. Thera believes Mackenzie is happy she spent that one Christmas with her father. It meant more to Bob to have them with him for that holiday than anyone could have realized. His heart was very full that beautiful Christmas day, because of his treasured daughter.

Thera was terribly ill about a year before Bob died. She was recovering from a dangerously high heart rate in March of 2010. Her heart was working way too hard. She underwent oblation surgery in order to slow her heart rate down. That was a grueling six-hour surgery her frail body had to endure. Thera held on to this life by a mere thread throughout that time. Her heart rate had to come down.

Bob called his mother and said, "Mom, I want to come see you." Still attached to her couch while trying to overcome the nausea, Thera asked her son what he wanted to do. Bob answered, "Nothing. I just want to sit with you, Mom, and spend time with you.'

"I was very sick. My heart rate had been around two hundred beats per minute. I was in and out of the hospital about seven times. They used shock treatment four times on my heart. I finally had oblation surgery to slow my heart rate down. Nothing worked. I pretty much lay on my couch from March to January, because I struggled to breathe. I couldn't go to church. Bob took the time to come visit me. He came and stayed with me for four days. We were relaxing and visiting and he said to me, 'Mom, nobody will ever know how many tears I've shed over Rick, Trish, Sadie and Dad. I really miss them.'

Over the course of those four special days, Bob expressed his love for Arlene. We went to Nick and Cara's once while Bob was with me. He talked of his dreams for his future, and all that he wanted for he and Arlene. He again expressed how much he missed his little granddaughter, his dad, brother and sister. It was obvious he looked forward to the day when he would be reunited with them, the day when they would ALL be together as a family never to be away from each other. The day will come when our family will ALL be in heaven once again."

Bob and Thera talked and laughed for four marvelous days. Thera said that those four days were filled with great memories she will always hold dear.

"Prior to his death, Bob had his priorities in order. His two children lived very active and strong in the church. Zachory served as a Bishop. With his soul mate by his side, my son had come to the realization that he once again wanted to become active in the Gospel of Jesus Christ. Bob had been working towards that with his Bishop, just as Trish did years before. His good Bishop shared with me that Bob had been going to church for about a year, watched conference, met with him every month, and that Bob had just started temple preparation classes so that he could go back to the Temple of our Redeemer once again. It is never too late to be welcomed back into the fold!

Bob was, and I know continues from heaven to be, very grateful for Lynette and the good mother that she is and has been to their children. When she married Brad, Bob was thankful for him. Bob appreciated the way Brad cared for Mackenzie and Zach."

Thera has a great love for Arlene. She shared with me that this very special daughter is a ministering angel to her as is Cara, Cathe and Millie. I know that Thera, and the rest of the family, would be ecstatic to have Arlene sealed eternally to Bob. I also know, without doubt, that this is Bob's wish. His love for Arlene is stronger than *till death do you part.* I have felt Bob's love for Arlene, and Arlene has expressed her love for Bob to me. Their love is eternal, and their bond as husband and wife is one that Bob yearns to have eternally with his beautiful sweetheart. Bob's actions to come back to the Gospel are proof of the desires of his heart for his family to be together forever, with his beautiful soul mate by his side enjoying their eternities together.

"My son came back. He knew that the teachings instilled in him by both his father and myself were true. Bob came back. My boy came back."

Memories of Bob from Nick

The peacemaker. Literally. I don't think in Bob's entire life he ever got in a fight, or was the center of an argument. He always seemed to be able to find the friendly way out of most situations. He had that sixth sense when trouble was arising. Bob was the only member of our immediate family who was born in a foreign country. With all the military travel, he was born in Germany.

Bob was the closest sibling to me in years, he being four years my senior. I had him as the brother that I could hang with sometimes. In our elementary years, he was in school with me. I traveled through junior high and high school alone, but not unrecognized, thanks to Bob. I was known as Huish's little brother. My big brother was really liked by most of the teachers, even the ones he didn't have as teachers! Those that knew him, who I crossed paths with, had a substantially higher expectation of me than my own ambitions. Bob paving the way before me made it real tough for me at times. It seemed like on the football field or running track was the only areas that I could pass his level of achievement. Bob spread friendship, peace and laughter to everyone around him. I was interested in anything sports related, nothing book related! Yep, he was a difficult act to follow.

Bob was a lot like our big brother Rick. Both of them excelled in debate, music, drama, and various other areas of school none of which were included in my forte. When I entered those classes, I could feel the mark of his presence still lingering. The teachers made me well aware of their high expectations based upon what they knew I was capable of, because of my good ole' big brother Bob.

Bob was a true friend. He had good, committed, life-long, devout friends. Lowery and Pete being a couple of them who stand out in my mind. They were the ones that Bob hung out with the most from school. Mom and Dad didn't have to micromanage Bob much. He seemed to know their limits pretty well, and for the most part stayed within them. With that being said, Bob did have a little rebellion in him every now and then. He was probably Dad's unconfirmed favorite, which nobody could blame Dad for that!

On one occasion he had decided it was time for a little *country fun* in the hallowed halls of the educational facility. School was pretty uneventful for Bob and his pals, so they decided to make it eventful. He and a couple of his buddies went to a local pig farmer, and gathered up a bunch of piglets. (Now, whether or not those piglets were purchased or borrowed was never confirmed.)

My big brother decided to make the break between classes an adventure to be remembered by all. He and his pals took those piglets, greased them up with Crisco, and then freed them in the halls just before the lunch bell. What happened next comes from varying stories. It didn't matter the title, teacher or student, since it took any who were game for trying to catch those little squealers. After a few hours and a lot of people corralling the piglets, they were finally captured. So were my brother and his partners in crime! I don't know who betrayed them, but I'm pretty sure Bob and all the culprits involved were under federal probation for the rest of the year! That prank was one of the most popular and memorable pranks to ever take place at that school. The piglets had resounding effects on my big brother's personal schedule adding points to his popularity!

During the summers while a teenager, Bob headed north in an attempt to satisfy his inner cowboy. He'd head out to the farm where mom was raised. Bob loved being there! It seemed to be his place of solace. Being with Grandpa and Grandma at the farm was an environment that he was comfortable in. Horses, old machinery and the simple life fit him. Bob never liked complicated things. My big brother did best in a setting of simplicity where there were more times of laughter than frustration or stress.

Our cousin Chris was Bob's partner at the farm. Both of them worked hard in the fields to keep up with our Grandpa and uncles. Mom and Dad would take us there on the weekends. Bob became a different kid there. Grandpa seemed to take a serious liking to him for sure. Mom was proud of Bob's accomplishments on the farm. Grandpa's pay for a summers worth of work was a new pair of Tony Lama boots for Bob and Chris, which seemed fair to them. After all, they were there for the fun! Throughout his life my big brother was a hard worker, always dependable. Bob learned many life lessons in those days on the farm. He applied those lessons learned in his daily life from that point on.

When there was a family riff or squabble between us siblings, Bob always did his best to quickly find a solution for the dispute. He had a *go-to* song whenever tempers would flare at home. He would sing the same church song *Love At Home* every time. Bob would start singing that song, and within a minute or two it seemed like the air would clear. His singing those words somehow put things in perspective, and the problems at hand just seemed smaller.

Bob struggled with stuttering. In his younger years, Mom worked diligently with him in order to help him get past some really difficult times due to the stutter. He found that if he talked with a rhythm he had fewer problems with his speech. With that knowledge, his love for singing became a part of him. He sang like a bird! When he sang he was free from the repetitive anchor that tested him. I admit we teased the heck out of him, so did his friends. But, Bob took it all in stride. He even made fun of himself sometimes, which just made us love him all the more.

He seemed to be able to approach anyone, strike up a conversation, and become a quick friend. He worked like a farmyard horse! He never had a problem getting a job. When he left any job, the door was always open for his return. We had a dune buggy. Bob worked two jobs while he went to school in order to pay for gas, and to work on his dune buggy. He was notorious for working so much that he had a hard time not falling asleep. This was not only at school, but while driving as well.

Bob's adventures in driving while sleeping almost rival the incident with the piglets! How he got home safe many nights after working until three or four in the morning were a mystery. Bob could tell you when he left work. As far as the drive home, the conditions of the streets, or what route he took? Nope. He usually had absolutely no memory of any of those. Anything about the drive home escaped his memory! All he knew was that he had left work and woke up in his bed the next morning. Honestly, at times he was a little scary to ride with.

When he moved to the Bay Area in San Francisco, he worked for a freight company. He lived in Napa and drove to the San Francisco airport every day. He worked the swing shift, which ended at about two o'clock in the morning. Bob told a story of how he left the airport one night, and the last thing he remembered was getting on the freeway towards Napa. He did say that he remembered briefly waking up at one point seeing his exit. The next thing he knew he was waking up late for work the next day!

Bob had sleeping disorders as a child. He was a sleepwalker. Evidently he kept Mom and Dad on their toes walking through the house at all hours of the night or in the wee hours of the morning. Sometimes he even left the house to tour the neighborhood. I guess Mom finally had enough. She came up with a 1950's fix. She took a pair of her nylons tying one end to the bedpost, and the other end to his ankle! Child Abuse? Where's CPS when you need them? Actually Mom was pretty genius, because her nylons evidently solved the problem. After that, Bob was scarred for life. It has been reported that he enjoyed being bound to a bed! (Just kidding.) But seriously, it did stop him from walking in his sleep and the nylons kept him in his bed. Boy, there are so many directions you could go with that innocent story!

I was hired for many of my early jobs specifically from Bob's reputation as a hard worker. I didn't mind working hard, none of us kids did. It's always been normal and is something that has always come natural for those of us linked to my parents. Dunford Bakery along with Little America Hotel was two of my most memorable jobs that I had with Bob. We had great times working together! Mom and Dad instilled good ethics within all of us at a young age, which proved to be very valuable. Jobs were plentiful for my siblings and me, as were the good references that followed. Bob took to heart the things Dad and Mom taught him. In most cases with the jobs he held, his bosses soon wanted a better position for him. That was appropriate, because that's just what Bob hoped for with everyone around him. He always wanted good things for the people in his life.

Our oldest brother Val instigated Bob's migration to the Bay area by recruiting him into becoming part of his custom pool business. Val had begun his business years earlier. My brothers quickly bonded, and between the two of them they built a very respectable business. Bob worked the northern Bay area to Napa, while Val focused on the Bay area and east Bay area. Bob became an instant hit in his area being regarded as one of the *go-to* guys for the wineries and owners of unique custom pools. Top wineries along with celebrities peppered his clientele list. They all adored him! He never promised anything he couldn't deliver. In fact, he always told them that perfection was something not to expect and that coming close to perfection was all he would guarantee. His clients made sure they were good clients for him. They knew that Bob worked diligently to exceed their expectations. He came as close to perfect as was possible.

I worked with Val and Bob for a couple of years. During that time I truly had some of the best work related experiences I've ever encountered. Both of my brothers have always taken such pride in everything they've done. Val still does today. This is a different time now. Bob is gone. If I could roll back the hands of time, I'd live those years all over again."

Messages from Bob's Children

Bob's daughter Mackenzie

My father was one of the kindest, most generous, and sincere people I've ever known. He had an uncanny way of making every person who knew him feel like he was his or her best friend. His sense of humor was endearing and drew people to him.

Above all, my dad loved his kids and adored his grandchildren. Oh, how he loved those grandchildren! He would get down on the floor with them and play, and play, and play. There was nothing that they could not get him to do. His eyes would sparkle with joy like nothing else when he spent time with them.

I count myself blessed to be his daughter and pray that I can be like him. Mackenzie

Bob's son Zachory

My dad had no motto, but was wise beyond his years. He had a heart of gold always giving more than he could spare. He is a legend! When I think of Dad I smile and easily turn my thoughts back to jokes he shared while driving down the road, or a story that he told me inspiring me to be better. I am one of many souls that are forever grateful Dad graced our lives with his. Zachory

From Val's daughter Lisa:

Uncle Bob was Dad's best friend. Being near him made anyone happy! I will always remember his mustache and cowboy boots. I admired how much he loved Arlene. They were so cute with each other. It was always entertaining to watch him eat Thanksgiving dinner. He was a great animal lover and when Sid came around, it was such an adorable friendship between the two of them. I miss being 'Niece Lees'. I know everyone misses his lightheartedness and his happy, positive, kind outlook on living.
Lisa

~Chapter Ten~

Nick - Selfless

With all the places the Huish family had lived, they had made a complete circle back to Provo. Sterling was an instructor at BYU for the young men who were going into the ROTC program. Thera was pregnant with her and Sterling's fifth and last child. Todd Nicholas Huish was born March 12, 1959. Nick was born at Utah Valley Hospital, which happened to be the same hospital where Nick's oldest brother Val was born. So many years later, Nick was also under the care of the same doctor as Val was.

"Sterling took me to the hospital early in the morning. The kids were home. The doctor informed us that it would be awhile before our baby would come. We decided that Sterling would go home and take over the morning routine of the Huish household. He left, but was ready to come back when it was time. Shortly after that, the doctor said, 'It looks like this baby is eager to enter this world.' I vividly remember looking out the window as the sun came up shedding light over the beautiful mountains in Provo. I have often thought that what I had seen at that moment, as that wonderful day began, epitomized Nick's life. Learning I was pregnant with Nick was quite a surprise at that time. But, what a blessing he has been in my life. I can't even tell you what a blessing my son has been!

Sterling was so excited about going into the delivery room with me. He would say, 'I finally get to be with you when one of our babies are born!' Nick arrived and I told my doctor that I felt so good I could just get up and go. He explained that he knew things had gone well, but told me I was going to rest. They took me back to my room where I showered and got all cleaned up. Sterling came back from taking care of the morning duties. Walking into my room, he found me lying in bed. He had no idea Nick had arrived! He was every bit as excited and thrilled at having Nick as I was! I was only in the hospital a couple of days.

I was so happy Nick was healthy, and that we had another little boy. But, I knew there would be a little girl at home that would be heartbroken. When Sterling went home to tell the children they had a new baby brother, Trish was standing at the window. He happily announced, 'It's another little boy!' Sterling later told me that tears just welled up in her eyes. Though Trish's disappointment didn't last for long!"

When Sterling and Thera took the newest member of their family home from the hospital, the first one wanting to hold him was Trish. It was love at first sight for Trish with Nick. Val, Rick and Bob were excited to have a new little brother, but oh, how Trish loved having Nick in the house! There were eleven years difference between Trish and Nick. Trish took being his big sister very seriously.

"Nick was a great Cub Scout, but there was no way he was going to be a Boy Scout. My son never wanted to leave home during those Boy Scout years, and Boy Scouts went to scout camp!"

96

As far as school goes, Nick was a great student. All the teachers loved him and he got good grades. In grade school he did what he had to do, no more. For church he did what he should do.

"When Nick got into high school, his studies became a pain in the butt to him. He loved football, and he was good at it. He wanted to swim, because his dad had received awards for swimming."

Nick's head and neck got hurt while playing in a football game. He had terrible headaches after that. Realizing he couldn't play anymore didn't help him want to push himself academically. His teachers explained that Nick was great at sports, but added that he wouldn't apply himself to studying.

The company that had hired Thera wanted her in Arizona. Nick decided he'd finish high school at their new location once they moved. He was put on the football team. He quickly moved up the ranks to the position he wanted. The headaches started again. While visiting with the principal it was determined that Nick was still injured and shouldn't be on the team.

"The principal told us that everyone loved Nick, but continued explaining that our son wouldn't stay in class and study. He then suggested that the best thing we could do as his parents was to take him out of school and let him go to work in sales because of his personality."

Shortly after, Nick was working in a men's clothing store. Following that, he got a job in a furniture store.

"Nick has always had a talent with being artistic. He started creating the furniture displays for the store. He did magnificently well!"

In his youth, Nick took it upon himself to become his mother's protector. He did this in so many different ways. Nick was intuitive to Thera's heart. He knew when she was hurting due to Rick's poor choices because of his addictions. In his volunteered role, one of the very first things he did was to begin shielding his mother from being hurt by Rick's actions.

"Nick took care of Rick. He would always protect me from seeing the messes his big brother made. He protected me as much as possible from seeing Rick when his big brother was a mess."

Nick married Cara at nineteen years old.

"Cara is a sweetheart! The relationship I share with her is one that I am humbled to have. She has been there through the best of the best and the worst of the worst with our family. How lucky our family is to have

her. She is such a special wife, mother, daughter, sister and aunt. She is a blessing to all of us!"

Nick and Cara blessed Sterling and Thera with two wonderful grandchildren, Adam and Nicole. Nick and Cara thankfully stayed close to Sterling and Thera by living near them, except for a few years when Nick worked for Val in California. Thera's youngest son and his family have been there to support Thera through all she has endured. Nick has always been able to get to his mother in a matter of minutes during her many times of desperate need. His love and dedication to his mother is unfailing. Nick's devotion to ALL his family, here and in heaven, surpasses the understanding of most.

"Nick has always been the first one to be there for me when I needed anything, or when something has happened. Val always called his little brother the good son."

Every time Thera has been sick, Nick has been there. Whenever she had to call 911, Nick would get to his mother's house as fast as the emergency teams did, sometimes beating them there!

"Once while in the hospital, I was given something in my IV to control my heart rate that I shouldn't have been given. Nick and Cara were sitting next to me. I could literally feel my body dying. I barely got the words out, 'Nick, I'm in trouble.' He ran out in the hall yelling for the nurse. From that experience, Nick now has a list of every medication I have ever been given, including the ones my body can't have. Always my protector."

Thera required a pacemaker, which the surgeon put in. It didn't work to help her, but instead caused much strain on her heart. Nick was with his mother supporting her. A second surgery was needed to replace the first pacer with a new one that fit the needs of Thera's heart. The surgeon was explaining everything about the new pacemaker to Thera and Nick.

"Everything went over my head. Nick addressed the surgeon and said, 'Now let me make sure I have this right.' He then repeated everything back to doctor perfectly. He made certain that he understood fully what the plan was to save my life. Nick has always done all in his power to do what he could for me. He has always kept me safe."

Nick has served his family unconditionally, expecting nothing in return. Nick sketched on a pad as he sat by his dying brother. He rarely left Rick's bedside. Nick took control of the situation to obtain justice for his big sister's murder. He wouldn't let Trish down! When his father died, he wouldn't allow his mother to go to the hospital without him being there for her to lean on. He was there when his father's body was wheeled out of the hospital room. Sterling was gone. Nick was there for his mother, as he held his father's hand and cried. When the family lost Bob, Nick went to Bob and Arlene's home. He cleaned it for Arlene while helping her through the shock of losing her husband. Nick is an example to all us of how to live a selfless life in the service of others.

"Verily I say unto you, inasmuch as ye have done it unto one of the least of these my brethren, ye have done it unto me."
Matthew 25:40

Those are the words of Jesus Christ. All of Sterling and Thera's children have thrived when it comes to service. The examples set by both of their parents became infused in the very core of their beings. I know that the mansion prepared by the Lord for this most amazing family is the grandest of grand!

"Nick and Cara are the most giving, caring people who continually serve others. Both are loving grandparents. I am thankful for my relationship I have with them, and their family. Nicole is a loving daughter, mother, and a loving granddaughter to me. Adam is a very attentive man. He reaches out to those in need following the example of his father. Nick has a tender heart like his dad. Both Nicole and Adam are incredible parents."

Val's thoughts on Nick

"Nick is our big dreamer. He has great ideas with talents that I envy. I am more proud of Nick right now than I have ever been. Because of our age difference, I didn't really know him when he was in Junior High or playing football. My youngest brother married young, but married well.

As he got older, he always had his lofty goals and visions. He did stocks, power point, wrote things for companies and developed brochures. The companies that utilized what Nick could do for them had growth. But, he didn't really get paid for creating that growth. For a while he sold motor homes.

There was a time that Nick was really having some financial struggles. Around the year 2000, I asked him to come help me with my business. I put him up in the house. For about three years he sold pools with me. He wrote programs for my company that I still use in my business today. He would take trips to Arizona to visit our parents.

Nick moved back to Arizona, and is now involved in a company where he oversees meetings for them. I told him that nobody could be happier for him than me. When I told my little brother, "I am so proud of you," Nick got tears in his eyes. He said, "You know Val, you telling me you are proud of me means

99

so much to me." He is an organizer like Trish. He is a talented fellow with a big heart! He and I like to hug people.

Nick has become a spiritual being. It took him awhile to accomplish this. He is very much in tune with the spirit. Great things happen around him. He reads his scriptures all the time. He has a great set of morals and standards. My little brother has really come into-his-own, and it has been rewarding for me to watch his growth.

I am grateful for all he has done for our family and I am proud he is my brother.

Val"

"Since Nick was our last child, he didn't feel that he knew Val very well. Val was doing things Nick couldn't do as a child. It is interesting how connected the two of them are now. They are so close. My two boys have done their best to fill a huge void that was inside both of them when, one by one, they lost their three siblings and their father."

Thera's Letter to Nick

Dear Nick,

I want you to have this letter from me to you. As I think back on the lives of each of you children, one would think that at eighty-six years of age much would be forgotten by me. But, memories burn clearly in my mind. Throughout the years, I have sent many letters of love and appreciation to each of you children. Although I have done this, there are many things that have been left unsaid. The faintest of ink is better than spoken words. A letter is tangible with written words that can be read by the receiver long after the sender is gone.

When you were born, you had three brothers and a sister at home. Your big sister was anxiously waiting to see if you were a sister for her! Those were the days when we did not know the sex of the baby until he or she was born. Trish was very sad when your dad announced that she had another brother. Yet, she was there with open arms to hold you when we brought you home from the hospital. She fell in love with you immediately!

What a blessing you have always been to her, both while she was here with us and after she was taken from us. The love you have for her children (actually for all of your nieces and nephews), along with the kindness you show to each of them is wonderful! I am amazed at how you and Val are able to share your love, your homes, and anything you are able to share in order to bless our family. You are both ideal examples of being your brother's keeper in so many ways.

100

Val and Bob used to tell me that you were the good son. They would say that you carried the majority of the load when anything happened, because you chose to live close to us. You have always been there to handle whatever has come along in my life, and we both know from experience that a lot seems to come along.

With you being the last of five children, much of our military life and travels were coming to an end by the time you reached your teenage years. Living in Utah gave you a chance to explore the hills, valleys, and even climb a mountain! Remember? You did leave a note that told me not to worry, and that you would be fine. Thank goodness, the rainstorm made you come home after you got soaked that night in your tent. Amazing that you even thought of climbing a mountain, when you couldn't stand to be away from your family and home for even one night with the scouts.

School was fun for you and you loved it. But, truth be told, what you enjoyed was your relationships you had developed with your teachers and your friends. Schoolwork was not your favorite thing. An injury that happened while you were playing football took you out of the game and school. The principal told us to get you into sales. How wise he was! You are like every one of your brothers and your sister. You are an amazing salesperson and great trainer. You know what your goals are, and you know how to achieve them. You have chosen to learn from the things you have done in the past. Your experiences have taught you so much along the way.

It had to be tough on you as you watched your big brother Rick, such a brilliant young man, become a victim of alcohol. Through his actions you witnessed him lose family, friends, integrity and morality. His uncontrolled dependency caused self-sabotage within him. You saw this deadly addictive disease in action. I recall how you made it your job to keep track of Rick. You cleaned up the situations he left behind those many times he disappeared from our lives. Whenever your brother retuned home, you loved him unconditionally and helped him in every way you possibly could.

Rick was finally admitted into a hospital to live out his last days. During his two months of being in and out of comas, he needed someone at his side at all times. I watched as you were always there for him. When the end came, you and Trish held his hands as his last breath left his body. You are very close to his sons, and they love you. I know Rick must look down with great love and appreciation for you.

What a great time we all had with Trish! We shared so many fun dinners, parties and trips. When you were young, your sister took care of you. As you grew older, the roles reversed and you always took care of your big sister. You made sure she was not mistreated by anyone, in any way. You knew many things about the man that tore her life away from us. You paid special attention to make sure all was okay with your big sister during those times she struggled in her marriage to him. Little did we know when we spent that last night in her home as they were leaving for Mexico, that in two days she would be dead. Her murderer joking with everyone that night and making their trip to Mexico sound so special. When we learned of your sister's murder, you knew, as did I that he was guilty of murdering her. We knew that his hands had ripped her away from all of us, from her children!

Our family goal: To have justice served, and see him pay the ultimate price for what he had done.

Nick, it was through your dedication and never-ending searching for clues that our family objective was accomplished for Trish. You were relentless in all that you did, and all that you did for your sister was incredible. Because you were able to get us on national television with our story, his accomplice was found and confessed the whole story.

Val and Bob were not able to be here unless they came for just a few days. But, our vision as Trish's family for the outcome was one in the same. Without Val's financial assistance, I could not have paid for the attorney who put the murderer of our Trish away for the rest of his mortal life. (The Lord will take care of putting him away in outer darkness for all eternity.) Bob and Arlene opened their home to missionaries from the Mormon Church, and even to this day they are remembered for their love and care of these young men and women serving away from home.

You filled both of your brothers' shoes for them since they lived in California. And, you did it twenty-four hours a day seven days a week. You selflessly gave of yourself. You did all the research, gaining evidence for your sister with a watchful eye making sure that your dad and me were all right. You, Cara and your children did all kinds of crazy antics to bring some happiness back into our lives. Your dad and I were so blessed to have you and your brothers who did all each of you could, in order to help lessen the pain of losing two children in a mere eighteen-month period.

The trial ahead was frightening. You were not able to be inside the courtroom, but you stood outside for four weeks awaiting the verdict. It came. Through your sacrifice Trish's murderer received the death sentence. We had no idea we would face a second trial ten years later.

During those ten years, you stood by my side through everything I faced. You were with me as they brought your father into a private waiting room after he died. We know he died because of incompetence after his surgery. I often think of Trish, a little girl ten-years old, waiting at the window to see if she had a new little sister. My son, I know the Savior knew we all would need YOU in our lives. You are the protector of those whom you love. You have proved that time and time again without fail. You protect those of your loved ones who are still in this mortal existence. You protect those who are near but have moved on from this life.

After all we had endured, you were excited to spend time in California working with Bob and Val. You saw it as a great opportunity that would allow you to spend more quality time with your two remaining brothers. You wanted to know both of them better, since they were older than you. So many times, we don't understand the reasons we make the choices we do. We cannot see the road ahead, or what may be around the next bend in life. There are those times when we make choices, and as we look back, we are so glad we made the right ones.

Your days in California were happy days you spent selling pools, helping Bob and Arlene redo their home and creating memories you will always cherish. The hours you spent working on their home was truly a delight. Bob loved everything you did. When I visited them, after you had stopped working in California, they were thrilled with their home!

It was another heart-wrenching day when I was leaving for an appointment, and you called asking me to come by your home. I knew as soon as I walked in that something terrible had happened. I was so right. You had to tell me Bob had been rushed to the hospital, and though he was alive, had died three times from sleep apnea. Our family watched and waited for six weeks to see if Bob would come back to us. He waited those six weeks until your big brother knew that we would all understand him leaving us. He was at peace knowing he could go home and be with Dad, Rick, Trish and Sadie.

Bob was a peacemaker. He never wanted anyone to feel bad. I know that his leaving this life was a bittersweet for him. As we sat in Val's home the evening before the funeral, it felt strange to realize that from our family of seven, there were now only three. I shall never forget the outstanding talks you and Val gave at your brother's service. I know Bob appreciated them so much. The church was packed that day with his family and friends. Those who knew Bob loved Bob.

You have the gift of art Nick. You possess the talent of sketching, drawing, painting and enhancing beauty with your ability to design. I have watched you create amazing brochures, folders, and advertising pieces for so many companies, receiving very little compensation in return for helping them. You have said many times that you were gaining a great education without going to college. Now, all of your experiences are truly paying off with your business, and I couldn't be more proud of you!

There is no way I can say thank you for all you have done for your mother. You have rushed me to the hospital, spent endless hours at my bedside and taken me in for so many trips to doctors who've tried to help me. I am impressed at how very well educated you became on all of my health history and challenges. There have been too many times to count that I was so sick that had you not been there for me, I am not sure I would be writing this letter of appreciation. I deeply love you and Cara for everything you have done to watch over me.

There is a closing to all things in this life. Knowing that if we have lived as Jesus taught, we will be together as an eternal family. This is the greatest blessing of all! My heart is filled with joy! The greatest gift you could have ever given me was your activity in the Gospel of Jesus Christ. You serve the Bishop well as his secretary, create beautiful programs for the people of your ward, and I know that those in your ward appreciate your hugs that you give to all. One of my life's most special days was the day I was able to be with you and Cara as you were sealed together for time and all eternity in the temple. Such a priceless blessing!

Thank you Nick and Cara for your endless love and care. May the Lord bless you that all of your desires for your family to be with you forever will become a reality.

Love you,
Mom

~Chapter Eleven~

Memories from Nick

The love of family gone is something very difficult to describe. I guess if it was just one family member missing, hours could be spent lamenting of times gone by with memories abounding of that person. When I try to assimilate thoughts, some good and some not, I'm simply overwhelmed. My brother Val and I are the bookends. He is the eldest sibling, and I the youngest. After Rick's death, the three of us kids used to question which way death would go in our family. Rick was the exact middle of the five of us. As a child, one doesn't really think of anything short of a long life for yourself, or any family members. It was just a non-existent thought in my world that I would lose so many whom I loved and needed.

Life will be grand! That was my thought as I envisioned family get-togethers every year, watching my brothers grow into dads and my sister grow into a mom. I just knew that I would become an uncle many times over. All these things would happen while watching mom and dad go into their golden years with abundance, witnessing their posterity continue to grow in numbers. It's just what one expects, right? It's what should happen.

I grew up in a military family where dad served our Country honorably. He fought not only in World War II, but did his time in the Korean and Vietnam wars as well. America was deeply rooted in my father's heart. Whenever the military was discussed around dad, it was like watching a dog's ears perk up when hearing his name called! Dad's stature grew by what seemed to be three or four inches every time.

Having this opportunity to reminisce of days gone by has definitely caused me to find the time to think about my childhood. I've traveled around the world in all different directions through the different places my father was stationed. The one commonality that comes to my mind, which provided me with security and safety as a child, is my family. In my opinion, the only thing any person has that really matters is family. Love and hate relationships with family members happen. But, we each must remember our time with those we love is undetermined, and must not be taken for granted.

As the youngest of five, I always knew that my older brothers and sister were there to protect me. I knew that my mom and dad loved me unconditionally. I'm sure that my perspective of growing up as the youngest is different from Val's perspective as the oldest. My siblings grew older before I was really able to understand what a family unit was. At times, I find myself looking back and wondering what parts of the family growth I missed out on by being the youngest. So much happened before I arrived. I've heard stories my entire life about things that took place, but I really don't have personal memories of many of them.

My perspective of family events that took place comes from the youngest child's point of view. I always looked up to everyone in my family. I have a special place in my heart for every event that took place, each happening at a different time, and in a different place. My experiences with my family have built the character of the man I am today. Each member has left their own unforgettable mark on my heart and brain. I can go back and reflect upon those memories of times spent with my family, and hopefully those recollections make me a better man.

With the quiet time in my home, which is not a normal situation, I've attempted to bring as many good memories to mind as possible. I'm writing them for Larina to integrate into this book. I don't know the family joys in the years prior to my birth other than through the stories I've been told. Sharing those is better left to those who lived those experiences. I have my memories that will never leave me.

Where does one begin in telling the story of a living angel, a modern day Joan of Arc per se? My mom is perfect in my eyes. She is my champion, comforter, challenger, and supporter. She is an incredible mother who would never give up on me, or anyone NO MATTER WHAT! Gifted with the ability of blessing our family by always making bad things okay, and good things even better. She took away the pain, and somehow made it okay to hurt when she couldn't take the pain away. She always has been the adhesive in our family unit. It is heart warming to call her **my** mom.

I've seen pictures of my mother during the fifties with her jet-black hair, and her cat eyeglasses. I have a faint memory of the young lady she was. The pride and strength she exuded was evident to those who knew her back then, and to all who have been blessed to know her throughout her life. I can only imagine the enchantment she must have had over my father. My father must have felt great pride, as she became his wife.

Somewhere in the process of growing from a child into adolescence, one can forget the importance of a mother. Then, the day arrives that each of us reaches a certain age where the realization of all that our mothers have done for us is realized. I have always been blessed from having my mother. I now recognize how important I am in her eyes, the eyes of the most important person in my life.

I know that there have been times when I have caused her hurt, which she has always returned with love. I learned the importance of compassion and the depth of gratitude from my mother. I experienced the fulfillment of life. And, I have felt the eternal joy family brings through the family my father and mother created. My mom, as perfect as she is, is untouchable as far as anyone attaining the levels she has attained in this life. It has taken awhile, but hopefully she understands that there is no way any of us could ever even begin to fill her shoes, or I should say her high heels?

Mom has this uncanny quality of somehow finding the good in anything bad. And, when I'm talking bad I'm talking all levels of bad. Her optimistic reasoning was spot on every time, no matter what was being faced. My mother is gifted with the ability to convert a loss into a gain; hurt into something that becomes an experience one can grow from. Through example and conversation from her genuine concern and caring, she causes those of us around her to ponder the possibilities found in any situation. She does this all while forecasting positive solutions.

The one unwavering position in her life that has held her together through all the adversities she has faced is her love for God and Christ. She is indisputably committed to them. Mom questions not the tribulations she has been given. She knows that each struggle has been given to her for personal growth as well as to strengthen her commitment for her beliefs. She has a sure knowledge that her struggles are stepping-stones, experiences that continue to remind her of the joys and blessings she has been given. Her viewpoint is not inhibited by the world, but rather is an enlightened perspective stemming from grace and dignity.

We traveled quite a bit until I was about fourteen. We visited some of the places where dad was stationed abroad and in America as well. I remember taking a lot of family road trips in the car, with the windows wide open. Mom and Dad would be settled up in the front seat. Val, Trish, and Rick lined up on the back seat. Bob and me? Well, we ended up anywhere we'd fit! Seat belts were a nuisance back then, and not a law. I remember spending a fair amount of time on the ledge under the rear window. One could only imagine how we survived! The road trips were rather joyous. In fact, I think we all looked forward to them.

Mom was the entertainment coordinator. She would keep us kids focused on various activities, so dad could focus on the road! Whenever the AM radio lost reception, she was prepared with all sorts of silly little games that kept the five of us siblings occupied for hours. As the game playing finished, mom would pull out her ukulele and begin playing a plethora of songs for the family to sing together. We had songs from all different venues consisting of synchronized multi-versed and two-part musical numbers. The family favorites were songs like Ol'Shanty, Five Foot Two, and Tan Shoes With Pink Shoe Laces. (I think that's the title!) We would sing for hours! Unbeknownst to us kids, mom had us all under control. There was a method to her madness! She was the one who made our trips harmonious.

To me, my childhood memories are one big story of *Never Never Land*! The military bases where we lived were far from that magical kingdom, but I always had such wonderful experiences! Looking back, it seemed everywhere we called home ended up being a great place to live. For a child, living a Military life can be very troublesome. Military families are never in one place much longer than two or three years. That was just about the length of time it took me to get to know the other children, and for them to get to know me. Then, just like that either they, or I, would be gone. Either way those friends from my childhood became a faint memory for me. For adults however, it is a perfect scenario! It seemed my folks never got close enough to the other parents to call them lifelong, close friends. But, they sure built up one heck of an address book collecting friends from all over the globe!

Moving so much caused some reservations in me. Insecurities surfaced when I had to walk into a brand new school not knowing a soul. I found myself doubting that I would ever find another friend, or thinking that none of the kids at school would like me. All my emotions would get built up, and it seemed as though it took an eternity to make friends at the new destination. When in reality, it may have taken a day or two! Mom was always the person pushing me, and my siblings, out the door. I can still hear her telling me that the new kids were all waiting to meet me. She never let any of us feel lonely. She wouldn't give us any time to feel sorry for ourselves. Mom took the position that there would always be another day for self-pity. Mind you, the *other* day was always *another* day away! Needless to say, the five of us adjusted with each move!

The military took us to foreign lands. My earliest memory of my mom was when we were living on the Kaduna Air Base in Okinawa, Japan. We had a two-bedroom home for the seven of us about the size of a shoebox! Mom made it home. She made sure that all the details of running a home were met, and that our family had the comforts we needed. We were all there, together.

Despite her always being very busy, mom was committed both to her family and to her faith. With that being said, she always supported my father by making sure there was always enough. At one time, she took on a job as a hostess at the NCO Club (non-commissioned officers). By doing that, additional money was brought in for the family. I don't recall ever wanting for anything. Looking back, I'm sure that it wasn't easy to provide for each other and five children while living mostly on a military budget. The life I led was the same one that everybody else had, or so I thought. I was raised to respect others and to be thankful for all that I had. God, family and faith came first. Everything else came after as far as the list of priorities goes. I was taught to have respect for my father and mother. Loving my four older siblings, even though at times they were stinky mean and quite pains, was an absolute rule. To be honest, I was probably the worst of all of us!

Before any of us dared to leave the house, mom would always make sure our clothes were clean and pressed. Our teeth had to be brushed and hair, without question, was combed. Our homes were always maintained and very clean. Mom accomplished this with work, and with the help of various housekeepers throughout my childhood. In Okinawa our housekeeper was Hachiko. Hachiko loved Mamasan who happened to be mom. She did everything she could to make sure the house was clean, and that Mamasan didn't have to worry about cooking when she came home from the NCO Club. I just remember Hachiko working and laughing all the time with mom.

Mom let me explore the fields around our house in Okinawa, which was good for me. It truly was an amazing place with all the makings for an incredible land of wonders! I would explore for hours finding the things that interested me. I imagine that by the fifth child, she had already learned to let her children fall. But this I know, my mother was always there to help us rise! She was a master at that. I couldn't possibly tell you how many cuts and scrapes my body underwent, only that each time I added another one she was there to make me feel better. Band-Aids and methylate, Watkins Methyl-Camphor and Petro-Carob Sauvé and liniment were all staples in our home. All these medical aides I am sure were found in the farmhouse she grew up in!

Oh yeah! And, of course good ole' Vicks. You know? The ointment in the blue bottle? That was a must for our colds. I vividly remember mom sitting on the side of my bed rubbing my chest and neck with Vicks, while at the same time singing a song to me. She did that with all of us kids whenever we were sick. I know for me, she always made me feel just a little bit better.

I had my share of illness as a child. I dealt with hay fever and headaches, along with various other issues. I suppose I was no different than most the kids my age back then. My headaches were not good, and they were plentiful. I don't know what caused them, but when they would come they would come with a vengeance. During those times, I would find myself in the arms of my mom. The pain was terrible. She would rub my temples on the sides of my forehead until I fell asleep. My mom seemed to be the only medication that worked. Thankfully, I outgrew those headaches. I can recall one particular time when I was in severe pain with one of them. All mom could do for me is walk around our home with me in her arms singing to me. How real are the feelings of comfort and security that come to me now thinking of my angel mother, as she did all she could to ease my pain. She must have walked with me for an hour, during which time she never stopped singing to me or rocking me in her arms.

We left Okinawa after a few years, and relocated stateside. Our destination was Bountiful, Utah. That is where most of my memories begin for me. Mom seemed to be so happy to be back in Utah, and in a home that was bigger than the shoebox! This home had two levels, one being the basement. Us four boys all slept in the basement while mom, dad and Trish slept upstairs. Rick and Val were in one bedroom downstairs, and Bob and I were in the other.

As usual, we had an impeccably clean home. Mom found a wonderful lady by the name of Mrs. Newman to help her. She was an older lady from Germany who spoke with a heavy accent. She loved to be with us. She would make sure the house was clean, and that meals were prepared when she was there. Mom loved Fridays with Mrs. Newman, because on Fridays Mrs. Newman would always bring our family a cake that had been made in a German Bakery. The cakes were frosted with chocolate frosting and had Marzipan wedges on the top. Mom loved those cakes!

I learned at a young age what charity meant through both my father and my mother. I learned what it meant to help others. The rewards that come from serving others can be monumental. I know that the extension of love and compassion affects the lives of those recipients in need. During the late 60's and 70's it was not politically correct to be pregnant without being married. Unfortunately, today we live in a very different mindset. Some call it acceptance. I'm not completely convinced of that. The moral fabric of society today is quite different now. Values and standards are substantially lower than they were back then.

Mom and Dad opened their home to young women who were pregnant without a marriage certificate. These young women were generally in their third trimester. They were with us for only a few months before the babies were born. This was an incredible learning experience for me. Although I am sure my brothers, being older, had different views. At my age, the girls were like having more big sisters. The only problem was that just as soon as I had bonded with them, they were ready to have their babies and leave. That seemed to be the case with the history of our family. Ties were created all over the world and then, just as soon as those relationships started to feel good, it was time to move on.

These young ladies were welcomed into a home that was full of love, laughter and tears. They became part of a unit that I'm sure left an impression on their lives. Mom would take them to the hospital when the time came for them to deliver the child, and then bring them home to recover for a few weeks. The girls came home alone since they were placing their babies up for adoption. The babies were placed in a home environment that was ready for them. Mom was there to comfort the broken heart, give them a shoulder to cry on and to help them reset their life clocks. It was a tough job, but mom was up to the challenge. Without doubt, my mother received as much as she gave.

Influencing one life for the positive, influences generations in the future.

As was always the case with mom, she couldn't sit still for a moment! Her brain was constantly figuring out how to generate extra income for the household. Bountiful is where she launched her extremely successful career in network marketing. For some of you, you associate that with multi-level marketing and have a negative opinion of that type of business. But it certainly wasn't negative for my mom, or our family.

Mom had been working as a hostess at Dee's Family Restaurant for the extra income our family needed. She was excellent at her job, and was able to communicate with people very well. One day a lady came into the restaurant to eat. Mom seated her and visited with her for a few minutes. The woman was very impressed with the way mom presented herself. She approached mom and asked if she had ever heard about the Figurette Bra. Mom was hooked! Suffice it to say that was the beginning of a lifelong and successful career for my mother in network marketing.

I had fun watching mom's career grow, because I was still at home. I witnessed all of her meetings in our home with people in and out by the carloads! Who would have thought that something that held a couple pounds of flesh (at the time, that's all it was to me!) could be so popular? Anyway, her success was so good that she soon started making more money than dad. Dad didn't complain!

It was amazing to see her in front of large groups of people, as she invited them to get involved with her in the bra business. She was exuberant! She became so passionate and full of life people were naturally attracted to her. She held the attention of everyone in the room. In order to boost her career further, she became a motivational junkie. She was the proud owner of just about every cassette tape made by any motivational speaker of that time. She also was an avid reader of self-help books written by authors such as Zig Ziglar, Napoleon Hill, and many others. These people who inspired others became members of the family! Looking back, I believe that step in her life was very positive and profound. It was not only amazing for her, but for the rest of our family also.

We were taught to not feel sorry for ourselves. Mom always had a positive attitude, no matter the situation. She wouldn't allow negativity to be a part of our household. As mom's career advanced, many awards followed. She was at the top of the sales charts with any of the companies she became affiliated with. One of the very first awards she received was a new car. I remember the look on mom's face when she told all of us that she had earned a new car. It took about a week before the grin was off her face! Having a new car was a first for us. All the cars we had in the past were pretty old and battered.

Mom and dad flew out to Iowa to pick up their car. I remember her shining face when she came home with her brand new, bright red Mercury Park Lane. It had a white vinyl top and was the talk of the neighborhood for weeks! Mom said that the night she picked up the car she kept going to the window and pulling back the drapes to make sure it was still there. She was worried that they would come to take it away. I soon learned that being in business was a pretty sweet deal.

The opportunity she was in seemed pretty simple. Ladies would come to the house, go down to the basement, try on bras, buy the bras, and leave! What a deal! SIGN ME UP! Mom's success came quick as a top producer. A couple years later, mom had earned enough money to build what would be called *The Hotel*. The house was built at the top of a street in a new neighborhood. That's when mom had arrived!

Mom made her mark, not only professionally, but I think as the woman she always wanted to be. Mom shared stories about when she was a little girl living in Promontory, Utah on a farm. She would look at the Sears & Roebuck Catalogs in amazement. She saw ladies all dressed up with fine hats and handbags. They looked like successful businesswomen. That's what she wanted to be. She wanted to become a successful businesswoman from the time she was a little girl looking through those catalogues. Can you imagine living in the middle of nowhere, back in the 30's and 40's dreaming of becoming a successful businesswoman? It's almost unfathomable that a little girl of that time in history would have had such lofty dreams. She wanted to get off of the farm she was raised on. Then she wanted to move out of the small town community she was raised in. Of course, my mom achieved her childhood goals!

Speaking of Promontory, I learned at a very early age that farm girls could hit, or in my mother's case spank. And spank hard too! Living on a farm one has to be extremely self-sufficient. I have a deep appreciation for the basic necessities and commodities that exist on a farm, and the value they hold to those who depend on them. For example, fuel is an important part of those commodities with its many uses like running tractors, pumps for irrigation, combines and swathes for cutting wheat and alfalfa. Those are just a few things that require fuel to operate.

My cousin, Darwin, and I had another use for fuel that I doubt had ever passed the mind of my grandfather. A simple stick with cloth wrapped around it, soaked in... yes, the valuable commodity of gasoline. Unfortunately, at the age of eight or so we didn't quite comprehend the potential flammability of fumes. Before Darwin and I put the hose back on the hand-operated pump, we lit a match to light the torch we had made. Needless to say the torch ignited and along with it the hose. After that, the pump also ignited. My brother, Bob, came out being the first to see the flames. He immediately ran to the farmhouse to get mom and grandma. Grandpa was in town. Both mom and grandma came flying out of the house racing to the work shed. The pump was consumed in flames. Grabbing shovels they started throwing scoops full of dirt on the flames. They worked tirelessly to extinguish the roaring flames to suffocate them. Darwin and I did what we could to help, but it seemed futile in comparison to their efforts. They prevailed in overcoming the flames, and saved the tank from being completely engulfed and exploding. Mom and grandma saved the farm.

During the war with the fire, another fire had been ignited. This fire didn't need gas or flammables. The fire I'm talking about is one where rage begins and there is no extinguishing it. Remember when I said farm girls could hit or spank? Well, I found out that day just exactly what a good old-fashioned lickin' was all about, and what a perfectly placed swat to the butt can do.

Mom laid into Darwin and me. I'm sure if a neighbor lived closer than two miles away Child Protection Services would have shown up Johnny-on-the-spot! We both were looking for something to cool our butts off after the punishment we took that day. And yes, it was well deserved! We all laugh about it today as we look back, but that could have been a catastrophe to the farm had it not been for the quick actions of Bob, and the heroic maneuvers of mom and grandma.

Mom's goal was not to become the best pie maker in the county, or the best dressmaker in the town. Her dream was to become a successful businesswoman. In those days with the frugal means available to her, her dream was like plotting a course for the moon without a rocket ship! But, that's the epitome of my mother and what her life has always been about. Facing adversity, showing no fear, having a plan and implementing that plan with conviction. That's her MO, her method of operation.

Mom's success continued in spite of all the personal loss of loved ones. It's difficult to even try to imagine her losing her spouse at eighteen and becoming a widow with two children under three, losing a son that was only thirty-six years old, losing a daughter to vehement murder, losing her second spouse from a surgery, and finally (or so we pray finally) losing yet another son from sleep apnea. The loss of two spouses, and three children would be a heavy load for anyone to carry. I know we all have our crosses to bear, but mom has borne hers with grace and strength. Mom has taught everyone around her the lessons she has learned from all she has endured. That lesson is simply this:

"It's not what happens to you, it's how you handle it."

With her conviction, tenacity and determination my mom powers through whatever comes her way. She always diligently looks for the lessons to be learned from each life experience.

In about 1972, we moved again. This time we located in Holiday, Utah about fifteen miles south of Bountiful. This move took us closer to Salt Lake City. By this time the only siblings in the house were Bob and I. We lived in an upscale neighborhood called Three Fountains East. It was a new condominium complex with a guard shack at the entrance. Nowadays places like where we lived are called gated communities. My brother Bob was not happy about the move. He had roots in the Bountiful community and had already started high school at Viewmont High there. He wasn't about to go to another high school. Mom's view on the matter differed from Bob's.

Through many negotiations, Bob finally coerced mom and dad into allowing him to drive to Viewmont everyday for school. The one stipulation mom placed on the deal was that Bob had to drive the dune buggy we had built. Unfortunately for Bob, our buggy was built for driving in the sand not snow. The top came down in the spring and summer, and was up in the fall and winter. The one catch was that the buggy didn't have a heater! It only took one winter for Bob to become a new student at Cottonwood High in Holiday. Mom was pretty much a genius at letting us learn our lessons. She always had an underlying plan to help us learn the lessons we needed to learn quicker!

I loved that area. It was my time! Bob was getting close to moving out. I was the ruler of the house, or at least that was what I thought. Nobody to haggle with, plus I had the choice of any bedroom I wanted. Mom kept me grounded and always tried to keep me in line. I know I gave my parents a run for their money as a teenager. I played all the sports in junior high and high school. Because of that, I had somewhat of a reputation to uphold. Mom was there to make sure that my head didn't swell too much, and that I remained somewhat humble. Unfortunately for me, I chose a path that had its ups and downs. A little more downs than I would have liked.

When I was fifteen, I somehow convinced mom that I was able and responsible enough to drive the car to both church and school. Her and dad's rule was to school and church ONLY. One wrong step, and I was barred from driving until I got my license. I toed the line at first, not even taking the long way home as an alternate route. I loved the freedom. Mom was the one who rewarded me for my responsible actions. On the other hand, she was also the one who made me suffer her wrath when I was irresponsible.

I distinctly recall one evening when my best friend Kelly Woodland and I had a party. We had kegs, and all our friends were there. Kelly's dad owned an apartment complex, and we had the party in the clubhouse. Kelly kept telling me to call my mom and dad to let them know that I was spending the night. To this day I'm still not sure why I didn't heed his advice. All I remember was falling asleep after a night of fun. Then as if in a dream sometime in the middle of the night, I woke to my mother's rather irritated voice. In a forced restrained voice she let me know in no uncertain terms that the night was over. Yeah, more than the night was over for me, that was for sure!

Needless to say, I was not of normal consciousness. I was rather dizzy and wobbly. The earth was rotating at a speed much higher than when I had retired earlier that evening. Dad didn't have to say much, as mom had firmly had taken the reins. She made me aware, as I sat at the counter in the kitchen, of their concerns. They had been up all night looking for me. Hospitals had been called to see if I was a patient there. They had called neighbors and other friends, waking them in order to see if any of them knew where I was. Mom completed the conversation by ending all my privileges that I had until she deemed it appropriate to dole them out as she saw fit to do. Short of school and work my activities were in her control. I don't remember exactly how many months it was before she allowed me the opportunity to regain my freedom, but I remember I thought I had learned what an eternity felt like!

I think out of all of us children, I was the one least likely to learn a lesson. I seemed to rather enjoy the voice of an outraged mother. My ninth, tenth and eleventh grade years seemed to be years that I was stretching my legs, or in other words sowing my oats. It was a rather confusing time for me. I had another friend named Scott Clinger. We were rather mischievous. Trouble found us without an invitation. We had this harebrained idea to climb Mount Olympus, which happened to be the largest mountain in the area. Yeah, I know, the name itself is daunting. The mountain is part of the Rocky Mountain Range and is about nine thousand feet in elevation. With no hiking experience, Scott and I decided to test our climbing skills. Skills that I might add were non-existent, because of never being used before! We were sure our parents would have other thoughts about us going on our journey, so we decided to leave a note and forgo their approval. We attempted the climb in the mid-morning. We weren't quite prepared for the ensuing storm that was forming. Back then there were no weather apps, or weather channels.

Realizing we were in danger, Mom called the Sheriffs department. Her brother Howard happened to be a private pilot. Both were enlisted in the full-scale search and rescue to find us. My mother's love was surely at the head of the organized plan. The Sheriffs department climbed the mountain, while Uncle Howard scoured the mountain from the air. Both parties searched until the sun had set, and it was dark. The rain started, and it didn't take long for us boys to hoof it down the mountain. I'll never forget the look on mom's face when she arrived to where the sheriff had us in his car. That was a look I never wanted to see again. Her eyes were filled with despair and fear. I watched as those emotions disappeared with the knowledge that her baby was recovered safely and would be coming home.

Messages from Nick's Children

Nick's daughter Nicole

Dad has always been the comedian. He made my friends laugh. Sometimes I used to think they came over to see him instead of me. My dad has a way of making us laugh even when we don't want to. He is also a great storyteller. I love hearing him tell stories about when he was growing up. With him being the youngest, he was always up to something that got him in trouble! He laughs about most things now, but at the time I am sure there were not a lot of laughs.

During my life at home, the one thing I remember most was feeling safe. I can remember one time specifically. I was on my way home from pom camp and the rain was a torrential downpour. I was scared to say the least. I thought my heart was going to jump out of my chest it was pounding so hard. Just a side note, weather terrifies me! I don't like thunderstorms or monsoons. And, yes, I know that I am in the minority on that point. Anyway, on the drive home I remember just closing my eyes knowing that my dad would get me home safe. And he did. When there were storms I can remember lying on the floor of my parent's room right next to their bed. No matter how bad the winds and rains were, I felt calm and peace lying by them.

Dad doesn't give up. He never gives up. There are so many examples of this throughout my life. The one that is the most prominent in my mind was when my Aunt Trish was murdered. My father was relentless in his pursuit to find justice for his sister. Now that I am older, and a parent myself, I see why he never gives up. He loves his family. He will stop at nothing to protect them and keep them safe.

He is an amazing father. I love him dearly. Even when he drives me crazy! I wouldn't have him any other way.
Nicole

Nick's son Adam

My father is kind, genuine and would do just about anything for anyone. My mother is amazing, loving, and she has truly kept us all together. Growing up I was always looking up to my father. He was the *cool* dad in our neighborhood. In the fifteen years of my playing sports, not once did my

parents ever miss a game showing their true dedication, love and compassion they have for me as their son. I am proud to call them Mom and Dad.
Adam

~Chapter Twelve~

From Little Dreamer to Successful Entrepreneur

"I started my career outside, because we didn't have indoor plumbing at the time. When I went to visit the outhouse, I was totally impressed with the Sears catalogue. You see we didn't have the luxury of toilet paper. Instead our duties were finished with the use of the Sears catalogue! During my 'duty time' I would look at the pictures of the ladies in their pretty dresses, high heels, hats, purses and suits. I made up my mind then and there that I would not work as hard as my mother. I wouldn't be a farmer's wife, though my father was an amazing man.

I remember well getting my first pair of silk stockings that my mother bought me. My mother would be given men's old suits and take them apart. She made clothes for us kids out of them. I had one dress and I learned to take very good care of that one dress."

Thera would practice walking. She would stand straight and tall, because she knew that the day would come when she would dress well and be a businesswoman. She started watching successful people and began mimicking things they did. The Sears catalogue, along with the example of prosperous people, was what she had during the great depression that instilled visions of success within her. Thera didn't have television or radio back then. In her community, the women were mothers and farmer's wives. She saw them all work so hard, just like her mother.

A dream was born in that dear little girl all those years ago. It all began because of the models she saw on the pages of the Sears catalogue portraying how she imagined herself being in the future. Thera determined from studying those pictures that the day would arrive when she would be a successful businesswoman.

For the most part, school was a horrible experience for Thera. She attended a one-room schoolhouse where there were a total of thirteen children combining all eight grades. The schoolteacher came out to Promontory. She boarded with someone while she taught school for nine months out of the year. She was a single woman, so all the cowboys would come to see her. Each time she went out to talk to the cowboys, she would ask Thera to teach the class.

"That was when I began to stand in front of people. I watched her and did my best to be as professional as my teacher was."

Thera didn't enjoy high school. In her opinion it was crowded with too many kids.

"I didn't like going to high school at all. I married Dorian at sixteen years old. There was never any talk of my attending college. My hard-working parents just couldn't afford anything like that. I admit I was a student who did not study. When I became pregnant and got married, I came to the realization and acceptance that I would be a homemaker like

my mother. I would be a mother just like my mother was, the greatest mom any son or daughter could ever have!"

As Thera expressed earlier in this book, if she would have remained married to Dorian, she knows she never would have accomplished all she was able to accomplish in her life.

"Marrying Sterling allowed me to travel the world with my husband, the man I loved, the man who never held me back. We did struggle during those years of getting him through college. When I married Sterling, I began a life associating with not only men who were educated, but also with women who were educated. I still considered myself as just a farmer's daughter, because the words of Mrs. Toland had never stopped going through my mind.

My exposure to education came as I watched Sterling graduate from college and go into the Air Force. The Air Force threw me into another stream of life that I found very interesting. The women would dress up, as I once dreamed of doing when I was a little girl. I started reading and studying more. I had exposure to people whom I could meet, greet and carry on conversations with. I would ask myself, 'How can I do this, and be professional?' I always walked tall and straight. I took pride in my appearance, while talking the very best I could. I listened to people, and learned from how they spoke."

Thera sought out the opportunity to do telephone soliciting when Sterling was in the Air Force. She did this to help bring in extra income to help their family. Her job was to set up appointments for the salesmen in the company. The salesmen would then go to the appointments Thera had scheduled for them, in order to sell stocks and bonds.

"I did this when my children were going to school. I had looked for a job I could do at home. I understood that being a mother was the role that needed to come first, along with being a wife and a homemaker. I would go to the sales meeting around nine o'clock a.m. to take my phone leads into all the salesmen. I made two percent of all that they made from the sales they got through my leads. The salesmen would stand in line to get the prospects I had created through my phone contacts, because my leads were quality leads that led to sales."

Thera learned how to use a telephone. In the sales meetings she would listen carefully to what was said. One day she thought to herself, "If my leads are so good and these guys are taking my leads and earning ten percent while I only earn two percent, why can't I do what they are doing and earn ten percent?"

"I made the decision to learn what the salesmen's job required, so that I could earn the ten percent for my family. That is exactly what I did! I ended up outselling every salesman in the company before the company shut down. I earned that ten percent, and I deserved that ten percent."

Tupperware was the big thing during that time. Thera had purchased some items from a representative. The woman continued working on her, doing her best to get Thera to sell Tupperware.

"I kept telling her I couldn't stand up in front of women to do a presentation. Finally, after her urging, I decided to try. I set up a party and it ended up being a huge success! I went home, went to bed, and was scared to death. It literally had made me sick to get up in front of those women. I had no self-confidence, because I had never had any professional training. After the success of my party, some of the women involved in the company tried to get me to be a manager. After feeling so inadequate even though I had experienced success, I wouldn't do it. I simply didn't want to. I sold a little Tupperware here and there. From doing that, I gained the experience needed to go out and do lots of little things. Those little things taught me valuable things in baby steps. I was prepared for my personal success because of those baby steps."

Sterling and Thera experienced wonderful things during the time they were married. Through his military career, they struggled to provide for their family. Thera's confidence had finally grown to a point to where she felt that she could build something on her own. That is when she started with the bra business experiencing great success, earning company cars, and big money.

In a blessing given to Joseph's mother, Thera's grandmother, she was told that she would leave this life when she chose to do so. She died at about one hundred years old and lived in her own place almost up until she passed away. She was a matter-of-fact kind of gal. Hmmm… I'm thinking Thera had just a bit of her grandmother in her! One day she notified all of her children that they could go through her things and buy them. She never gave anything away. She then informed her children that she was going to move in with her daughter, Dorothy.

"One evening grandmother told Dorothy, 'It's time for me to go. I'm ready to go.' Up to the day she died, she always had her hair done. I am named after her daughter Thera who died at the age of eighteen. I was the first grandchild, so I was named after my Aunt Thera. Grandma would dress in bright colors. As a child, I saw my grandmother always dress in bright reds, pinks, purples and all the other colors. I always remember her with white hair. She was a farmer's wife, but she was also a lady. I open my closet now to bright colors and think, 'I'm just like Grandma!' I

have been very blessed in my life to have had the influences of my mother and grandmothers."

Those of us who know Thera are very blessed to have her influence in our lives. Thera's posterity will forever have her qualities instilled within them. She will forever be a part of who they are. Just like her grandmother, Thera most certainly is one very special lady!

"Any woman can be a wonderful wife and a stay-at-home mother raising her children, while at the same time earning an incredible income, experiencing being a successful businesswoman. As a woman, you can be your own boss and fulfill your priorities to your family first. This is accomplished by taking control of your own life. Every woman can be a successful wife, mother and entrepreneur!"

Thera now earns $15,000 to $17,000 a month at 86 years of age! Both her boys are so proud of their mother.

"Nick calls me and asks, 'How did you do this month, mom?' When I die, Nick and Val will take over my business. I am so grateful I have it to leave to them, and my family. I have been successful. With my priorities in order, I had lost everything monetary. I did this as a mother sacrificing whatever was necessary in order to prove my daughter's murderer was guilty of violently taking her precious life. When I lost Sterling, I also lost everything including my home. Anyone can pick up broken pieces, and put a better masterpiece together than the one they had before. Anyone can!

I am a mom first and foremost. I never dreamed I could do all the things I have done, been where I have been and experienced such great joy in the process!"

Life passes quickly. Decide who you want to be and become that person. Don't be idle in your growth; move forward in your life. Decide what makes you happy, what you are passionate about and follow your dreams! YOU are responsible for making your dreams come true. Don't settle for less. YOU have the power to bring your visions to life!

"This Life doesn't hand anything to you, so get to work. Our world is glorious! It is filled with incredible opportunities. Find yours!"

~Chapter Thirteen~

Rick's Death

"Watching as the horrifying effects from years of alcohol addiction literally ravaged my son's body, was this mother's greatest anguish up until that point in my life. Rick deteriorating away before my very eyes was almost more than I could bear."

Rick found a level of peace and happiness when he met Millie. The two married, but were only married for five months before Rick died. After they got home from their honeymoon, Thera's son went into the hospital twice. The third time, he never came out. Millie was constantly by her husband's side. Millie, Sterling, Thera, Trish and Nick were with him. The doctor told the family that there was so much ammonia inside of him that, even if Rick opened his eyes, he would be a vegetable not recognizing any of them. Rick did open his eyes and he recognized every one of them. Even though his body was failing, he was still a genius with his intelligence. Millie was a registered nurse. She would clarify and update Thera on everything that was put into Rick's file by the medical team taking care of him.

"Millie was an angel who blessed our family. I was oblivious. She would explain everything to me. There I was, a mother, not understanding what was happening to my son. Thankfully I had Millie. It was such a terrible and tragic situation. Rick's children didn't know him. We knew him as this happy wonderful child and young man. There was no relationship that developed between he and his boys, because of the disease that consumed their father."

Millie and Rick were married May 1st, 1989. Rick passed away just three months later on the 3rd of August. Millie said that in those three months she and Rick shared a wonderful spiritual marriage. Thera informed me that Millie is her daughter.

"A nurse came out of the intensive care where Rick was. I recognized the look on her face. It was the same look that was on my father's face when he gave me the news that Dorian had been killed. The nurse was thoughtful and kind. She put her hands out to me and said, 'This is the hardest part of my job, to tell parents that their child is going to die. There is nothing more we can do. Your son will probably die today.' Because of the years of alcohol addiction, Rick's liver was gone. He was bleeding internally and everything in his body was shutting down."

Rick was in the hospital for six weeks before he lost the battle for his life. During that time he was in and out of comas. The family would take turns being with him. Millie would play music and hold him massaging his dying body. It was tremendously hard on Thera's heart watching her cherished son suffer such excruciating pain. She sat by his side praying for her boy, and loving him.

"I would walk up and down the hospital hall with my heart heavy while I thought, 'I wonder if my son will die today.' One Sunday at church they were singing a song. I began to cry. I prayed and asked, 'Why do I have to go through all this? Why does Rick have to go through all this? Why did he make the choices he made that have brought him to this point?' Then I stopped myself. 'Wait a minute. I can't ever put a question mark where God puts a period.' That was when I knew I had to get out and talk to people. I had so many opportunities to talk to young people and help educate them on the disease that destroys lives.

There was a billboard that had a picture of a guy leaning back with a beer in his hand. It said, 'Life doesn't get better than this.' Let me tell you what it is really like when one's body is dying from alcohol. My son's stomach would swell from the internal bleeding. He would throw up blood, though too weak to move. His organs shut down. The lining of his organs ruptured causing the bleeding. Rick would beg for water, but they wouldn't give him any water. They don't give dying alcoholics water for some reason. When the nurse left, I would give my son water and let him suck on ice chips."

In the hospital Nick would sit by Rick's side sketching pictures, beautiful pictures! He and Trish were there with Rick. They shared with their mother that Rick didn't have long.

"I couldn't be in the room and watch my son die. I was in the waiting room with Millie. Nick and Trish were with Rick."

I cannot begin to imagine the emotions within Thera while she waited in that hospital waiting room. I remember well reading a very profound book on the life and ministry of Jesus Christ. The title of the book is *Jesus the Christ* written by James E. Talmage. I would like to share the author's thoughts of the feelings of God, when His only begotten son suffered and was crucified. I now quote from that powerfully enlightening book:

"Our Father had with him his Son, our Redeemer, in the eternal worlds, faithful and true for ages, standing in a place of trust and honor, and the Father loved him dearly, and yet he allowed this well-beloved Son to descend from his place of glory and honor, where millions did him homage, down to the earth, a condescension that is not within the power of man to conceive. He came to receive the insult, the abuse, and the crown of thorns. God heard the cry of his Son in that moment of great grief and agony, in the garden when, it is said, the pores of his body opened and drops of blood stood upon him, and he cried out: "Father, if thou be willing, remove this cup from me."

I ask you, what father and mother could stand by and listen to the cry of their children in distress, in this world, and not render aid and assistance? I have heard of mothers throwing themselves into raging streams when they could not swim a stroke to save their drowning children, rushing into burning buildings, to rescue those whom they loved.

We cannot stand by and listen to those cries without it touching our hearts. The Lord has not given us the power to save our own. He has given us faith, and we submit to the inevitable, but he had the power to save, and he loved his Son, and he could have saved him. He might have rescued him from the insult of the crowds. He might have rescued him when the crown of thorns was placed upon his head. He might have rescued him when the Son, hanging between the two thieves, was mocked with, "Save thyself, and come down from the cross. He saved others; himself he cannot save." He listened to all this. He saw His Son condemned; he saw him drag the cross through the streets of Jerusalem and faint under its load. He saw that Son finally upon Calvary; he saw his body stretched out upon the wooden cross; he saw the cruel nails driven through hands and feet, and the blows that broke the skin, tore the flesh, and let out the life's blood of his Son. He looked upon that.

The life's blood of his Beloved Son went out. His Father looked on with great grief and agony over his Beloved Son, until there seems to have come a moment when even our Savior cried out in despair: "My God, my God, why hast thou forsaken me?"

In that hour I think I can see our dear Father behind the veil looking upon these dying struggles until even he could not endure it any longer; and, like the mother who bids farewell to her dying child, has to be taken out of the room, so as not to look upon the last struggles, so he bowed his head, and hid in some part of his universe, his great heart almost breaking for the love that he had for his Son.

Oh, in that moment when he might have saved his Son, I thank him and praise him that he did not fail us, for he had not only the love of his Son in mind, but he also had love for us. I rejoice that he did not interfere, and that his love for us made it possible for him to endure to look upon the sufferings of his Son and give him finally to us, our Savior and our Redeemer. Without him, without his sacrifice, we would have remained, and we would never have come glorified into his presence. And so this is what it cost, in part, for our Father in Heaven to give the gift of his Son unto men."

"My son was utterly exhausted from suffering the effects of his earthly prolonged addiction to alcohol. His body could not endure anymore. Trish and Nick held their brother's hands when Rick's choice spirit left his abused mortal body. How can one possibly describe the anguished, grief stricken, plagued and tortured heart of this mother?"

Rick fought an inward battle so intensely, but in the end the scars from that battle took him from those who loved him, from those whom he loved. Rick was Thera and Sterling's first child to succumb to death. He truly was a remarkable person, a multifaceted and talented individual. Rick had many aspirations he was not able to achieve in this life. How humbling that we can live each day of our lives knowing of the perfect love that God, even our Father in Heaven, and His Son Jesus Christ have for us. We can see and feel of their love when we acknowledge all that is good in our lives. Through them, and the immeasurable sacrifices both made in our behalf, Rick now experiences indescribable joy as he continues on his eternal journey freed from his worldly vulnerabilities.

"At Rick's viewing Diana was concerned about her children viewing a body. She was cautious about how they went to the casket. I reached over and took my grandson Shane's hand. He really loved his Uncle Rick. We walked over and looked at Rick's body. Shane looked up at me and said, 'Grandma how come you smile all the time no matter how bad things are?' That came from my grandson. From the mouths of babes."

I am sure Shane learned a lifelong lesson from his beautiful grandmother that day. What a gift it has been for me to write this book. In so doing, I have learned so many lessons from Thera that I will remember forever. Her trust in God and in His plan remains unshaken.

"I can only imagine the joy Rick must feel as he watches over Casey, Corey and Cobey from heaven. I know he watches over them, their wives and their children. Casey is the father to three children, Corey is the father to six sons, and Cobey is the father to two children. Rick has eleven amazing grandchildren who I know he loves. Rick is proud of his boys and the men they are today. Rick has a deep love and appreciation for Sonja, for the mother she is to the boys and the grandmother she is to those eleven wonderful grandchildren! Those three boys show great respect, and I know their father couldn't be prouder!

Corey found out that his father's class reunion was happening. He reached out and asked his father's schoolmates to share any memories they had of him. The response was great! I was so pleased when Corey wondered about his father's past. He was amazed when I handed him all the letters Rick had sent me. I had kept every one of them, because I knew the day would come when they would end up in the hands of Rick's boys."

I asked Thera her thoughts about people that seem to breeze through life without cares and trials, not having to endure things like she has had to endure.

"As a spirit I knew I could handle anything that I would have to do here on earth. I simply said, 'Where do I sign? I'm in!' I didn't fully understand what I had agreed to back then in the pre-existence. I am thankful for corners. Corners allow each of us the opportunity to recover from an event, without knowing what we will have to face next. When

Rick died, I knew that the experience was the worst thing in my life. Then a mere eighteen months later Trish was murdered. I lost Sterling. I lost Bob. Heavenly Father and Jesus Christ know us. We each have our own set of trials to endure. Corners are a gift."

Memories of Rick's final days, from Nick

In the last years of Rick's life, he managed to see the hurt he had caused. He recognized the wrong choices he had made. Unfortunately, as is the case many times, that knowledge came too late to save his life. All of his struggles had caught up with him. His life was at the end of the hourglass. He met and married his second wife Millie. She loved him in spite of his downfalls. She was committed to him and he to her. It was tender to see the happiness that my brother finally had found with Millie, the fulfillment that overcame his spirit.

In his final days here on earth, his body systematically decided that it had had enough. It was tired, and was shutting down. Rick was in a fight. We spent just over thirty days in the hospital with him. He was in and out of a coma. The ammonia build-up in his body was severe due to the lack of his liver functioning properly. He would wake up for an hour or two then slip back into the coma.

Trish and I sat with him, as did Millie, Mom and Dad. We were with him for hours and hours on end waiting and praying that somehow his body would take a turn for the better. Rick surely felt the love and compassion that surrounded him. We all were with him daily. We cared for him, cleaned him and made sure he had plenty of music to listen to.

Life came to an end for my brother at the young age of thirty-six on August 3rd 1989. Trish and I were in the room with him, just the three of us brothers and sister. It was so surreal. There we were sitting in a room where all the thoughts of growing old together became a distant, unrealistic dream. Rick was dying. Our brother was dying right in front of us. We were stroking his hair as he struggled to open his eyes every now and then. Rick's time was at hand. I knew that Val and Bob wished they could be there. I knew they would want to say something to him.

I got up knowing that we needed to include them in some way. So, I told Trish that I was going to call them. I let her know they needed to know that things didn't look so well for Rick, and to find out what they would like to tell him before he left us. I went to a phone where we could talk, called them, and they were both on the line. I explained to them that Rick could go at any minute. I asked them both if they had anything they wanted to tell our brother. It was silent for a moment. Val and Bob both shared that they wanted him to know how much they loved him, that they were going to miss him, that they were okay, and it was alright for him to leave. I know that may sound a little odd, but it felt like Rick was holding on because we all couldn't let him go.

In our minds we knew that it was time to let Rick know that if it was time for him to quit fighting, it was okay. He was tired. Upon returning to the room where Rick and Trish were, I looked at Trish and she said, "He's gone." I looked over at the heart monitor and there was a slight heartbeat. I said "Trish he's not gone. Look at his heart monitor." She responded that his heart had stopped when I walked out of the room. I sat on the bed Rick was in, and lifted his head. I quietly said to him, "Rick, Val and Bob love you deeply. And, it's okay." With that, he opened his eyes for a brief moment giving us a very faint, beautiful Rick smile. I was happy to know that he knew he was loved, and that he left this world with nothing but love surrounding him.

~Chapter Fourteen~

Trish's Death

"The night of Sterling's barbershop chorus, Trish was supposed to be sitting with me as she always did. She loved to listen to her father sing and perform! I thought of my daughter as I sat in the audience, and said a prayer that she was safe."

Thera's beautiful daughter was safe. Trish was in the arms of our Redeemer. Rick had escorted his big sister *home*.

Bob and Arleen had come from California to attend Sterling's performance with the barbershop choir he sang in. When Sterling's performance ended, they all went home. Shortly after, Thera answered the phone to a collect call from the enemy that Trish had been married to. He was calling from Mexico, where he had taken his wife and children for a vacation, a vacation of which he had strategically calculated and prearranged every detail to murder his wife. After answering the phone, the enemy told Thera that he needed to talk to both her and Sterling. Thera immediately sent Bob to go get his father. She put the phone down waiting for Sterling to come.

"In those moments the Spirit let me know, 'He is calling to tell you that Trish is dead. Be careful what you say to him; he murdered her.' I knew exactly what he was going to say. Still, the words pierced my soul to my very core. 'I'm calling to tell you Trish is dead.' I put my hands down between my knees to keep them from trembling. I was in shock. I knew this man was capable of many things, but never thought he would be capable of murder. Through divine revelation as Trish's mother, I absolutely knew that the man Trish had been married to had taken her life."

The speakerphone was on as he talked to us like one who was speaking memorized words. Sterling was in a state of shock. His little girl was gone. Bob and Arlene were shocked. Thera felt a rush of traumatized emotions as only a mother could feel. Trish's life was violently taken on the 23rd of February 1991, by her husband's bloodied hands. Sterling and Thera lost their beloved daughter. Val, Bob, and Nick, along with their wives, lost their treasured sister. Marsha, Thera and Hayden lost their beautiful mother. Trish's nieces and nephews lost their amazing aunt. Grief piercingly ripped through the hearts of the entire family. Feeling the loss extended to all who knew and loved Trish. Her influence reached far beyond what any of us can comprehend.

"I had just lost Rick eighteen months earlier. I knew from experience that my daughter was gone. I'm sure I was in shock, but even being in shock my mind fixated on, 'What do I have to do to make this right for my daughter, and my grandchildren?' I will tell you that I did not grieve for Trish in the beginning. I knew what Trish wanted. I was focused on the mission at hand, the mission I knew my daughter needed me to do. I was

driven with the charge, as Trish's mother, to bring justice for my daughter's murder to those who had ended her life tearing her beautiful light away from her cherished children, and all of our family."

When Nick arrived, Thera told her son that she had to go outside. She announced that she needed to go for a walk.

"When we were alone I turned to my son and said, 'Nick, I want to tell you something. I haven't spoken it to anyone yet.' Nick said, 'I know Mom. We are both thinking the same thing.' Then I said out loud, 'He murdered Trish.' As I continued to walk, my mind was impressed with two thoughts:

1. I have to get Trish's children away from him, so they are safe.
2. I will see that he goes to prison for taking Trish's life."

Memories from Nick on Trish's Death

The man Trish was married to decided selfishly to take Trish's beautiful smile away, and to extinguish the light we all loved so much. He concocted a demented, twisted plan with the transsexual he was having an affair with to murder Trish. Her time was up in his mind. She was in the way. He was too proud to do the manly thing, and walk away from what he had no more. Trish's life had progressed so much further ahead of his. She had the greatest respect amongst her peers and community. So many people loved my big sister!

The coward was evil, drowning in the water looking for a life preserver. Fired from his job for stealing, while having an affair with a transvestite, he had no place to go. No place that is except for my mom and Trish's extremely successful business, and Trish's big fat life insurance policy that went with it. He could have walked away, and spent the rest of his days in Mexico as he had planned with the transvestite that helped him take Trish away. But, he had to have ALL the money first. He didn't care how he got it, or whom he hurt in the process just as long as he walked away with everything Trish and my mom had worked so hard for.

The last time I told my sister I loved her was before she left with her little family on that fateful trip to Mexico. Her husband had determined Rocky Point would be the place where Trish would leave this life. Through warped premeditated planning, even to the point of making a medieval-time weapon, he accomplished what he set out to accomplish. Through one horrendous blow to her stomach and thirteen repulsive blows to her head, he deprived his own children of their loving mother. He had computed every detail including place, time and method. He had designed everything down to the vile act of sending their little children into the room before anyone else, to find their beloved mother. He would finally have control of my sister.

132

Trish's murderer made personal choices in his life that created a self-serving, miserable, professionally scourged and evil man. No matter what, he was going to have the last say, the last word. He thought his plan was brilliant. In his immoral, criminal mind he was going to walk away a free man, and take with him every penny of my sister's insurance money along with her share of TNT. I can tell you now, with incomparable sorrow, the only part of his plan that went without a glitch was his plan for ending my sister's life.

I love you Sis, Nick

The enemy told Sterling he wanted to talk to Thera in person. Thera stipulated that the only way she would see him was if Sterling and also the Bishop were present. That was arranged.

"The man that murdered my daughter came into the room. He held his arms out to me. I demanded, 'Don't you touch me!' Sterling and the Bishop were there with me. I looked into that man's face and said, 'You murdered my daughter.' I watched as he began to sweat profusely."

The tragic death of such a beautiful, vibrant woman had hit the community hard. So many people were at Trish's funeral.

"I've often thought about when Nick was born, and how much Trish wanted him to be a little sister. I remember her falling in love with him at first sight! How humble that Heavenly Father sent us our son! I shall never forget his promise to his big sister, as he stood next to her casket holding her lifeless hand. 'Sis, I'll find out who did this to you, and they will be brought to justice.'"

Two Stake Presidents spoke, as did Thera for Trish's funeral. While sharing her message she said, 'I know the person or persons who did this will be brought to justice very quickly.' Then, with all the love that overflowed from her mother's heart for her child Thera invited everyone present to go home and pray that those who murdered Trish would be brought to justice.

After the service, the procession of cars lined up following the hearse that carried Trish's body. On the way to the cemetery the rain came down in torrents! Over a foot of water soaked the cemetery grounds. Trish's freshly dug grave filled with so much water it prevented her casket from being lowered into her grave. They couldn't bury her. A dedicatory prayer was offered over the gravesite. The prayer blessed the place her body is now laid to rest until the glorious resurrection day, when her spirit and perfected body will once again be reunited. Jesus Christ will come again to the earth for His miraculous second coming, bringing to pass the magnificent resurrection!

The casket holding Trish's body was once again placed into the hearse. The police escorted everyone back to the church. A meal was served with about two hundred of the closest family and friends in attendance.

Afterwards Trish's body was then returned to the mortuary where it lay for two days, until the rainwater cleared from her grave.

During those two days, she was a very busy girl from the other side of the veil! With Thera's invitation for those at her daughter's funeral to pray that justice would be served, amazing things happened. Prayers were heard and answered. A loving Father opened the heavens allowing Trish, and many others from heaven, to influence those whose testimonies would help put the murderer away. Prayer is such a gift! Perhaps fifty to sixty leads were shared with the Gilbert police. Every lead pointed to the enemy. They **all** said to check him out.

Thera's grieving process flooded her soul after the funeral was over. Her still scarred heart from losing her son was invaded now with a new, immensely deep, fresh wound from losing her daughter. The pain was almost more than she could bear. But, more agony was to come for Thera. Trish's murderer wouldn't allow Thera to be with her grandchildren. The precious three children whom Thera loved with all of her heart who had just lost their mom. He wouldn't let her even see them. He had taken their mother's life. The children were innocent, clueless as to the gross monster he was and what he had done. Of course, the cowardly enemy did all in his manipulative power to turn the children, and so many others, against Thera.

Thera was alone when the all-consuming grief debilitated her, overshadowing her tender heart. It was a terrible time. Thera's grief stricken soul yearned for both her son and daughter. Her heartache was magnified a thousand fold with the almost unbearable agony caused from the enemy not allowing her to see her grandchildren. Surely their beautiful faces would have helped to fill the intense void in their grandmother's world. Thera sat completely alone and helpless at her desk.

"I prayed. I asked what I could do to see my grandchildren. I asked what I was supposed to do next to bring about justice for Trish. I knew, without doubt, that those were the two things my daughter needed me to do."

Trish had been taking voice lessons. The Sunday before Trish was murdered she went to Thera's Ward. Thera was teaching a lesson and had asked her daughter to come and sing the song *Because I Have Been Given Much* to go along with her lesson. Trish singing that song enhanced the spirit that was already present from Thera's lesson. Everyone in attendance witnessed something very special. The spirit touched each soul in the room.

"I sat at my desk feeling overwhelming heartache. I then opened one of the doors of my desk, and a tape fell out landing right in front of me on top of my desk. I took the tape and put it in the player. It was my angel Trish singing a song! I didn't move as tears streamed down my cheeks. The song she was singing was about crying. The words to the song were

134

saying that it's okay to cry, that Heavenly Father loves us, and that He'll take care of us. Trish was sending me a message through that song. Trish was telling me that no matter how many tears I cry, or how alone I feel... I am not alone. We are never alone! I cherish that sacred time between the two of us, when my daughter lifted my heavy heart with her heavenly song."

Trish lovingly communicated with her mourning mother, consoling Thera's grieving heart. The grip of death itself could not keep Trish from doing so. The veil between this life and the next is indeed thin. Thera has no recollection of her daughter ever giving her that tape. Yet, Trish's tape was the *only* thing that fell out of the above shelf in Thera's desk.

"No matter how hard it was for me everyday I got up, dressed up, and showed up. I was consumed with what needed to happen to save my daughter's children. I was consumed with what needed to happen in order to put the evil man in prison that had brutally ended their mother's life. I couldn't eat. I lived on nutritious shakes. Nick was the unyielding investigator, following the criminal's every move, and tracking every lead. Without Nick's dedication to his sister and to our quest, justice may have never been served. Trish was at the forefront of everything that took place after she was murdered."

Someone sent Thera the book, *When You Are Out Of Apples*. Within the pages of that book, she found five questions that put everything into a new perspective. Those questions blessed Thera by giving her the strength to push forward with her mission.

"I posted the book's five questions on my desk where I could see them each day. Every time I would start to doubt that I could even get through another day, I would ask myself those questions. There was no time to feel sorry for me, or to wallow in a pity-party. I was Trish's mother. I was Marsha, Thera and Hayden's grandmother. There was no one who could replace me. As Trish's mother it was my job, first and foremost, to make sure her children were safe and taken care of. Secondly, that justice would be served."

The five questions that continue to bless Thera with even greater wisdom today are:

1) What am I feeling?
2) Where does this feeling come from?
3) What am I going to do with it?
4) How long do I want it to last?
5) What will I replace it with?

135

These five questions, when answered honestly, can provide you with the insight as to how to overcome any struggle. Do you want profound knowledge from Thera? When you are in the midst of troubles, your focus *must* change. All of your negative thoughts and feelings must be replaced with positive thoughts and feelings. Asking yourself the five questions will allow you the ability to move forward in a positive direction away from the most traumatic of tribulations.

"I am a bottom line, as a matter of fact kind of person. I knew what had happened to my girl, and I knew what I had to do. That was it. I had to save my grandchildren, and get the one who took Trish away from us put in prison. I wouldn't stop until both were achieved. There were no other options."

Thera's quest was a process that obsessed her. It got to the point that every thought she had was geared toward protecting her grandchildren, and getting Trish's murderer before a jury with the proof needed to put him behind bars. Her ultimate goal was that of getting the children safely home with her and Sterling.

"I often look back on those times. I was not exhausted. It was like I was filled with some sort of energy from living each day on sheer adrenalin. I was focused with blinders on. I had no time to think about me. If Sterling would try to comfort me, I would simply let him know that I was fine. Perhaps, both Sterling and I needed for Sterling to comfort me. How I would love his comfort now!"

While Trish was still alive loving her children and her life, her enemy made many desperate attempts to sway his wife into signing legal papers naming him as beneficiary of her insurance policy and inheritor of her portion of TNT. Despite his attempts he was transparent, and Trish wisely wouldn't do it. She had found out about her husband's affair. She had let certain family members know that she was planning on starting divorce proceedings against him. The enemy was also aware of that fact. Trish made sure her Last Will and Testament was clear, her mother was the beneficiary of all of her holdings if anything happened to her. She also made sure that her will stated that it was her wish that, in the case of her death, Val would raise her children.

After Trish's murderer carried out his vile plans and irreversible actions, he was greedy for money. Thera knew what he had done, as did so many others who knew him personally. Despite this knowledge Thera would pay the TNT business expenses first, and then send the enemy half of the business profits each month because he had the children. Thera gave him thousands of dollars to make sure he had money to provide for her and Sterling's three grandchildren, and to insure that the children would not do without. I am sure her three grandchildren never saw a penny of that money. Thera didn't have to give him anything at all. It was her choice to do so for her grandchildren. Of course, Thera's giving wasn't public knowledge. He never spoke of the money Thera was generously giving him for the children. Rather, he continued in his futile attempts to poison Thera's world by doing all in his power to attack and defame her character.

"Here I was making sure that he had money for my grandchildren. He lied to Marsha, Thera and Hayden telling them that they had to sell their toys in order for them to have food to eat. He was playing his church ward as well. When we got wind of this, we sent proof to the church leaders showing the checks that I had sent to him. Every month I would send him half of the profit I was earning from Trish's and my business. Those checks were around seven to nine thousand dollars each month. The evidence showed that he had in fact signed and cashed every check from that first month on."

Thera's only goal in giving him the money was to make sure the children had everything they needed, and some spending money for what they wanted. Thera later found out that during the time she was giving him money, he was telling everyone that she was a crazy, greedy witch. This corrupt man was so focused on playing the sad widower to the world that he couldn't possibly cover all of his sickening plans and actions. He was so twisted in all his lies, as he played the role of victim, which he had assigned himself to play, that he couldn't keep track of all the deceit he spewed from his mouth. Frantic to get his hands on innocent Trish's money after he murdered her, he took Thera to court. His evil never ceased!

"The enemy finally succeeded in getting the courts to take everything Trish and I had worked for. I was taken into the judge's chamber, with no opportunity to say one word. I was informed that all of my business had been placed into a receivership as of that day.
The judge threatened me. I quote his words, 'If you use one penny more of the money, show up on Monday with your toothbrush because I will throw your butt (only he didn't use the word butt) in jail.' Those were the exact words the judge used. I had been dedicated to paying half of the profit to provide for my grandchildren for about six or seven months at that point in time, but wasn't able to even explain that fact to the judge. Nor was I able to show the proof that I had that showed that the enemy had cashed every check for himself.
I came out of the meeting in a state of shock. I remember that I nearly passed out. I was so frightened at what the man who had murdered my daughter had just done to Sterling and me. That horrible man sat there

with his attorney, and had also invited the press to manipulate the situation so that he would come out looking like the poor victim.

You know, all these things have been buried so deep in my soul, and yet when the door is opened, it is a floodgate. It is terrible to be poisoned by one so evil, and feel as helpless as I felt that day.

The court took my monthly check and gave me a small amount. He also got a check. Though relentless, he never got the business. Because of him, the courts took everything from me. Val stepped in and gave me money for my attorney. Matol then paid all the attorney bills for me to prove Trish's murderer's guilt. Once he was found guilty, I started to pay Matol back by only getting a third of my checks. Matol kept two thirds of my earnings in order for me to pay back the money they gave me. I paid back every penny borrowed to get justice for Trish."

Thera went into survival mode. She had no life other than taking the actions needed in achieving her two objectives for Trish and her grandchildren. From everything I have learned, I believe Trish was by Nick's side through every selfless sacrifice he made in her behalf. No rock was left unturned by her wonderful little brother. It was through Nick's perseverance, commitment and devotion that the evil hell-bound human, who stole Trish's beautiful life from this earth, will breathe only prison air for the rest of his mortal existence. God's righteous justice will take care of sending this vile creature to hell for all eternity.

When any family faces grave circumstances, the family must work together supporting each other in order to endure those circumstances. It is through love, kindness, understanding, patience, respect, and yes, through sacrifice that families are able to travel straight through the storms of this life. Those families that follow the map of qualities just shared, will come out of the storm *together* into the warmth of the sunshine once again. Thera and her family have proved that scenario time and time again.

"Every thought I had was geared towards getting those children home SAFE with me and Sterling. I knew Trish wouldn't rest until that was accomplished, because of her love for her children. I was fully aware that the only way to achieve that vital goal was to keep pushing forward. I will tell you I was like a tiger that had been let out of its cage!"

The trial started. Sterling, Thera and Val sat in court to hear the verdict. Nick was not allowed in the courtroom, because he had been involved in every aspect of putting away his sister's murderer. He had been a public face in the case. The attorneys knew that it was Nick that had gathered the evidence in order for the trial to take place. Thera had asked to be able to sit at the very end of the row.

"I wanted to sit on the end so as to be close to Marsha. I did this so that I could put my arms around her if the verdict came in guilty. With her having been in fourteen different foster homes, the thought of her not having her mother or father hurt my heart. I needed my granddaughter, that I loved and still love so much, to know that somehow things were going to be ok. I wanted her to understand that she was (as she still is), a very special member of our family. I prayed for her to feel how much we all loved her and that we would take care of her. The first time the judge said he was guilty my focus was to get to my granddaughter.

But, it didn't work that way. My old secretary, who I trusted once upon a time, ended up being an awful person. She was right behind Marsha. My secretary had been in cahoots with Trish's murderer for a long time. The man who took my daughter's life, and also the secretary, both did their best to brainwash the children against me. I didn't get to hold my granddaughter in my arms that day. Marsha struggled with feeling as though she was a part of the family. She felt a great deal of pain, because she had not only lost her mother, but also her father after the guilty verdict came in."

The tormenting ordeal Thera had endured of grief, sleepless nights, tears, loneliness and heavy sorrow was *finally* coming to a close. Even so, she didn't allow herself to savor a moment of relief over the guilty verdict that she, Sterling, Val, Bob and Nick had all exhausted themselves to hear. There was a beautiful young lady named Marsha in the courtroom that day who was precious to her grandmother. She was Thera's priority. I wonder if our sweet Thera's mind ever takes a rest? In writing this book, I certainly have grown to know and love one of the most unselfish souls to ever be born.

"Trish was murdered in February. For almost a year I was isolated from her children, which caused me more sadness than I could ever express. Behind the scenes our family sacrificed endless hours, and spent insurmountable dollars fighting a battle to bring justified conviction to Trish's murderer, and save her precious children from the enemy. I was finally reunited with them in December, after the man that murdered my daughter was finally arrested. Our grandchildren had survived a nightmare beyond what any child should ever have to endure."

Selfless Thera was focused on only one thing in the courtroom, Marsha. Thera's concern for others seems to somehow take on the sufferer's feelings. Whenever that has happened, she has felt as though it is her responsibility to do all in her power to make everything okay. With all the battles Thera has had to fight, all the losses she has endured, all the heartache she has felt, it is no wonder that she does what needs to be done when it needs to be done.

139

"Whether it's good or bad, I have lived my life with laser focus. If something needs doing, I do it. If someone needs me, I'm there for him or her. If I set a goal, I achieve it. Our daughter's children, Sterling and I's grandchildren, had been through so much. We both needed to be there for them."

Sterling and Thera had two of Trish's children come and live with them for about one year. As loving grandparents, both did everything in their power to succor Trish's traumatized children after the unimaginable tragedy they had lived through.

Thera was troubled with remorse. Each time she thought of what Trish had gone through, she felt a penetrating pain that deeply pierced her heart. Thera struggled with the fact that, as close as she and Trish were as mother and daughter, she didn't feel that Trish was in danger. She felt she should have sensed something, that she should have known something was wrong. This guilt haunted her, along with all the awful things Thera was going through at that time.

"Sterling and I went to the temple for the first time after losing Trish. I sat in the peaceful temple, yet I didn't feel peace. My head was bowed. When I put my head up to watch the wonderful film, the beautiful clouds were moving across the screen. I saw Rick's face within those clouds. It was my Rick. I closed my eyes. I heard his voice. He spoke to me, 'You don't need to worry Mom. I was with Trish. She wasn't alone. Don't you remember she held my hand when I died? Trish was on one side; Nick was on the other. I was with Trish every moment, and I took her home.' Miracles and compassion from our loving heavenly parents allowed Rick to bring me that message in the holy temple. The terrible remorse I had felt for not being there for Trish was completely gone as I left the temple that day."

Trish's wish for her children was honored after the concentrated crusade to save her precious children and bring justice for her senseless murder. After two of her children spent time with their choice grandparents, Val became Thera and Hayden's father. What a blessing he has been to each of them! I know that Trish is happy with the outcome of the intense battle fought by her parents and brothers for her and her children's behalf. I am sure Trish's light vibrantly shines in the heavens, never again to be dimmed.

Thera understood that there was only one more thing that she had to do for herself, and for Trish. Perhaps this last thing was the hardest thing of all. Thera had to forgive.

"I looked at those five questions.

1)   What am I feeling?

140

2) *Where does this feeling come from?*
3) *What am I going to do with it?*
4) *How long do I want it to last?*
5) *What will I replace it with?*

I knew the answer to the last question. I had to replace every negative feeling I was feeling with forgiveness. I sat down on Trish's birthday and I wrote a letter to both of the people who murdered my daughter. I explained in the letters that writing to them was my gift to Trish, and to me. To the man Trish had been married to, I wrote:

> *I forgive you. I hope that one day you can find it in your heart to write a letter to your children explaining why you murdered their mother, and ask their forgiveness. But, that is your choice. There will be a day when you will meet your maker, and your final judgment will come from Him. That is not for me to do. For me and for Trish, I forgive you for everything. I have no malice in my heart towards you. I wish you the best for the rest of the time you have left on this earth.*
> *Thera"*

In order for one to heal and truly move forward, one must forgive. Bitterness, anger, and hatred are poisons to the human soul. An unforgiving person becomes hardened. It is as if a cloud of darkness overshadows their heart affecting their very outlook on life. Negative thoughts prevent one from experiencing happiness and joy. Don't we all want happiness and joy? Harboring malice towards another sadly causes one to become callous. Many times health issues ensue. Over time, people holding onto their pain, which has been caused by another's actions, can forget how to love those God has given them to love. Forgiveness brings healing and freedom to a scarred soul.

"After the war we had fearlessly fought for Trish and her children, I had a dream. Though it wasn't like a dream. It was real in every way. I was sitting at an airport behind where people are checked in. Trish came around the corner absolutely beautiful! I exclaimed, 'Trish what are you doing here?' Her answer brought me the peace which had escaped my soul since she was taken from me, 'Mom, I want you to know everything is wonderful. I want you to go on...'"

~Chapter Fifteen~

Joseph and Doran's Death's

"Father had a stroke while walking thru his fields, as he caressed his grains with his fingers. Being the John Wayne man he was Daddy could fight the winds and rains, but he couldn't fight the loss of the use of his arms. Mother would go to the nursing home and spend all day long sitting with him. It was such a mental strain on her that she eventually went into a form of dementia. My mother lived for her husband and her children.

When daddy died there were not many tears from mother, or any of us for that matter. We all knew whom our dad was and that he was only happy when he was active with his family, in his fields, or taking care of his animals. Daddy raised us knowing that one does not eat until their animals were fed and taken care of. Daddy was completely coherent until the moment he died.

He passed away peacefully in the nursing home about two and a half to three years after his stroke. His stroke had paralyzed one side of his body, which was very hard for Daddy always being the active man that he was. As the end drew near, he was slipping in and out of comas. He would wake up and talk about his parents, along with so many other people whom we knew were there with him from heaven. I knew Rick was among them, because he had left us just ten months earlier. Our loved ones were with Daddy to take him home on June 15, 1990."

Doran was with Joseph when he passed. She had sadness, but also a sense of joy for her husband that she loved so much. This amazing woman knew him better than anyone else on the earth. She had witnessed her bigger than life husband become debilitated and she felt how difficult that was for him. She was deeply aware of Joseph's feelings of helplessness. She too was helpless in giving him relief from the pain she knew invaded his heart.

"When Daddy died, after his grand reunion welcoming him home, I am sure that he went to the sacred ground Heavenly Father had prepared just for him and mother. I can just see my Daddy smiling as he walked with both arms outstretched feeling the soft, sweet grains of heaven glide through his fingers."

Joseph had an old red pickup truck. He wanted to be buried in his truck. He would tell his family, 'When I die, bury me in my truck because it has never left me in a hole yet.' At his funeral instead of flowers on his casket, the family had his saddle on it.

Doran ended up being placed in a facility where she went into her own world. Thera shared that her mother didn't recognize any of her family. One of Thera's sisters lived near to where Doran was. She would go sing to their mother, and do her hair once a week. There just wasn't a lot anyone could do for her. Dementia is a terrible disease not only for the person suffering from it, but also for the loved ones.

Thera would go see her mother when she was in town, but Doran didn't know or recognize her daughter. This was hard on Thera. It was hard on all of the children not to be known by their mother. Doran was the woman who had cherished, loved, protected and lived for them their entire lives.

"Mother could take on anything! She was a tiger when it came to protecting her family and home. But, at the same time my mother had a very tender heart. In her last days, there were tears in her eyes. I could see her fear and I could hardly stand that. She loved her hair combed when my sisters and I were little. We combed mother's hair at the end. That simple act calmed her before she returned to heaven."

Those caring for Doran had suggested putting food lines in her. She was sipping little sips of water, so the family opted not to have her go through the stress of inserting the lines and the discomfort that would follow from having them. Doran Morella Howard Nicholas passed from this life into the strong arms of her loving husband a little over ten years after she lost him. Joseph and Doran's sweet reunion happened on the 27th day of November, in the year 2000. Thera's parents will never be parted again.

"We missed her, but she had been gone from us for a long time before she died. When she left us, her mind was freed! We all knew where Mother was, and how relieved and happy she was to be with Daddy again. I believe her tears were from her inability to speak to us. One time for a pacemaker surgery, I lay on the table listening to the medical team around me talking about me. I tried to speak out to tell them to please make sure I was unconscious for the surgery, because I was in a state of waking up. I couldn't communicate to any of them. I felt panicked. I liken that experience to what mother was probably experiencing being completely out of control, feeling alone, not knowing anyone, and not being able to communicate to any of us around her."

When Thera shared her experience with Nick, he explained to his mother that because of her age the anesthesiologist woke her immediately upon the completion of her surgery. Nick assured Thera that she wasn't awake until after the surgery.

"Daddy and mother are buried side by side in Ogden, Utah. They are extremely happy in heaven now that they are together again. I know that both are released from the physical and mental ailments they endured the last few years of their lives here. When I look at the pictures in my bedroom of my mother and father, I feel great joy! I think of my parents in heaven. I am sure that they smile as they walk hand in hand through their serene, stunning heavenly meadows. And, I know that every once in awhile Daddy takes Mother up in his arms for a dance! I think of my

Sterling. Oh, the love that will overflow from my heart when I will once again be in his arms, as Mother is in Daddy's."

The veil is thin between those of us living in mortality, and those who have passed on to the next phase of eternity. A devoted parent's love transcends the division between this life and the next. It matters not whether the parent, or the child, returns to heaven first. The love of a caring parent for their child is never broken. There is an eternal connection between the two and the bond only grows until they are reunited once again.

All five of Thera's treasured children feel of their mother's great love for them. Thera's three children of whom have been taken from her, unquestionably feel of their mother's love for them as they reside in heaven. Thera has been surrounded by both Joseph's and Doran's love, during times where grief has nearly consumed her soul. She feels her noble parents near her expressing that they continue loving her as their daughter, as well as *all* of their posterity. These two beautiful people, who are the Patriarch and Matriarch of quite an awesome brood, love and watch over their amazing family each day. Thank you Joseph and Doran for your choice examples that inspire us. We know you will be blessed forever!

~Chapter Sixteen~

Sterling's Death

Before I begin this chapter, I would like to share that Sterling Huish was, and still is, a great man! As I stated earlier, I have known both Thera and Sterling since just after they lost Trish. Sterling was a bit prone to not taking care of himself. He didn't always do the things the doctors told him he needed to do.

"Sterling had stomach problems, which created heart problems. Both Sterling and I were working at the temple when he finally agreed to go into a cardiologist for a stress test. The doctor recommended my husband get an angiogram. Through that test, it was determined that Sterling needed to have his aortic valve replaced."

Sterling stayed in the hospital for a couple of days before the surgeon performed the surgery. Thera's wonderful husband wanted a Priesthood blessing. He requested that their good home teachers come to the hospital to give him his blessing. In the LDS church, men are called to be home teachers. The women are called to be visiting teachers to other women in the ward area they reside in. With each man's personal acceptance of the calling to be a home teacher, they are then assigned a home teaching partner who has also accepted the call to serve. The two receive a list of a few families to visit monthly, to watch over those families making sure they are not in need. Both of the programs of home and visiting teaching are certainly inspired. Generations of families have benefited through the services given from faithful members, who magnify their callings in these capacities. Once Sterling had his blessing he still had concerns, but seemed more ready to go into surgery.

The doctor informed Thera that her husband's operation would last about three hours. Upon its completion, the surgeon told the family that things went well and that Sterling would be just fine. The cardiologist explained that he had used tissue from Sterling's body to do what needed to be done, and that an artificial valve had not been needed. This was back in 2001.

"Sterling remained unconscious. We were concerned that he wasn't awake yet. The nurse that was supposed to be caring for Sterling had just returned from her honeymoon. We could hear her laughing and telling her fellow workers all about the events of her life. We asked her why he wasn't awake. She told us that she would wake him in two to three hours, and that it would be best to let him rest through the night. She said that we should go home and come back in the morning. Nick asked her what the tube was that was coming out of his father's nose filled with blood. She explained that is was cleaning out his lungs assuring us he would be fine while adding, 'I'll be right here with him.'"

Thera and Nick left their phone numbers. Then, they hesitantly left this most adored man in both of their lives. Sterling was their rock. Once at home, Thera didn't go to bed. She just lay on the couch. She stayed by the phone. Nick, always doing what needed to be done, called to check on his father at around ten o'clock. He called his mom after he had gotten the update on his dad from the nurse and said, "Mom, Dad is still not awake. He should be awake by now, but the nurse assured me that everything is okay. She said that we could come in the morning to see him." Thera knew Nick had checked on Sterling so she lay down to go to sleep. A little over an hour later, Thera's phone rang once again. This time it wasn't Nick.

"It was the hospital calling. The voice informed me, 'Your husband has coded.' With my heart pounding I asked, 'Are you telling me my husband has died?' The voice answered, 'Well, yes. But, we revived him. The surgeon is on his way, but there may be some complications.' I immediately called Nick. 'Nick I think something serious has happened to Dad. I just got a call from the hospital telling us to come as quickly as we can. I'm heading for the hospital right now.'"

Nick told his mother she couldn't drive alone. He, Cara and their two children met Thera near the freeway. They went to the hospital together. Upon their arrival, they rushed through the ICU doors. A full medical staff surrounded Sterling's bed. Nick asked his mother, Cara, and the children to wait. He moved quickly towards his father. The surgeon who had operated on Sterling stopped him. Nick and the surgeon walked over to Thera. The surgeon told them that they shouldn't have come in the ICU the way they did. Thera looked at him and with a rush of emotion she said, "Don't you tell me what I should or shouldn't do!" Thera adamantly questioned, "What happened to my husband?" The surgeon took them into a room where he explained that Sterling had blood in his chest, and they didn't know where it was coming from. He continued, "We are taking him back into surgery as soon as the anesthesiologist gets here. I'll go take care of all of this and be back out to let you know how it goes as soon as I finish."

"I looked at the doctor, and had a horrible feeling inside. I felt that Sterling was gone, that he had passed away. We didn't get to see him. They ushered all of us into the waiting room where I said, 'I think Dad is gone.' I could hear the desperation in my son's voice as he responded, 'Mom, you can't say that.' 'Nick, I think he is with Rick and Trish.' I knew when they rolled Sterling, the love of my life, into surgery that he wouldn't come back to us. Everyone in the family was trying to reassure me. I couldn't shake the sick feeling invading the pit of my stomach that I had lost him."

Thera sat, waiting. The others paced the floor. The family waited for what seemed like forever. Around two-thirty a.m. the door opened.

"When I looked up and saw 'the look' on the doctor's face. I knew that my Sterling was dead. It was the look from one who has to tell someone that his or her loved one is gone. The surgeon walked in, took his cap off and didn't say a word. He didn't have to say anything. I knew all too well the expression on his face and what that expression meant. His face showed the same emotions that I had seen too many times before on the faces of those who had told me that one of my loved ones had passed away. I broke the silence, 'He's gone isn't he?' He answered, 'We put all the blood we could back into him, but we couldn't bring him back.'"

When a catheter had been inserted to measure Sterling's blood pressure, the process was not done correctly. A hole was ripped in walls of Thera's husband's pulmonary vein. The blood from the rupture went directly into his lungs and chest cavity. We all know that after surgery comes recovery. The patient spends a *short* amount of time in the recovery area in order for the nurses to make sure the patient is coherent, and doing well after the procedure. THE PATIENT WAKES UP! I am in awe how those responsible for the life of this wonderful man could have possibly thought he was all right.

"On June 23, 2001 they brought Sterling to us in a bed. We all gathered around him, holding his still warm hands, and kissing him."

Thera, Nick, Cara, Nicole and Adam received a tender mercy from Heavenly Father amid the acute devastation. Sterling did not leave his body until we were together at the hospital. The five of them were able to surround Sterling's warm body. With his spirit still near, they each said their good-byes to this noble and wonderful man whose legacy every family member carries proudly.

"One thing I thought about as I looked down at my dear Sterling lying there, was how much he had wanted to be able to forgive the evil man who murdered our daughter. Sterling would say to me, 'I hope one day before I die, that I will be able to forgive him.' Thera sadly continued with these words, 'That day never came.'"

A strong feeling came over me as Thera shared her thoughts with me. There are times when a spirit can be equally linked between this life and the next. We who remain here do not know what experiences our loved one is having when this happens. Times such as these can be very profound for the person in the *in between* state. Intubation literally attaches a spirit to its mortal body, which it has resided within throughout life here, by a mere thread. The person's spirit is still present and close to their body.

149

I witnessed this firsthand as my big brother lay in a hospital bed on life-support. I shared with Thera my personal experience after she told me that Sterling had not forgiven the man who ended their daughter's life. One of my brother's beautiful daughters lived in Hawaii. She needed time to get from there to Denver in order to be with her father before he passed. During the time it took her to travel to him, his other six children were around him. Each had sacred time with their father, and he with them. Sheah was able to arrive before her father was called *home*. She too was able to say her final good-byes to her dad.

Though there was no response from my brother, Larry's children spoke to him. Each child expressed things to their father *that they needed to share with him, and that he needed to hear* before he left this mortal existence. I could feel his presence in the room. I could honestly feel Larry's amazing love for each of his precious children. Our loving Father in Heaven blessed my brother, and his children, with tender time together for so many reasons that surpass earthly understanding. However, my dear big brother now understands and our devoted Heavenly Father understood all along. Their time together was necessary, and that is why Larry lingered here before he returned *home*.

I knew that Sterling wanted his sweet wife to know that he had indeed been able to forgive the man that took their daughter's life. I explained that from the time Sterling did not wake up after the first surgery to the time that he was pronounced dead, he had experienced many amazing things! When my dear Uncle Josh passed, my sweet aunt and their daughter shared that as they sat by his bed he would say the names of loved ones passed. He was speaking to them. They were there with him just as Rick was there with Trish, just as both Rick and Trish were there for their father. My uncle Joshy spoke to my beautiful grandmother, his angel mother, as he repeated "Mama" numerous times.

In my mind I captured a glimpse of Sterling, his spirit still linked to his body. I could see his smile through his tears, as this loving father's eyes gazed upon his treasured daughter dressed in white radiating her magnificent light before her dad! The veil is thin when one is close to death. Sterling could see his girl standing in front of him for the very first time since she had been taken from him.

I believe it was at the very moment his and Trish's eyes met that this father, who adored his daughter, was able to forgive the man whose hands had robbed her of her life. You see my friends, yet another tender mercy. Sterling was able to forgive. Giving forgiveness allowed him to be released from the bondage of bitterness before he died. Trish was waiting to take her father home when his *appointed time* arrived. In Trish's eyes, I could see her undeniable love and adoration for her father, her hero. Oh, the tears of joy Sterling shared with his daughter, his son, and his little great granddaughter!

I shared with Thera my personal experience of when I lost my brother, as well as the vision I had seen in my mind of her husband and their daughter. I finished and Thera resounded with, "I agree! I completely agree!" I heard elated relief in her voice. Thera received the comforting knowledge that our kind and gracious Heavenly Father had blessed her husband with the opportunity, while still in this mortal life, to forgive. Once Sterling was able to impart his forgiveness, he was ready to join all his loved ones in the heavens.

We do not know God's plan for us as his children. But, both Thera and I testify that God is our Eternal Father who knows and loves each one of us individually as His children. Jesus Christ is the Son of God whose ability to love surpasses all in this mortal existence. They fully understand our needs just as they did Sterling's and Larry's needs in the final hours of both of their lives.

The all-encompassing power of the Atonement of our Elder brother Jesus Christ, combined with personal repentance, enables us to be forgiven of our every sin and weakness. With that most priceless gift of being forgiven, are we not also to forgive those around us? This is such a powerful lesson we each must learn for ourselves. Through the Atonement of Him, who is the only perfect being ever to have walked the earth taking upon Himself our sins and every heartache we will ever feel, we are assured immortality. His invaluable Atonement provides us with the opportunity to call upon Him. By doing this, we receive strength from the Son of God, our Elder Brother, who has experienced *every mortal* infirmity, anguish and burden from the beginning of our world.

Our Father in Heaven and His Son understood Sterling's struggle to forgive the man who had violently ripped his precious daughter's life from her. They understood completely. Both know well our lives, our feelings, our hurts, our personal struggles, and our heartaches. Heavenly Father knows us as His children, for He is, after all, our Father. Jesus knows us as his younger brothers and sisters, for He is our Elder Brother. Their love for us is pure; it is divine.

As Sterling's spirit lingered between two spheres of existence, that of mortality and that of the spirit world, Heavenly Father blessed Thera's husband with the critical time Sterling needed to forgive. Our loving Father allowed Sterling to see Trish. Sterling then opened his heart to the Lord's healing that comes through forgiving another. How liberating for this wonderful husband, father, grandfather and great grandfather to finally have such a heavy burden lifted from his soul! Sterling's tears were not only tears of joy, but also tears from experiencing the sweet release that comes to each of us when we simply forgive. Noble Sterling was then ready to return with Rick, Trish and Sadie... *home.*

"We said our good-byes to the most amazing man I had ever known in my life. We asked him to take our love to Trish and Rick. I knew that my husband was already there with them. They were having a beautiful reunion while I sat down dazed in the rocking chair by his bed. I was exhausted in every possible way one can be exhausted. I watched Nick,

Cara and the children as they surrounded their father and grandfather with tears streaming down their faces. I watched my son. Nick said to me. 'Mom, I don't understand this. Why have we lost so many people?'"

Thera looked at Nick, her child who was once again by his mother's side. His face bereaved with grief. In that moment, Thera's mind remembered. Nick had held his big brother's hand when death took Rick. Nick held his big sisters hand as her body lay still in her casket making a near impossible promise to her, a promise that he fulfilled. Thera watched as her son's emotions overflowed with the debilitating grief from his heart. Nick was unable to hide in his expression the intensity of the pain flooding his soul from no longer having his dad with him.

"As I looked at my son with such appreciation I thought, 'How much more?'"

Someone gave Thera a bag with Sterling's clothes. His body was being moved to the coroner. Sterling's wife, son, daughter-in-law, and two grandchildren walked slowly out of the hospital in the wee hours of the morning. Their hearts heavily weighted down with grief.

"We left the hospital empty, without him."

Thera felt the intense void of emptiness overcome her soul. The emptiness had felt different with the loss of each loved one, but losing Sterling brought emotions she had never before experienced. Thera was not naive to death's repercussions. She once again found herself thrown into survival mode. She had walked into the doors of that hospital with her loving soul mate, husband, lover and best friend. She walked out intensely alone. A new enormous void existed within her heart that, once upon a time, overflowed with a love and joy only Sterling had the power to fill.

"I knew my very world would never be the same again."

Though crushed beyond measure and utterly exhausted, Thera found herself thinking out loud as they all walked from the hospital, "Our choir director is going to be broken-hearted! Sterling carried the voices of the entire choir. I will never be able to sit next to him and hear his beautiful voice singing the hymns."

"The night Sterling died I went back to the house. I went upstairs to his office and set up a table. I spent probably six months up in that office putting together a memory book. I had everyone write me memories of their dad and grandpa. I put a scrapbook together. That book is so special to me! I made scrapbooks for Rick and Trish when I lost them. Sterling and I had a little dog whose name was Barney. Sterling always

had our dog sit in the chair with him. Barney grieved and grieved for his master when Sterling didn't come home."

The mortuary picked up Sterling's body. They notified Thera that in their opinion Sterling died from accidental death. Nick wanted to know what the death certificate said. He was informed that it said that his father had died from an aortic valve replacement surgery. Nick called the coroner and asked for an autopsy.

"The autopsy report showed that there was a huge hole that had literally been punctured through Sterling's pulmonary vein with the catheter made to take accurate blood pressure. My husband bled to death; he had not been cared for properly. Sterling's death certificate stated that my husband had died from an aortic valve replacement surgery. Sterling didn't die from surgery, my husband died from neglect. Winning a medical legal suit for negligence is almost impossible. There was not one attorney who would take our case and help us. My husband died from negligence, but we had nobody that would help us prove that. I didn't know how I was going to handle everything I was facing."

Before Sterling's surgery, the family was preparing for the second trial against the man that murdered Trish. Sterling's life insurance policy had lapsed. Sterling and Thera were so emotionally spent on the upcoming trial they simply didn't re-instate his policy, though they intended to. Thera did not have one penny of insurance.

"With Sterling's death I realized no matter how hard anyone tries to fix things, not everything is fixable. I thought, 'What am I going to do? I have no insurance.' Sterling's check paid our house payment. I basically had only Sterling's Air Force retirement check to live on. My business wasn't doing well at that time with the second trial coming up in just a few weeks. My energy had been spent preparing for that, not engaging in my business."

Thera's check with Matol went to pay the legal fees up to that point, while Sterling's military retirement and social security provided for their living. Thera had no more money to pay for the legal costs. She was doing what needed to be done for her family. She was living her priorities. At that time, the owners of Matol helped pick up the legal fees needed to convict Trish's murderer. Thera told them that once he was convicted, they could keep two-thirds of her checks to pay back her debt. Of course, Thera paid back every cent.

"When Sterling died it was devastating to Bob. Bob already missed Rick and Trish so much. Now, he had lost his father. Bob told me that nobody could ever know how much he cried over Rick, Trish and his dad."

Bob had been all right with his dad having surgery. He was relieved after getting Nick's call and being updated that his father's surgery had gone well. Bob was awakened at about three in the morning to Nick's second phone call. Arlene kept hearing Bob say, "No, this can't be." Bob felt anger that his father was gone. Both Bob and Arlene cried and prayed together. Then Bob took some time for himself.

He went outside, and looked up at the stars through the tears that continued from his eyes. Arlene shared with me that when Rick died, Bob had picked out a star for his big brother. When Trish died, he picked out a special star just for his big sister. He did the same for his father that night. Bob prayed. He talked to Rick and to Trish. Feeling so small beneath the vast heavens, he pleaded to his two heavenly siblings, "Please take care of Dad." Bob's heart felt the loss of his father deeply. After packing, he and Arlene left for Arizona. When they arrived, Thera threw her arms around her son. He held his mother tight in his arms. Both cried.

Thera, always strong, was shakily trying to hold herself together as best as she could. She reaped strength from her three boys being with her. All of them cried freely together. Val, Bob and Nick went with their mother to take care of all the details and necessary arrangements for their father's service. I know Sterling was proud as he watched his sons give support and strength to not only their mother, but also to each other and the rest of the family.

"My boys are amazing boys!"

Thera decided she wanted Sterling's funeral to take place at the church they had attended for many years. There was an abundance of wonderful family and friends in attendance to support her. Sterling had touched all of their lives in a positive way.

"Sterling's service was like a big family reunion. Family and friends traveled from Utah and Idaho. Sterling's service was a celebration of his life! Of course Val and Bob came from California. I recall the service being extremely hard for Bob. He shed so many tears that day."

Being a member of the a cappella barbershop chorus, Sterling had suit jackets in all colors that he wore for different performances. Val, Bob and Nick each picked out one of his jackets to wear. Sterling's boys wore their dad's suit coats proudly the day they bid their father farewell.

Bob's daughter Mackenzie sang a beautiful song entitled *His Hands*. Before she sang the song she asked her father, "If I stop, will you help me Dad?" Sweet Mackenzie loved her grandfather so much. All of the grandchildren loved their grandfather. This special granddaughter was singing and began to cry. She looked at her father through her tear-filled eyes. Bob immediately stood up from his seat joining Mackenzie. Their voices blended like the voices of two angels in honor of the man they both loved so deeply!

"It was one of the most tender, beautiful moments I have ever witnessed."

In sharing that experience of Thera's with you, I can visualize her sitting at her beloved husband's service. However, that is not all. I also visualize Sterling with Rick, Trish and little Sadie. The four of them sitting close, holding hands, as they too witness the tender scene... together.

"Sterling and I had raised a family, lived all over the world, and together had survived the loss of two of our children. He sang with his barbershop choir for about twenty years. When Sterling's casket was wheeled in, an a cappella barbershop chorus sang. It was beautiful! Everyone in the audience was thrilled to hear this choir sing, because we all knew of Sterling's passion for singing. I know he is very happy with the final celebration we had for him."

The family was so happy that Sterling's barbershop choir sang! At the end of the day's events, the family was together. They all reminisced. There wasn't a lot of sadness that night. Each member of Sterling's family understood that families are forever.

"When we were in the military, our family would travel all over. I would get out my ukulele. Sterling would sing with the children and me. We would sing and sing! That night after his service, the kids wanted to sing like we had done so many years before during those times in the car. We sang: Old Shanty Town, Tan Shoes With Pink Shoe Laces, church hymns and songs of the '60s. Old Shanty Town was so fun on those trips, because Sterling and I would sing one part and the kids another.

When I go to church and sing the hymns without my husband next to me, the tears just come. We spent all of our lives together! My first Sunday back after I lost him I cried during the songs. I had to get up and leave the meeting. My heart hurt terribly without my eternal companion next to me, his beautiful tenor voice filling my soul. It was so hard for me. Oh how my soul ached to hear his pure angelic voice singing those songs! I yearn for that every Sunday. I think Sunday is the day of the week I miss him the most. Sundays will always be difficult on me, until we are together again."

A year had passed since Thera lost her beloved husband. During that time, she made his memory book and went through everything in the house.

Thera knew that she had to downsize. Lots of books and CD's were taken to a second hand store. Thera gave away all the things that the kids didn't want.

"It took me about six months to clean everything out. After I had gone through everything and had kept those things that were the most special to me, I tried to put the house up for sale. We had taken a second out on the house in order to continue fighting the battle for Trish and the children. Sterling and I had to borrow that money. We were so close to achieving justice for our daughter and closure for our dear grandchildren. I didn't have the money to pay back the second we had taken out on our home after I lost Sterling, so I eventually just had to leave the home.

That is when I learned that a house is not a home unless you make it a home. Sterling and I had so many wonderful memories that we created together living in that home for the years we lived there. I packed up, closed the door, and walked away from a house that was no longer our home. I took my treasured memories with me."

Thera had started looking for a new home about six months after her husband's death. She knew that she had to move closer to Nick and Cara.

"I was all alone. Things change when one is alone. My future completely changed. All of the wonderful special things Sterling and I did together wouldn't happen anymore. I was suddenly doing everything for myself. I have often thought of how kind our Heavenly Father was when he took Sterling before me. Women are caretakers. I found myself imagining how difficult it would have been on Sterling had I been called home first. Sterling wouldn't have had me there to support, love and care for him. As devastating as it was to suddenly be alone, I knew that the transition was smoother for me to endure than it would have been for him had I have been the one called home."

Thera quickly understood that she needed a place where she wouldn't have any responsibilities outside and she needed a home with minimal maintenance inside.

"I didn't want to have to fix anything up."

She found a home in a gated community that she loved. Val gave his mother the money for the down payment, and Thera had the contractors build her a brand new home. It goes without saying that she paid Val back the money he gave to her. Val purchased the home in his name, but Thera made all the payments with her business income. Her name is on the title.

"Sterling died on the 23rd of June, 2001. Trish's murderer's court, where he was finally sentenced to life in prison happened just a few months later. I moved into my new home the beginning of July 2002. It was a year of difficult adjustments for me without having Sterling by my side. I settled down in my new home, living only about a mile and a half away from Nick and Cara. How grateful I am for my wonderful children! I am humbled that as I have grown older I have had Nick near me, and Val and Bob were both a mere phone call away. Nick's care and attentiveness to my needs has been a great blessing for me in my life. Val and Bob living in California were no different in their loving me, and being there for me as their mother, they just weren't nearby. Nick and Cara have been by my side through the worst of the worst and they are the best of the best."

Two to three months after his father's death, Bob had a dream that he shared with his dear wife, Arlene. "Me, Mom, Val and Nick were sitting in a restaurant eating dinner. All of the sudden, dad walked in wearing a bright white suit. I said, 'Dad what are you doing here?' He answered, 'Son, it's beautiful up here! Don't worry. Don't cry. Be happy for us!"

After Sterling came to Bob and told him how beautiful it was in heaven, Bob dealt with his father's death a lot better. Both Bob and Arlene would talk about Sterling, and both would cry. But after Bob saw his dad, like when Thera saw Trish, it was a good cry.

Sterling and Thera were blessed with a fulfilling fifty-year marriage. They had their struggles like any other couple, but their love and respect for each other, their children, their country and their resolute dedication to the Lord brought them fifty years of joy through even the severest of tribulations. I can see them holding hands, laughing with each other, dancing on the dance floor, and simply loving each other. Sterling and Thera's love, life together, and family are eternal.

"Sterling and I were married for fifty years. Our life together was a wonderful celebration with family and friends. I look at the world today and find myself wondering... How families will have a happy, fulfilled life as a family unit? How many married couples will make each other and their children the priorities necessary to stay together for fifty years? Sterling and I went against all odds in creating and achieving our happily ever after. As I quietly sit here in my home office today, I look around at the walls. I feel a great peace and love in this room. The walls are filled with cherished pictures. I can see the faces and smiles of Sterling, our children, grandchildren and great grandchildren. I have a wall dedicated to the man I adore and love with all of my heart. On Sterling's wall I can see, within the portrait and through his medals of honor, his years of service in the military to our country. While sitting here talking to you, Larina, I look around me and am reverenced as I see a lifetime of stories

157

within the pictures and special occasion items framed here. Yes, I love this room. I love my family. Forever is going to be perfect."

~Chapter Seventeen~

Pops
(Memories of Sterling from Nick)

As a young boy, my dad was a hero in my eyes. My dad continues to be my hero today. As an officer in the U.S. Air Force, he seemed to stand ten feet tall in his uniform! He looked much taller than his actual five foot ten-inch frame because of his posture, the way he walked, and the way he acted whenever he wore his uniform. My father was proud to serve his country as an American serviceman. He held The United States of America close to his heart his entire life. When the Star Spangled Banner played he would stand at attention, whether in uniform or not, addressing the flag with the proper respect all while singing our National Anthem with pride and dignity.

Dad was a true Patriot. I remember going through the gates at the different Base's we lived on. We would approach the guards at the gates, and my father seemed to sit a little taller. The guards would look at the sticker on the car, look at him and immediately stand at attention saluting him. He would dutifully solute back at them. Watching my dad in that capacity was usually the highlight of my day!

Pops was a very compassionate man. Mind you he did have a little temper on him, but he seemed to be able to keep it in check. Remembering all of us siblings back in the day, I think I was a little more whacked-out than the rest of our crew that he raised! The funny thing was he would get mad for something we had done, let us know in no uncertain terms that we had screwed up, and then within a short period of time come back to tell us just how much he loved us. Dad couldn't stay mad for any length of time.

I think stubbing his toe was the only thing he would stay mad at and dad was the grand master of stubbing his toes! At the slightest possibility of a piece of furniture being in the way, his toes would find it! Pops was famously known for his crazy antics after a stubbing occurrence. This mostly happened while he was in his pajamas typically in the morning or just before bedtime. Dad would catch a toe, scream out, grab his foot, hop around on the other foot balancing until he could find a place to sit, and then throw his head back for more affect! Okay, I gotta tell you, I'm laughing hysterically right now just thinking about him yelling, "Godfrey David! Oh my Lord!" or any other descriptive adjective he could use without swearing! He kept his tongue in check as well as his temper. I can't begin to tell you how many times that happened over his lifetime.

Dad was always there no matter his schedule. He made it a point to be there for his children for our different events. The only time I recall that he wasn't able to be at one of my important events was when I was to be baptized. I was eight years old. My dad was halfway around the world in Vietnam during the war. Mom asked me if I wanted someone else to baptize me. I remember feeling that it just wouldn't be the same if my father weren't the one performing my baptism. So, I decided to wait until his return. That decision was the right one. A few months later my dad was home, and my hero baptized me.

When we moved from Bountiful to Salt Lake City, I attended junior high school at Bonneville Junior High. I was on the track team running the 440 and the 100-yard races. I also ran the mile relay and the long jump. I always heard a familiar voice in the crowd. In between events dad would make his way down through the stands to come and tell me how well I had performed, while he rubbed my legs down with liniment. I will always remember those moments my dad spent with me on the field. While the other guys were trying to keep their muscles loose by doing their various maneuvers, I had Dad. Those were always times where I remember feeling special. It evidently helped because I seemed to be able to fair pretty well considering the amount of events I competed in.

He was the same way with me in football. He was on the front line at every game! We all recognized his voice through the noise of the crowd. His cheering was not only for me, but for all my teammates as well. It seemed like there was only three or four parents who were there for all the games. My dad was one of the dedicated few. He supported not only me, but also all the guys whose parents were absent. Dad loved watching me play football. We moved from Utah to Arizona and were living in Scottsdale. I had dropped out of High School before we had made the move.

Dad had some tricks up his sleeve. Shortly after we got settled dad asked me to go for a ride with him. We lived pretty close to a high school. He knew that in my mind I was done with school and ready to make it in the great big world. Pops had other plans for me, and they didn't match up with mine. He wanted to get me through high school. I got in the car and we ended up at the high school. It just so happened that the coach was holding tryouts for the football team. Go figure! We got out of the car, walked the track and talked. Dad was wise. Our talk wasn't about anything in particular just a father-son talk about life with the successes and failures we all go through. We kept getting distracted watching the players on the field.

Dad walked over to the coach and talked with him for a few minutes then came back over to me. I asked what they had talked about. He nonchalantly said that they were discussing the team, and where they were lacking in strength. Wouldn't ya know? They were weak in their defensive backfield. Hmmmm... The exact position I played in Utah! Dad went on to let me know that I wouldn't be interested since I was no longer interested in school. At that time, I had no idea what he was doing. I was oblivious! But, my dad succeeded. A week later I was on the field playing with the team!

I want to expound on my father and his short-term memory anger. During high school I worked as a bus boy, then advanced to a waiter. I loved the waiter job. I made great tips and had cash in my pocket all the time! The bad side to the job was I didn't usually get home till midnight or after. On the weekends I was even later. On a weekend one night after work, I had picked up a buddy of mine. He needed a ride home from his job. We started for home and about halfway there a cat ran out in front of the car. It was a dimly lit street in the middle of a tree-lined area, so it was very dark. I swerved to miss the cat, and went onto the shoulder of the road. The area had about a four-inch drop-off that was gravel mixed with dirt. It had very little if any traction. I tried to make it back on the road, but we slid sideways towards a telephone pole. I was able to get the car under control and straighten our path of direction. Unfortunately, before we could even react, the pole was in the middle of the car. I hit it head on at about forty-five miles per hour. Neither my friend nor I had our belts on. Wearing seatbelts wasn't the law then.

All I remember was the slow motion impact with glass shattering and blasting everywhere, then silence. It was so quiet it was eerie. I sat there for a moment stunned, then attempted to start the car. My attempt was unsuccessful, of course. Starting that car would have been impossible with half the engine shoved up against the firewall, and the transmission buckling up through the floor. We had no communication, no cell phones back then. We had been traveling on a back road. Fortunately, a car came by about thirty minutes later, and the people left to call the police. Neither my buddy nor me had a scratch on us. We were in shock and in disbelief at what had just happened. The police came, called the tow truck, and then took both of us home.

When I arrived home about two hours past my normal arrival time, the police officer walked me in the house. Mom was standing in the kitchen. Dad was in their bedroom right around the corner. The police officer said that I wasn't in any trouble and went on to explain that I had been in an accident and had totaled the car. Mom's face went blank. My dad's voice came from the bedroom, "You did what?" The police officer left, leaving me to deal with my father on my own. Mom sat there looking at me, as dad did his best to make sure I understood the very meaning of what it meant to be grounded. I'm sure the neighbors from two blocks over learned the definition of being grounded that night! I was sent to bed after a thorough ten-minute tongue-lashing. By that time it was about three o'clock in the morning.

About four hours later I heard my name whispered in my ear. I felt warm wet tears on my cheek. It was dad. He had gotten up and taken a trip to the lot where the car had been towed. I can imagine his emotions as he stood there seeing the condition of the car. He had spoken to the driver who was the one that pulled the mangled mess from the telephone pole. Waking up to my dad that morning, I could see that he was clearly humbled. He asked me to sit up so we could talk. I remember him embracing me. It was an embrace like none I had ever felt before. There was so much love behind it. Dad was trying to talk to me. His words were mingled with crying and tears. He was doing his best to say how sorry he was for his harshness and scolding. He expressed how much he loved me and how grateful he was that I was still alive.

The car was totaled. According to both the police officer and the tow truck driver it was an absolute miracle that either of us boys lived through the impact, let alone walked away without a scratch. Dad explained all this to me. The two of us sat there for about ten minutes, father and son, appreciating life just a little more than the day before. I got up so he could take me to see the unsalvageable remains.

I always knew my Pops was in my corner. I'm pretty sure all my siblings knew that he was also in their corner. He was the guy that us kids feared when we had done something wrong, but the father that we knew we could always depend on no matter what. He had our backs. As I said before, even though he was mad he never could stay mad for long. Our father let his children know how much he loved us. Dad's love for all of us was evident every day of our lives. He had a large soft spot for us kids, and it didn't take much for that to kick in, even amidst a crisis we had caused.

Pops had the voice of an angel. He sang all the time, and I mean ALL THE TIME! He was born with an insatiable desire for music, a keen ear for sound, and the ability to harmonize to just about any song he was interested in. His talent in music was a gift he loved to share! He sang in school and in the military. In his later years he sang with the Phabulous Phoenicians, which was a barbershop choir. He enjoyed traveling and singing with the various bands and groups that he was involved with. He sang in Seattle, Washington at the Worlds Fair in 1962 with the military choir. Later in his life, while a part of the Phoenicians, he travelled all over the country and to Canada in order to compete. One year the Phoenicians became the international champions. It was a total triumph for my dad! In his eyes he had made it to the big league being a member of an internationally recognized body of voices. I have to admit they were impressive.

As far back as I can remember, dad was always listening to music at every available opportunity. When we lived in the orient, he felt like he was in heaven with their technology. He purchased the best in reel-to-reel tape recorders; turn tables, amps, speakers, and any other device that played all his records. He'd lie in front of those huge speakers listening to music for hours on end. I remember well the voices of Frank Sinatra, Nat King Cole, Sammy Davis Jr., Dean Martin, Ray Caniff, Burt Bacharach, along with all the other popular names from the Big Band era. Dad used to cringe with a lot of the music us kids would play. When we played any rock and roll, or current music of the time, we could almost see him have a complete internal melt down! He would say, "Your generation today doesn't know what real music is. How do you understand a word they're saying?" It was fun times back then to torment him. Now, I can totally see his point! I love the music of my father's era. Its no wonder those songs are being recorded by artists of today. Dad, you definitely knew that of which you spoke!

It was a pleasure to be with my father as he aged. He never lost his amazing voice. His patience wore a little thinner at times, but all in all he aged well. We would give him a hard time about his knuckles on his hands. He had such large knuckles that they made his fingers point in different directions. When he'd point, we'd look in the direction his crooked finger was aiming towards. We'd try to see what he was pointing at, but we'd usually end up having to ask him what it was he wanted us to see!

Pops also loved his little dogs. His favorite one being Barney, a little pure white Shih Tzu who went everywhere with him. Dad's driving scared the heck out of anyone who rode with him, except that little dog. All dad had to do was pick up the keys, and that dog was at the door waiting to hit the road with his master! That all ended after dad got in a wreck. The next time Barney heard the keys, he started to run towards the door suddenly making an abrupt about-face turn down the hallway to get into the bedroom. He wanted nothing to do with that ride stuff anymore!

Dad pretty much kept his health conditions to himself. We weren't really ever sure how he was fairing, until we got a phone call. Mom and dad were on a cruise to the Mediterranean. Dad had what they thought was a minor heart attack. The phone call was to tell us that they were getting off the ship to find a flight home. We had to get our parents out of the country they were in so that tests could be done on dad to find out what the real issues were. A private jet ambulance service was set in place. Four hours later, they were home safe and sound. We later found that it wasn't a heart attack, but rather the beginning signs of a heart attack.

Later that year dad was scheduled for surgery. He had Aortic Stenosis, which is the hardening of the aortic heart valve. He had to have his aortic heart valve replaced. Because he was seventy-six years old, I was under the understanding that for those his age having the specific surgery was not uncommon. Though for some, facing a surgery such as the one dad needed, was more difficult than for others. Dad was in the difficult group. He went through all the required testing, and I could see him failing a bit. He seemed to be a little less in the now and his attention span seemed to lessen. But boy, could he still sing!

The time finally came for him to have the needed procedure. Mom, Cara my wife, and I went to Phoenix Memorial Hospital the morning of the 20th of June 2001. My dad was scheduled for surgery. The nurses came into the waiting room and called his name. Dad stood up with Mom, and together they walked back to the pre-op area. Cara and I sat in the waiting area until they completed all they had to do in prepping him for the surgery. Finally they let us know we could go back and see him before the surgery. I remember vividly walking down the hall into the pre-op area. It looked like there was five or six other patients either going into surgery or coming out.

We slipped into the cubicle where they had my father. Mom was by his side. They were holding hands. The mood was gloomy. Dad was looking at the ceiling, and Mom at the floor. I could see the anxiety in the face of my father. Who wouldn't be anxious or concerned facing what he was facing? I tried to lighten the mood with some light-hearted comments and jokes. I remembered how dad was there for me when I was a kid, and had to have a bunch of warts cut off my hands and fingers. I wanted my dad to stay in the room, but they wouldn't let him. I tore the place apart until they let my dad back in. He calmed me, and held me the entire time until they completed the procedure. His comfort was all I needed. I knew somehow deep inside, my amazing dad was feeling the same way about this operation that I had felt those years before.

I bent over and told him how much I loved him, as he had done for me so many times throughout my entire life. I tried to comfort him by telling him that he was in good hands; that his Father in Heaven would be guiding the surgeon's hands. I held him in my arms for a few minutes the way he held me the morning after my accident. It was time. I asked him if he was scared. My father responded with, "Not so much scared as worried." He then smiled his awesome dad smile assuring me it was all good. Mom gave him a kiss, then Cara, and then myself again. The last thing I said to my father in this life was, "I love you, Pops."

The surgery was scheduled for about two hours, depending on what they had to do to fit the new valve in place. Obviously every minute to those of us waiting seemed to be hours, and the hours seemed like forever. If you've ever had a loved one in a critical surgery, you know the feeling I'm talking about. It unequivocally is a terribly trying time, one that is extremely painstaking on the nerves. Finally the surgeon emerged to talk with us. I actually watched as the fear left my mom's face when the doctor sat down and said, "It was the most successful surgery of the day. His valve was the identical size of the new valve and we had to do very little prep. The fit was perfect. All went very well." We asked the prognosis and recovery. He felt that dad would recover very rapidly, and be home within a day or two. What a relief! We'd take him home to finish his complete recovery after a day or two stay in the hospital. My Pops would be on his feet within a week! We were counting our blessings. We thanked his guardian angels, and our Heavenly Father.

Dad was in the ICU. The medical staff anticipated he would be unconscious for the next couple of hours. By this time it was about one or two in the afternoon. We were all tired. The nurse told us to go get a bite to eat and then come back. She assured us that he should be awake by then, and would want to have us with him when he woke up. We were back in about forty-five minutes. When we returned he was moving a little and mumbling just enough so we could hear him, but we couldn't understand a word he was trying to say.

At about six o'clock that evening there was a switch in the nursing staff for the ICU. The new nurse came in and introduced herself. She checked his vitals and dressings and left the room. We noticed what seemed to be fresh blood in a drain tube from his chest, and called her back into the room. She reassured us that the blood was normal and that it was there for a purpose. For some reason, she gave him more narcotics to slow Dad's waking process. It wasn't that he was asking for them. He was never able to wake up enough to tell us what he needed; she just gave them to him. With the dose she gave him, we could see that he was going to be out of it for at least four or five more hours. We had small talk with her, and found that she had just returned from a 30-day vacation. At one point, I remember her saying that it was going to be fun staying up all night after thirty days of a normal sleep cycle. She reassured us that in the ICU no patient is ever left alone, and that someone would be with Dad throughout the night. With that she invited us to go home and get some rest so we could be there in the early morning.

I admit getting some rest sounded good, after the long day we'd had. By then it was about eight o'clock. I was thinking, "In bed by nine, up by six, and to the hospital by seven." I thought that was a pretty good timing plan, one that would allow all of us the chance to get plenty of rest in order to be there for dad the next day. We'll follow that plan, and see dad in the morning. A few hours later, I was sleeping in my bed. I woke to a voice, "Dad. Dad! Wake up, it's Grandma." Waking up from a deep slumber, I looked around to see my son with the phone in his hand. I thought I had overslept. Taking the phone I said, "I'm sorry mom! We'll be there as soon as we can." I heard my mother from the other end of the phone trying to get words out as she said, "Nick, I think something serious has happened to Dad. I just got a call from the hospital to come as quickly as we can." I looked at the clock and replayed what she had just said in my mind. Things didn't sound good. It was midnight. Reality set in.

It was only a matter of a couple of minutes before we were all dressed and out the door. We met up with Mom on the side of the road. I jumped in her car, and Cara drove ours with the kids. We pulled up to the hospital at about twelve thirty in the morning. I remember going through the emergency doors with my family in tow. We looked frantically for someone to help us, but the desk was empty. We went to the ICU. We could see a room filled with doctors and nurses working and moving around at a pretty fast pace. I told Mom to stay with Cara and the Kids and I'd find out what was going on. I headed toward the room.

The doctor who had performed dad's surgery hours earlier emerged from the room. He stopped me saying that my father was in there and they were working on him. He told me that I needed to go back to the waiting room. Mom was by us now, both of us refusing to go anywhere without knowing what was happening. He explained that dad had coded, and that he was bleeding internally. They didn't know where the blood was coming from. The anesthesiologist was on his way and they would be performing surgery to find the bleed in a matter of minutes.

We went to the waiting room, and I did my best to explain the current circumstances. We sat and prayed. And, prayed. And, prayed. The time was agonizing. I called my brothers, Val and Bob, and informed them of the situation. Dad had the combined prayers of our family members. I did what I could to help get my mind off the possibilities currently happening in that operating room. An hour passed; then two. Finally the doctor emerged. As long as I live, I will never forget his walk or his look. The surgeon's walk was slow. I didn't want to see the look on his face, because his facial expression told me everything I didn't want to know.

This was happening. I didn't want to be there! He gradually made his way over to mom, slowly removed his surgical cap, and knelt down in front of her.

"I'm sorry Mrs. Huish. I did everything I could possibly do. Your husband was bleeding faster than we could get blood into him, and we were unable to stop the bleeding."

What???? Not my Dad! Not my Pops! He was fine three hours ago what happened?

The truth about what happened came out after we demanded that a full autopsy be performed. Which, by the way, was bypassed because he was under a doctor's care at the time of death. The findings were that Dad had died from loss of blood from his pulmonary artery being punctured. How did that happen? I did my due diligence to get the answer. A catheter is placed in the lung to measure blood pressure. This type of catheter is called a Swans Gath Catheter, or a wedge catheter. It has a little balloon at the end of it. The Swans Gath Catheter is inflated in order to take the blood pressure of a patient. It has the most accurate pressure reading, and is used frequently for major surgeries. The catheter is inserted then inflated so that the blood pressure results show. If the balloon is not deflated before it is removed, the consequences can be catastrophic, like the tragic case of my helpless father.

The fact of the matter is, that my father died due to a lack of concentration from those charged with his care while he lay unconscious at their mercy. An amazing husband, father, grandfather, and man lost his priceless life because of their careless negligence.

Nick's Words to His Father

I see you every day, Dad. I recognize you in so many of the things I do. As I grow older, I observe the qualities in me that I remember in you. I am your son; thank you for being my father. I love you and constantly miss you. I know we will be together again. I have this knowledge because I know of our Heavenly Father's plan. I have now accomplished those things that you wished I had done for my own happiness while you were still here on this earth with me. Dad, they are now done. I live each day with a purpose. That purpose is to have all of us together throughout the eternities. I live my life in obedience to God's commandments so that we will meet and embrace, as father and son once again, at heaven's door.

I love you, Pops.

~Chapter Eighteen~

Sadie's Death

Zachory called his father. He told Bob that Sadie had been showing sporadic symptoms of drooling, headaches, unbalance, fatigue and speech changes. On March 3, 2008, this sweet little girl was taken to the hospital for tests, where she was diagnosed with DIPG - Diffuse Intrinsic Pontine Glioma, which is brain stem cancer. Precious Sadie had an inoperable cancerous tumor on the lowest stem-like part of her brain. Both father and son were crying during that phone call. Sadie was Zachory and Tiffany's oldest daughter. This special little one was Bob's oldest granddaughter. Sadie loved her Grandpa, and Grandpa loved Sadie! Both had such a beautiful bond between them. It was the worst night of Bob's life.

"Bob called and shared the extremely sad news with me. Bob asked, 'What do we do Mom? How do we fix this?' I answered, 'Bob, there's no way we can fix anything. We can support and love, but this is in God's hands. The outcome is up to HIM.' The tumor Sadie had would take her life."

Sadie knew every apostle. When she was asked what she wanted, she said that she wanted to meet Thomas S. Monson, the President and Prophet of the Church of Jesus Christ of Latter-day Saints. Sadie wanted for President Monson to give her a special priesthood blessing. Though she was so young, she was one of the most spiritual children her family and those who knew her had ever known.

Sadie wanted to attend the dedication of the Ochre Mountain Temple in Utah. She was so ill and weak. She couldn't speak, so she would bat her beautiful eyes as she was wheeled through to see the lovely rooms. Sadie went through each room feeling the peaceful healing spirit of the Lord's House. She was determined she was going through before she went to heaven. Determination is an amazing quality that is passed down from generation to generation. Sadie is after all Thera's great-granddaughter.

"I remember thinking what can I do to help? I would send her cards, and call her on the phone. I went to visit Zach, Tiffany and the girls for three days. There was a constant stream of people bringing gifts. Though I felt I couldn't make a difference physically, I continued praying constantly for my family and precious great-granddaughter. I was very sick myself. I sat on the couch and played games, and we put puzzles together. Sadie loved puzzles!"

Zach and Tiffany fixed one room in their home with a heavenly theme. Then, they fixed another room. There was something to do with the scriptures in every room. They were teaching the children the Plan of Salvation each time their daughters would go into a room. When they took the kids into the Celestial Kingdom room, there were pictures of family members who had passed on. It was an incredible experience for their children and for all of us.

Before Sadie passed away, Zach and Tiffany asked their oldest daughter if they ever had another baby what would her name choice be for the baby? They had three little girls at that time. Sadie picked out a boys name, and Shiloh for a girl. From heaven, Sadie now watches over her four little sisters Olivia, Samantha, Shilo, and Sarah.

Bob and Arlene drove from Napa, California, to Eagle Mountain, Utah, pretty much every other weekend. After making that trip for sixteen months, Bob and Arlene were on their way home when the call came in that Sadie had lost the battle she had been fighting. Sadie's life was one of love. She was both the selfless giver and the recipient of love. When Heavenly Father called His valiant little daughter home, Sadie's parents held her. Sadie passed from the tender arms of her mother, as she entered the gentle arms of her Elder Brother, Jesus. With the news, Bob and Arlene were heartbroken. This loving and bereaved grandfather and grandmother pulled over to the side of the road to cry and pray. Because of all of his losses, Bob knew well that he would never hold his beloved Sadie in his arms again in this life. Both he and Arlene needed a few minutes together to mourn the loss of a new heavenly angel, of whom they, along with so many others, cherished.

"I called my grandson and granddaughter. With all of the experiences I had in losing loved ones, I explained to both of them that they had their other children who needed them, and that they needed to move forward. I reminded them that they had done everything humanly possible for their Sadie, and that they mustn't question what had happened. Sadie was happy!"

I have asked permission to share part of Miss Sadie's obituary as it describes her magnificent light that shone here, and still shines bright in heaven!

Sadie Brynne Huish 1/3/2003 ~ 6/25/2009

Our sweet Sadie passed away after a 16-month battle with brain cancer - a rare brainstem tumor called a DIPG. Sadie Brynne Huish was born on January 3, 2003 in Murray, Utah to Zachory and Tiffany Huish. From an early age she showed such intelligence and obedience. She loved puzzles, drawing, painting, and crafts. She was always quick to ask questions and was always striving to learn more. She enjoyed school, and learning to play the violin. She also liked dance and soccer. She was extremely compassionate; she never liked seeing anyone sad, and would do anything to try to make him or her happy.

Sadie had a giant testimony of the gospel, and a great love for Jesus and the Prophet. She was a loyal and dear friend to all around her. She showed such maturity, patience and bravery in her fight, and seemed to have a profound influence on all who followed her battle. She was an amazing big sister to Olivia and Samantha, and considered them to be her best pals. She also had a great love and appreciation for her dear cousins. She was such a beautiful little gal, inside and out. She taught us all so much in her short time here, and has changed the lives of so many. We are so proud of our Sadie. Our hearts are broken, yet we are so thankful she is healed in the arms of the Savior, surrounded in Heaven by loving family, and little pals who have walked the same road. A celebration of Sadie's life will take place on Wednesday, July 1, 2009.

"I would read the uplifting blog Tiffany created to bless lives through the experiences of her baby girl, Sadie. I attended the funeral and it was beautiful with amazing music. Sadie's parents and grandparents spoke. Recordings of Sadie's infectious laughter were shared. Sadie's passing was a sweet release from her diseased body. Zach and Tiffany have kept Sadie's memory alive in so many ways. They are engaged in supporting research for the type of tumor that took their daughter's life. I knew that our Sadie was welcomed 'home' by loved ones who were there to greet her. I knew that Sterling, Rick, and Trish were there to hold this sweetest little new angel in their arms. Yes, Sadie Brynne was a happy girl!"

Bob's outlook on death was that he wasn't afraid of it at all. He knew that when it would be his time to go, that everything would be okay. He fully understood that whenever that time arrived, he would once again be reunited with those of his family who had died before him. He had no doubt that his father, big brother, and big sister would be there to hold him tight and welcome him home. He knew that Sadie would be there to greet him with her beautiful smile! That she would throw her arms around her grandpa, and laugh the laugh he had longed to hear while they were separated.

"Bob spoke at Sadie's service. He came to the realization that he needed to get his life in order. His Bishop explained to me that Bob had been taking temple preparation classes to help him get ready to go back to the temple in order to gain the eternal blessings available for his family. Bob's Bishop expressed to me that my son was ready to do great things. I know he is doing great things in heaven! Bob placed the Lord as a priority before he journeyed home. Knowing that, has been a great comfort and gift to me as his mother."

~Chapter Nineteen~

Bob's Death

Bob was happy with his life. He was happy all the time! But one morning, Arlene woke to gurgling sounds coming from her husband lying in their bed next to her. She tried to wake him to no avail. She called 911 and did CPR on him. When the paramedics arrived, Bob was gone. His body was in full cardiac arrest with no heartbeat. Those trained to save lives used a defibrillator. Putting the paddles on his chest, they shocked Bob's heart three times before it began beating again.

"I was on my way to a presentation when Nick called and told me I should come to his house before my appointment. As I went in, Nick had the same look on his face as my father when he returned bringing me the news that Dorian and Mr. Toland had died in the plane wreckage. I knew that something was terribly wrong. Nick said, 'I need to talk to you, Mom.' He shared with me what had happened. My son died. Bob had already touched heaven. I know that Bob chose to come back so everyone could have peace and say goodbye."

Obstructive sleep apnea (OSA) is a common problem that affects a person's breathing during sleep. One with OSA has times during sleep in which oxygen cannot flow normally into the lungs. The block, or obstruction in airflow, is usually caused by the collapse of the soft tissues in the upper airway located in the back of the throat and tongue during sleep. Evidence shows that over time, this sleep disorder disease known as sleep apnea can increase the risk of death in adults. These findings strongly suggest that treatment may help lessen the risk of dying from cardiovascular heart disease also.

Bob's brain had begun the process of dying, because sometime during the night his breathing airways were blocked from his having sleep apnea. Without enough oxygen, his body went into full cardiac arrest. This means his heart completely stopped beating. When one dies in this mortal existence, the spirit leaves the body. Bob's spirit had left his body, but was brought back by the use of defibrillators shocking his non-beating heart with electric currents strong enough to start it beating again. As his mother expressed to us in such a perfect way, Bob had already *touched heaven.*

By the fourth or fifth day, Thera knew that Bob wasn't going to come back. On the phone everyday, she and Nick told Bob how much they loved him. Val struggled tremendously with the situation, because of the closeness he and Bob shared. As brothers and partners, he and Bob shared so much together. They were building six to seven pools at the time of Bob's tragedy. Val shared his feelings with his Mom and told her, "There's nothing I can do." Thera responded with, "I know. You must get up, dress up and show up." Nick went to Bob and Arlene's for a week to help, and to support in any way he could. Thera was ill and not able to go.

Bob was on life support for six weeks during which time he never regained consciousness. He was on a respirator and had a feeding tube.

When they would try taking him off of life support, he would do fine for a little while, but soon it became necessary for them to put Bob back on the respirator. When a person is on life support with severe brain damage due to lack of oxygen, their body can have what is called involuntary actions. To a grieving waiting family, these actions are often viewed as hope that their loved one will come back to them. About a week to a week and a half after the morning Arlene had awakened to her husband barely breathing, Bob's eyes opened. Once that happened, the doctors ordered another brain scan. The scan showed that Bob's brain was dying more and more. With each of the still pictures, more gray would appear in them. The gray areas on the films were the parts of Bob's brain that were already dead, or dying. The doctors then let the family know that there was nothing more they could do for this good man.

I have some knowledge with regards to all of this through a dear friend, Ken Matthews. He was my big brother's best friend. Ken and his wife, Lesli, have both been dedicated servants in the medical field for many years. Ken was our family's ministering angel during the course of my big brother Larry's passing, as Millie was to Thera during the time of Rick's departure. Ken was by our side keeping our family informed as to what was happening to Larry's body during his transition from this life into the next. Like Bob, Larry also went into full cardiac arrest, and was brought back. His body, too, was fully dependent upon a ventilator to live. My big brother passed away about twenty minutes after his life support was turned off.

For weeks, Arlene kept telling Bob that it was okay for him to go. Doing her best to convince not only him, but herself as well, that she would be fine. She let him know that she understood. She would tell him that Sadie would be the first one to run up and greet him. After six weeks, Arlene decided that she was going to have Bob taken to a nursing home. The first night in the nursing home, Arlene was not allowed to stay with Bob. This was very difficult for her. She spoke to Thera about it, and Thera expressed that maybe Bob needed some alone time. This loving mother reminded Arlene that Bob always had someone by his side since the episode happened, and that he hadn't yet been alone.

Arlene's Thoughts

"I would hold Bob's hand, and pray with him. I asked God to strengthen me and lead me in the right direction that I needed to be going. After spending the day with Bob, I got to my car and realized I had left my phone. I went back to his room to get my phone. The staff was in with him cleaning him up. I knew at that moment that was not what my husband wanted. I finally was thinking clearly. He and I had talked about what we wanted should anything happen to either of us. We had both promised each other that we would never let each other live that way. It was on that night, through that experience, that I made the decision to let Bob go. He deserved to have me give him his life back.

The next day the comfort care doctor came in to see me. I told her that I was ready. I heard myself speaking the words, fully understanding what they meant, as my heart ached within me. I continued expressing to the doctor that I was ready for my husband to go *home*, and be healthy again."

Arlene is thankful that she forgot her phone that night. She was able to see Bob through a new perspective. She was able to see him through his eyes and she knew without any doubt what her beloved husband wanted. Bob came back to his body leaving the unfathomable beauty and love that engulfed his being while *touching* our heavenly home. This peaceable man, so full of love, selflessly stayed until his family was ready to let him go. A special fast was called for Bob where family members and friends participated.

Fasting is something that happens once a month for members of the LDS faith. Those fasting miss two meals and typically don't eat for twenty-four hours. This takes place on the first Sunday of each month. They pray sincerely to God for whatever it is they are fasting for. This special fast for Bob took place on a Sunday. Bob was freed from the bonds that held him to his mortal body at about two o'clock in the morning the next day on April 16, 2012.

"How typical of my son, being such a good peacemaker, that he honored his entire family and his friends with his presence until he realized that they all were ready to let him go. When dear Arlene placed him in that nursing home, my boy finally had his alone time. I can hear my son's voice. I know that he said, 'Dad, I'm ready to go with you now.'"

This choice, kind man passed peacefully while his loved ones safely slept in their own beds. Everyone had been able to say good-bye to him on Sunday evening. What a sweet reunion this loving man had with his father, brother, sister, granddaughter, and Elder Brother, Jesus Christ. I am sure precious Sadie ran with outstretched arms leaping into the devoted arms of her grandfather. Joseph and Doran were there to welcome their grandson home, along with so many others.

Early Monday morning Thera answered the phone with a grieving wife on the other end. Thera had already lived through burying two of her five children and her husband. Though extremely difficult, Thera and Arlene understood that Bob had experienced a peaceful passing.

"After we lost Sterling, Val lost his little brother and Nick lost his big brother. Both of my boys were grief-stricken. I thought how Nick went to Bob's side while Bob lay in a hospital bed. Nick worked selflessly to prepare Bob and Arlene's home so that it would be ready whenever Bob

could come home. But, that didn't happen; his big brother never made it back to his home here."

The family held a viewing on Friday. Zachory and Mackenzie asked if they could put special white temple clothing in the casket for their father. Bob was buried in jeans, his usual attire, but his children lovingly placed temple clothing neatly folded in a white cloth envelope with him in his casket.

"I looked at my son as he lay silent in his casket. Because of all he had endured the six weeks prior, his body was just skin and bones. I remember saying to Nick, 'I have cried, and cried, and cried over so many. I just don't have a lot of tears left. I know Bob is where he is supposed to be.'"

Saturday was the day of Bob's funeral service. It was held in a huge Mormon Chapel. The majority of the people who attended were not members of the church. All those in attendance were people whose lives had been touched by Bob because of the man he was. Over six hundred people came to honor this man who worked hard, loved his family, lived a humble life, and brought laughter and happiness to others. It was standing room only for many who attended. The service lasted about two hours. Val and Nick both spoke, and two of Bob's little grandchildren sang the song Bob loved and sang every time there was any conflict growing up. The song was *Love At Home*. Arlene stood up to speak. She spoke of fun things. When she would share something tender, a tear would run down her cheek. She held Sid, Bob's faithful little pal, in her arms. This small dog, also grieving for his master, would reach up his little head and lick away Arlene's tears.

"Val and Nick were heartbroken at the loss of Bob. There had just been the three of them left out of the five siblings. Rick and Trish had already left us. The boys used to joke about which way death would travel. If it went up, Val would be the next to go. If it went down it would be Bob next."

Val, Bob, and Nick used to tease Thera by telling her that she would walk on all three of their graves. Thera told her sons not to joke about that.

"Bob and Val had worked together for about twenty-five years. They would have their business meetings at Sam's Club while eating hot dogs. Val shared with me that after Bob's death he was at Sam's Club. He said to himself, 'I'm okay. I can do this.' He bought a hot dog; the tears just came. The emptiness was overwhelming for him."

Bob's body was transferred to Utah. The family flew in on Monday. On Tuesday morning they met at the cemetery for Bob's graveside service. Bob's body now rests next to Sadie's grave until the glorious second coming of our Messiah, even Jesus Christ. The resurrection will indeed take place creating the grandest reunion in all of history!

"Bob loves his children! I know that my son has great joy with the way they live their lives and the choices they have made. He is with Sadie, and he is proud of his posterity! I often think of Bob's grandchildren and what they are missing out on by not having their grandfather here with them. But, I know death cannot keep loved ones from those they love. Bob is near, and he is there for all of us when we need him.

Bob always lived his life in a peaceful way. He taught that every problem could be solved with kindness rather than contention. He taught his children never to be angry or hateful. He taught all of us that there was always a peaceful solution that could be created instead of a hurtful one."

Thera had received a card from a woman at church. She in turn, forwarded it to Arlene. Arlene expressed how much she appreciated her sending the card, and that the message within it had helped her. After Thera had given a talk in church, the kind woman wrote these words in the card, "Thera, after all you've been through you still get up, get dressed and show up. I know that is what you are doing, even though your heart aches."

"Arlene was having an extremely difficult time. I told Arlene, 'I understand what you are doing holding that little dog and smelling Bob's robe. But the most important thing you can do is move forward as fast as you can. Pretty soon you get through the first month, the first Christmas, and then a few years have passed. Those who die are near. They are never really gone. Never.'"

Even though Arlene moved to Georgia, farther away from Thera, she remains an important member of the Huish family. Arlene felt a natural emotion many of us feel when we lose a loved one. When Arlene lost Bob, she felt anger along with the hurt and the heartache. Thera explained to Arlene that there was one thing Arlene needed to learn. That lesson was that when a loved one is lost, everyone is there for you. They are there for you for a while that is.

"You get meals, flowers, books, cards and visits. Then once your loved one is buried, everyone begins living life again. After a loss, it is an extremely difficult time. When someone dear passes, those of us left behind have the choice to wallow in self-pity or move forward. No matter how hard it is, one must move forward."

From Arlene

Bob's relationship with his mom was a perfect one. He would call his mom all the time. He had very tender feelings for his mother, who is a loving and caring mom. Thera is a mother that would do anything for her children, and her children would do anything for her. I know Bob continues to love his beautiful mother from heaven, as I continue to love her here.

"Bob would just go and do whatever needed to be done. He was never one to walk away from a job, or come up with any excuses as to why he couldn't accomplish something. When anyone asked him to do something, it was as good as done. Bob lived his life as a trustworthy and loyal man in every way."

Nick's Words

Time is something this family seems to have put to the test with Rick passing at thirty-six years old, Trish at forty-one, Sadie at six, Dad at seventy-six, and Bob at fifty-six. Val, Bob and I used to joke about which direction death would come. The answer came all too soon. Almost to the date of his birth, Bob's life came to an unexpected and unanswered end. I can tell you from experience, that telling my mother that another one of her children was gravely ill was almost as difficult as having to tell her that one had been taken from her.

My mother's strength and dedication to her beliefs of the life hereafter, has been humbling to witness. She has endured the death of so many! Numerous times she has braved devastating events. Many of those times were while she faced her own personal severe health issues that she was fighting to live through.

I find myself considering the unfolding of events that took place when we lost Bob. Mom was in the middle of life-threatening issues with her heart. She was in AFIB, or Atrial Fibrillation. This means that her heart wasn't beating properly. She was desperately ill and in constant pain. Multiple procedures were required in order to save her life. Mom was on massive amounts of medications to try and get her heart rate into a safe rhythm. Some medications had adverse effects. Mom continued being strong through it all. It was April of 2012, when she was going through everything that I just described. I'm sure she was enduring so much more than any of us knew.

Amid all of the health challenges and physical pain mom was going through, my mother lost another child to death. My big brother, Bob, passed away from sleep apnea at just fifty-six years old. His wonderful soul mate Arlene tried desperately to save his life as she heard him gasp for air. She valiantly performed CPR on Bob and kept him alive until just before the paramedics arrived. Through electric shock Bob was brought back, but he never fully regained consciousness. Sadly, he left us to join our other siblings, father, and his beautiful little granddaughter, Sadie.

One loss has been no greater than another in our family. Each loss has left those of us living with lifelong permanent wounds.

"Nick wrote a poem for Bob when he passed called 'Close'. Bob was working so hard on himself in order to get everything taken care of. His goal was to be able to have good standing in the LDS Church, and to be able to go back to the Temple. My son knew that by doing these two things he and his family would be blessed to live eternally in the heavens together, never to be parted again. In Nick's poem for Bob, coming close is good enough. This is true for all of us. Coming close is good enough because Jesus Christ will make up everything we are lacking, if we will only let Him. Bob let Him.

I knew when Bob returned to heaven that there were so many happy people there to greet him! Bob loved his grandpa, my father. He loved to go and work the farm with Daddy, and Daddy loved Bob to come to the farm. My father used to say that no hired hand could accomplish what Bob accomplished. Daddy had a great influence on my boy's life. I am sure that there was one happy grandpa in heaven when Bob walked through those pearly gates!

I feel very much at peace over Bob's death. I think of him and I smile. Bob always made me laugh, so I think of him when I laugh at funny things. I love my son. I am humbled to be his mother."

**The best way to have a little bit of heaven in your home,
is to have someone you love in heaven.**

~Chapter Twenty~

Messages from Thera's Grandchildren

~Message from Cy~

Grandma Thera is a one of a kind sort of person, woman, daughter, sister, mother, grandmother, and member of the Church. I know well her testimony of truth. I love and appreciate her for all that she has taught me through her example in life and for the impact she has had on mine.

Grandma is the woman who gave me my father. Could she have possibly known, as a young mother, what influence she would have in the lives of generations to come? I am grateful for the things she taught her children and what they have passed on to their children. She has been an example of faith in the Lord Jesus Christ and His restored church on earth today. She is an example of an unending devotion to family and the eternal potential a family has. She is also an example of what love and concern for others can accomplish. Grandma is bold, honest, kind, strong, caring, devoted, energetic, faithful and has always seemed to know she is destined for wonderful things to come.

I will always remember the time Grandma found me at the airport. I was very young taking my first flight. I didn't understand why I had been put on an airplane alone. I remember the kind people who watched out for me and took me up to the cockpit to meet the pilots, and all the fun it was to be on a plane. I even remember wondering as I saw what was beyond the clouds for the first time, "Is this where Heavenly Father lives?" I hoped I'd get a chance to see Him and that maybe he'd even wave back at me. When I landed in Salt Lake City, I think the people from the airline took me to an office behind their terminal counter. I was worried about where I was and wondered where my Mom and Dad were. They kept telling me it would be fine, but it wasn't fine until my Grandma showed up.

Grandma,

There are so many things we don't know about what comes next, but Heavenly Father is kind and has hidden wonderful hints of the joys that will soon be yours in their fullness. While here through our family, in marriage, and through our children we only get a small taste of the happiness that awaits us. You will not only reunite with those who have gone on from your earthly family, but you will know the joys of countless ancestors and experience what it is like to have a family that will become numberless.

The joy of being a child of beloved parents will be found again. This will happen not only by reuniting you with your parents, but their parents also, and so on back to our beloved first parents of our mortal bodies, Adam & Eve. I also know that you shall feel the true joy of having your memories restored of our heavenly life, and our Heavenly Parents. You will be received in their warm loving embrace while hearing their words, "Well done, dear daughter." You will experience the peace that comes to those who have lived this life well.

181

You have truly accomplished your mission here. We will all miss you when you return home someday taking your smile with you. We are all eternal beings that are destined for eternal beginnings. I love you, Grandma. I'm so glad I am your first grandchild. I must have been in a hurry to get here, so I could have as much time as possible with you. ;)

Cy and Stacey Toland

~Message from Lisa~

My Grandma, Thera Huish, has experienced things in her life that I couldn't possibly begin to comprehend. Nor can I understand what it has felt like for her to endure all that she has endured. I remember being young and hearing how my dad's father, Dorian, had been killed in a plane crash when my Dad was just a toddler. Grandma had become a single mother with two children at eighteen years old. I have watched her live through Rick's death, Trish's murder, Grandpa's death and Bob's death. There have been many times I wondered, "How would I feel and what type of person would I be if I had lost two husbands and three children?" It's unimaginable.

I remember that Grandma and Trish looked so much alike they could have been sisters. And, I remember how close they were. They were truly best friends.

I admire my grandmother's strength and resiliency. She has held her head high through it all! When she takes on a business venture, she is determined to be successful and she puts her heart into all she does. She loves her children, grandchildren, and great grandchildren. I think that it is wonderful that she will have the story of her life in writing, so those who don't know her will have the special chance to get to know her more intimately. I love you Grandma.

Lisa

~Message from Nicole~

Gram,

Where do I begin? You have been such a big part of my life from the beginning. I can remember when I was a little girl coming over to your house. We would take those little irons and run them along the circle and oval rugs on your floor. Who knew kids could entertain themselves with irons?

Starting at such a young age, I witnessed struggles that you had to deal with like losing Rick. Then, just eighteen months later, losing Trish and after Trish your parents. Little did I know you had already seen heartache at the young age of eighteen. Later in life you again were met with extreme trials and heartache with Grandpa's death, losing Sadie, and Bob's passing.

I have always wondered why our family has witnessed more death than any other family I know. Why has God let this happen? How have you stayed so strong through it all? I mean, literally. I think I would have crumbled had I been you, but not you. Through it all, you have maintained composure and been a pillar of strength in our family. I can only assume that the strength you have comes from a strong faith in God. I think I would have been mad at Him or questioned Him if I were in your shoes. Maybe you have, maybe you haven't. I just know that your strength is something that I hope to have, if ever I encounter just half of the trials that you have.

There are so many great memories I have with you. I loved the trip we took with all the cousins up to the mountains. We had a blast together! I will never forget the night you made navy bean soup and none of us wanted to eat it. You looked at us and said, "This is dinner. You eat it, or get nothing. Your choice." At the time I couldn't stomach it but now I LOVE bean soup. I also remember our Disneyland trip that we all went on right after Trish adopted Marsha. That was another fun time with family. The cruise you took Thera and I on was amazing as well.

The trips were fun, but I loved just visiting you at your house most of all. I can remember spinning on whatever that thing was in your backyard. I would get so dizzy, but it was so much fun! Let's not leave out your awesome breathing exercises you were so into doing. Did you know that the woman's video has been brought back to life on Facebook? I saw it the other day and laughed. I think some of my favorite times were just spending time laying my head on your lap and having you tickle my back and head. Those quiet times were the best, and they are memories I will always treasure.

Gram, you are a great storyteller! Oh, how I will never forget the story of how as a little girl growing up on the farm you killed your mom's favorite rooster. And you did it with a sunflower! That was amazing. But I think the lesson I learned from all your stories about growing up on the farm, was that you were a hard worker. Hard work is important to you. I know you value those who do the work and achieve success because of their efforts. Your Figurette Bra stories were the best. And of course, the many stories you have of my dad's childhood are precious and quite hilarious. I don't know how you dealt with four boys. They definitely kept you on your toes! You always had some crazy quote too that you would say. I think the one I will never forget and still can't figure out is "A dollar three eighty".

I want you to know that I have always admired you. You are a beautiful soul. The love you have for your children and family is fierce. The strength you have is amazing. Your gift for reaching people is awesome. And, your ability as a salesperson is, well, unrivaled. Honestly, I believe that you could sell anything to anyone. I know we joke a lot with you about this. But it really is a part of your being and has proven to bring extreme success throughout your life.

You have carried yourself with poise, grace and beauty through both the happiness and the trials of your life. You have taught me many lessons. I hope that I can continue to teach those lessons to my children and so on. In my eyes, your legacy you will one day leave to all of us is *love*. And really, is there anything more important?

Thank you for your example, your love, and your vibrant spirit. Never again in this world will I have the pleasure of meeting another Thera Huish. You are one of kind, Gram. I love you moistest infinity.
Always-
Colie

~Message from Mackenzie~

My grandmother is one of the most determined women I have been privileged to know. One thing that can be said of Thera Huish is that she endures well until the end. She has carried her trials and life experiences with faith, hope, and grace. She has endured more than her share, but that has not dampened her optimism on life. Both her optimism and endurance she credits to her faith in the Savior. Her knowledge and testimony of the things of eternity have come to my mind during my own trials and given me strength.

Her focus, especially in her business endeavors, is inspiring. As I was beginning my journey of being self-employed, she was especially encouraging. Grandma let me know that she was proud of my endeavors. The stories of her Figurette Bra days and KM days both entertain and inspire. I have always been touched to know that she is my cheerleader and mentor.

I adore her outspoken nature. As a family, we always know where she stands when it comes to her thoughts and beliefs on issues that are important to her. The political emails always make me smile whether or not I agree. She is fearless!

Thank you, Grandma, for being a wonderful example and touching as many lives as you have. I am blessed to be your granddaughter and am thankful for the trail you have blazed for us to follow. Generations to come will benefit from the life you have lived. And, generations to come will speak of you with joy and reverence. I love you.
Mackenzie

~Message from Corey~

To My Grandmother,
When I was little, you were always there. You were smart, strong, and someone I could depend on. There are so many great memories I have of spending time with you and Grandpa. From playing Matchbox cars on your brown circular rug in the living room, to swimming in the pool, to spending time together for the holidays. These are some of the most precious moments of my life. You have always shown us unconditional love and support through all of our trials and tribulations.

You are the strongest person I know, the steadiest person. The one that always knows that life goes on and that there will be bumps and bruises, both physically and mentally. But at the end of the day, you approach life with a smile on your face and an understanding that life's imperfections are what make it great. As I grew, I started to appreciate your example more and more and to lean on you for guidance and acceptance.

You've battled and won, in everything! I never doubt your strength. *You're still so strong!* I can honestly say that I am a better man and father for having you in my life. With all my Heart and Love,
Corey

~Message from Zachory~

My Grandmother is one of my heroes. She has always been anchored to her high principles. Even when life has challenged her and given her every reason to give up, she never quits. I greatly admire that quality in her and hope I can develop that quality to even a fraction of what she has. She is a *cheerful warrior* who has influenced so many people for good in her life.

She is a farmer. My uncle Val told me that he once asked her how she has endured so many trials, so many losses in her life. Her response was that we all have to learn to be farmers. Regardless of what the weather is farmers have to get up, get out of bed, and get to work! It doesn't matter if it is raining, snowing, or blistering hot farmers keep working the land. They don't get discouraged they just keep sowing, plowing, and praying. They have to have faith that the long-term outcome of their labors will yield a meaningful crop. I think this analogy explains who my Grandma is. She is a true farmer.

Her example of faith in the Savior and faith in the covenants she has made with Him has influenced and blessed not only me, but also the many generations that will come after me.

One of my favorite memories of my Grandma was the week we spent at Lake Powell. While we were there I can recall how she observed the Sabbath. I can remember the waves of the lake lapping against the houseboat she had rented for our entire family, and I remember how important keeping the Sabbath was to her. I will never forget that example of faith.

Through my eyes, she is an example of what it means to fulfill the measure of our creation. My grandmother came to do a very specific work in her life, and she has done that work so well. To me that is the greatest accomplishment any of us can achieve. I will always be grateful for the example she has set to never give up and to turn my will over to the Lord's will.

Grandma,
You will never know the influence you have had on my life. I will forever be grateful for you and for your example of faith. Thank you for taking the time you have taken over the years for me. Thank you for the cards, the calls, the trips and most importantly you and your faithfulness. Whenever your time comes and you get to go home, give everyone a big hug from me. :) I love you Grandma!

185

Zac

~Message from Thera~

I love my grandmother with my all my heart. She is who I am named after and I could only hope to be half the woman she is. She continuously inspires me, motivates me, loves me, and is there for me no matter what. My grandma is one constant I have always had in my life. She has been the greatest source of strength and love I have had through some really tough childhood experiences.

I see my mother in her and she sees her daughter in me. The two of us have always had a special bond. She is by leaps and bounds the strongest and most determined woman I know, excelling at everything she puts her mind to. There is no one quite like her! I had the privilege of being with my mother and my grandmother. This allowed me the great opportunity to experience their hard work, dedication and business smarts firsthand. They really were a dynamic duo!

My grandmother leaves an impression on everyone she comes in contact with and one cannot help but love her tenacity. I have a friend whose mother purchased Figurette Bras from my grandmother thirty years ago! To this day, every time I see her she asks me how my Grandma Thera is. This lady is always genuinely concerned with how Grandma is doing and expresses that she would love to see her. Even the people, who have had a mere brief interaction with her, walk away with a lasting impression.

Grandma's positivity is contagious! She is an extremely spiritual and uplifting woman no matter what pain or struggles she may be going through. I remember so many special conversations with her on the phone. They usually began with an enthusiastic, "Tell me the most wonderful thing that happened to you today," booming from her end of the line!

As a typical teenager, I usually just wanted to complain about something to her. But, Grandma always found a way to turn the conversation around getting me to not even think about my complaints that I thought so valid only minutes before. One of her favorite lines she used to accomplish this was, "You will get glad in the same pants you got mad in, might as well be sooner than later!" She has a no nonsense way of finding the good and forgetting the bad. She is never one to dwell on anything negative. Never.

All of our lives, as a family, have been full of special experiences with Grandma. I remember so many of them we shared together! From our road trips up to Provo to Aunt Janet's, to the family cruise we all went on. I loved our amazing trip to Hawaii for the women's conference. My grandma has filled my life with so much joy and so many rich experiences. I have even loved having special time to bond with her over our shared love of *witch* doctors. Ha! I am always up for trying a new naturopathic doctor. Which by the way, I learned all about from my Grandma.

I strongly believe my life could have taken another turn without her influence. My grandmother has truly been my saving grace. So much of who I am is credited to this amazing lady I get to call Grandma. I owe her so much.

Grandma,

I love you. You have been a rock for me when I felt so alone. I have always felt so incredibly loved and cherished by you. Thank you for fighting for me and loving me unconditionally. It is hard for me to imagine the time when you will not be here physically any longer. Your spirit is so fierce and strong! We joke that you will outlive all of us. I know that when the day comes and you are once again reunited with those of our family, who we love and miss so very much, you will live on through us. You and Grandpa have created such an incredible legacy together. You will not be forgotten, for your influence will be magnified daily from all of us who are blessed to be your family. I love you so much, Grandma!
Thera

~Message from Lee~

My feelings for Thera Huish have changed throughout my life. My maternal grandmother passed on during my infancy, so Thera was the only grandmother that I knew growing up. As a child there were all of the normal *grand mothering* and spoiling going on. I loved going to visit Grandma!

Later on, distance grew during the time leading up to the divorce of my parents. Too often this is natural happening with a divorce. Words become careless; emotions more guarded. But as time passed, I grew both in age and understanding. Life events helped to close that gap. I am blessed to have a Grandmother like mine and regret the wasted time and lost years that passed.

My grandmother's influence on my life was mostly indirect, she being the mother of my father Val Toland. Her parenting of him affected his fathering techniques. My father is a great dad that always does his best for his family and friends. As long as I can remember he has been the foundation of our family. He has found ways to serve us and always provide for us. When a son grows and becomes a great man, it says lot about his mother.

Distance kept my interactions with my grandparents mostly to holidays, celebrations, family gatherings, and funerals. We had far too many of the latter and not enough of the rest. But Grandma Huish was always welcoming and happy to see family whenever we were together.

As I grow older I reflect on one of the things that really impresses me about my grandmother, which is the times she has lived through. She grew up on a farm and basically lived a life not far removed from that of others who lived hundreds of years ago. She now lives and thrives in the Internet age. The changes that occurred to the world in her lifetime are just amazing:

- The Great Depression

- WWII
- Space Flights / Moon Landings
- The invention of TV
- The personal computer revolution
- The creation of the internet

Regardless of what the world looked like, my grandmother was willing to learn and work to make life better for her and her family.

Technological change was not the only area where she was open to change. One of my favorite singers growing up was Enya, because the music helped me during my turbulent teenage years. When I would share this music with her, she took the time to actually listen and experience the music with me. I hope to be as open to life and the changes that come with the passing of time, as my grandmother has always been.

Dear Grandma,

Thank you for being the person you are. For living the life you were given in the way you have lived it. Thank you for seeking out the best in people and for your example in business. And, thank you for your example during times of tragedy.

Regardless of whether or not life experiences were up or down, you have kept going while always looking for the lessons to be learned. I am happy you have financial success and that you touch lives in a positive way. I hope that you are able to enjoy every moment to come in your life.

Lee Toland

~Message from Cobey~

Caring, loving, sincere, charismatic, passionate, energetic, motivated, strong work ethic, focused, and driven are just a few qualities that my Grandma possesses. I have always looked up to her and, although I do not get to see her as much as I would like to, I realize I am very fortunate to have such a great grandmother. Knowing where she came from in life and how she has excelled has helped me with both my personal life and career. She has helped me understand that in order to get what I want I must work hard, stay focused, and stay positive even when things may look bleak. My Grandmother is also someone who brings out the best in people. She is a great mentor and leader.

Though she has had many unfortunate life events over the years, I feel those events have only brought us closer as a family and made her stronger. She is role model in all of our eyes.

Cobey

~Message from Marsha~

188

My grandmother has always been a great example of grace, loyalty and unconditional love. I have learned many things from her. The lesson that stands out the most is the true meaning of forgiveness. I have become a better person because of her and the example she has always set for me.

I have a deep respect for her; she has always been the rock of our family. My grandmother is a loving woman with strong morals and faith. She has shown that to me in every way possible. I have learned how to handle situations better, how to forgive and how to be more understanding. She is very driven in her career. She will do what she is engaged in the best that she can, and she always rises to the top. She could sell ice to an Eskimo! Really. I do think she could.

I remember her selling KM with my mom. Together they were amazing! They would hire us, and the neighborhood kids, to assemble their newsletters. We thought that was the greatest thing ever. We were having fun and making a few dollars that we could take up to Water & Ice to get a shaved ice. I loved listening to my grandmother's stories of her farm life as a girl, and of course the stories of her and my mother's Figurette bra career. Oh man, little did I know she still had a stash of those bras. By the time she was done with me I felt like Madonna!

I wish I could have been blessed with memories of her from my childhood, but I am so grateful for the ones I do have. I learned what a real family was when I was fourteen. While most the kids around me at that age were trying to become more independent from family, I was fully grasping a hold of a very loving family. My family. My grandmother took me and loved me just as she loved all of her other grandchildren.

I will always remember so many things about her. One of those memories is when I was sitting in her house in my Grandpa's rocker. I just sat there listening to her play the piano. If anyone didn't clap fast enough after she would finish playing she would say, "A little appreciation." Still to this day, I will stop and listen to someone playing the piano and *always* say thank you when they are done. My grandmother taught me that little things do mean so much.

Another vivid memory is hearing her breathing exercises that she would do. I seriously thought that she was dying the first time I heard them! Now that video has reappeared on Facebook. It was so funny, because most of us grandkids had *grandma comments* about her in the comment section.

I loved spending time with her on our weekly temple trips, going to Charleston's for dinner and then seeing a play. Little moments like doing her hair and having that one-on-one time will forever be cherished!

I got to spend lots of time with her when she first started suffering from heart problems. She continued doing her best to be strong and independent, but I know that her just knowing that I was there, made both of us feel better. I got to put together her scrapbook of all the mementos that she had collected over the years. I loved doing that. I got to learn so much more about her, my mom and the rest of the family. With me being adopted, and not growing up in the family since birth, I missed some of the small things. Those family memory books truly brought the past that I had missed to life for me!

Grams,

You will never know the influence that you have had on me. It is very difficult for me to even try to put my feelings into words. I will forever cherish the memories that I have shared with you. You have taught me some very useful life lessons. I know there are some I have ignored; I am after all human!

You have been thru so much in your life. I admire the way you handle things, the way you forgive and the way you love. You are such a strong person. With all life has thrown at you, you have always pushed on and made it through. Through the death and despair you have kept your head held high. I have watched you go through things with poise and grace. You are the woman I strive to be.

Thank you for all you have done for me and all you continue to do. I know that when your life here is over, I will be very sad! But, I also know that your legacy will live on for generations to come. I love you!
Marsha

~Message from Danielle~

Grams,

There is so much that I would like to say but all I can really say is *I wish* and *Thank you*. I wish I could have been in your life sooner. I wish that I could see you more often to listen to your wonderful stories. I wish that our lives weren't so busy and that we could talk more. I wish that I could be holding your hand to tell you something.... Thank you! Thank you for your unconditional love. Thank you for including and accepting me as family. Thank you for inspiring me to be the best wife, mother, daughter, granddaughter, sister and most of all the best self that I can be. Thank you for showing me that I can do **anything** if I set my mind to it. Thank you for showing me how to get up, when life knocks me down. Thank you for being Val's mother. He is my father and you are my grandmother.

I love you so very, very much! I am so grateful for having you in my life. And I regret that I don't tell you that as often as I should. You are a strong, beautiful, amazing woman and I hope someday I can be just like you.
Danielle

~Message from Adam~

When I look at my grandmother, I see inspiration. The things she has been required to go through nobody should have to endure. Listening to her play the piano has always been a treat for me. I remember when I was little I would ask her to play a Beethoven song. She laughed every time, but she always played one for me and I always listened. I have watched her at her highest points and been by her bedside at the worst of times. I truly love her.

Pretty Lady,

Where do I start? You have always been such a huge part of my life for so long. I remember back when we used to come over to your house and we would pick all the trees clean of the fruit. Hayden and I always wanted to crush all of Gramp's coke cans. Both of us boys would run around that house causing so much trouble! I will never forget the smell of your house, cars, clothes and anything that you are around has. You also would always say as soon as we came over, "Have you had your KM today?"

When I was only six years old you lost your first child, Uncle Rick. Then, less than two years later you lost Aunt Trish. I was too young to wonder what else you would have to go through. It was my senior year of high school when you lost Gramps. That was a day I will never forget. When that happened I was old enough think, "Why do we have reunions at funerals?" Uncle Bob died and I really thought to myself, "Why does someone as remarkable as my grandmother have to endure so many losses?" Parents should never have to bury their children, something you have done three times over. You are the strongest most amazing lady I have ever known. I am thankful to be your grandson.

There are so many great things we have done as a family. Besides all of the trips and adventures, the one thing I will never forget is in the houseboat at Lake Powell. You decided to ask me to dance. But it wasn't a slow dance it was more of a shimmy shake kind of dance. You kept saying, "Come on Adam! Shake it baby!" I will never forget that!

Going to the cemetery with you is another memory that will always remain with me. You and I would always go together. It was *our time.* You told me so many stories when we would go. I will miss that when you join our family in heaven. I am so glad that Colton has been able to spend time with you. I know that he is young but listening to him say, "How you feeling Grandma Ferra?" is such a joy!

Thank you for always being the best grandmother anyone has ever had. Thank you for showing us right from wrong. I am grateful to you for always being there for me, and being such a pivotal part of my life. I could never live up to what you have accomplished. There will always be a special place in my heart just for you! I love you
Adam

~Chapter Twenty-One~

Straighten Your Crown

"When tragedy strikes, there is only one thing to do. You have to dig in your heels and KEEP ON GOING! I learned this from mother delving into work whenever she had a problem, or when life would seemingly get the best of her. It was always during those times that she would wholeheartedly engage in work by digging in her garden, cooking in her kitchen, cleaning, washing clothes, sewing, crocheting, or doing so many other things. Mama would always immerse herself in working whenever she faced trying times."

I recognized a pattern in Thera's life. Thera is an incredibly strong-willed woman. She has faced the most extreme of hardships, one right after the other, and she has faced them head on without hesitation.

"My life has never been about me. It has always been about the situations I have found myself in no matter what those situations were. When my first husband died, I knew that I was on my own. I was a very young widow with two babies to care for. When I walked down the street of our small town with my two children just after Dorian's death, not one person spoke to me. I thought that I could just die because I didn't know what I was going to do. Through that experience I came to the realization that nobody was going to get my life in order, except for me. It was when my first husband died that I became the way that I am. Through that first death, I learned that no matter what happened in my life I could, and would, always get myself through it."

I truly believe this amazing lady has been thrown into a state of survival mode for much of her life. Most of us go into survival mode when tragedy strikes, or for many other reasons involving stress. Thera's focus has always been on what she has had to face at any given time and enduring it. She has lived pouring her energy into whatever *current* situation she found herself in for her family.

"With everything and anything I face, I look at the situation and think, 'How can I fix it?' I don't have all the answers. There are certain things that each one of us must turn over to the Lord. Death is one of those things."

Grief is a part of our growing process for what our Father in Heaven has in store for us. We know that even Jesus was familiar with grief.

"He was a man familiar with grief and sorrows."

Isaiah 53:4

With each loss Thera prayed for peace. She prayed for the strength to stay strong for other members of the family who needed help getting through what the family was facing. She was always able to find peace within herself for whoever had been called home. Having that peace enter her heart took longer with some than with others she had lost. For example, in Trish's case. Thera knew Trish's children needed to be safe in order to bring peace to their mother, to her daughter. Getting justice for what happened to Trish was not what brought Trish peace, though it brought some peace and closure to her family still here who love her. Trish fully understood that God will have His justice on the evil and the wicked. The Day of Judgment will come.

With each death, Thera found peace from her faith. Faith is a beautiful gift! If you've had your faith shaken, as most of us have at one time or another in our lives, perhaps through Thera's story you can open your heart just enough to allow your faith to grow. Even the tiniest bit can allow your pain to be replaced with peace. Thera has proven this over and over again in her life. You do have the power to open your heart and grow your own faith, if you chose to do so. Faith in knowing that somehow, someway everything will be all right brings peace through tribulations. Faith in God's plan allows us to live life, not without sorrows, but with an inner calm and joy. Faith opens the heavens.

"I rejoice in the knowledge I have of knowing my heavenly angels are in a place where they can see everything with open eyes. I know in our times of need, our loved ones, who have left us in the mortal sense, come to comfort and strengthen those of us who remain. Those who die love us even more than they did while they were alive! I know Heavenly Father loves us. He is a good and loving God who knows when we are hurting. I know from personal experience that during those times of need in my life, He sends a tender mercy. I have felt the presence of those of my loved ones who dwell the other side of the veil. I find joy while reflecting on the good things we shared together during their lives here. I am no different than any of God's children. He loves me no more than anyone else. Tender mercies can come to any, through faith in His Son, Jesus Christ."

Many of the things we go through happen because of the personal choices of those around us. We have no control over another's choices. Even a toddler will often test the waters when told not to do something. It is a difficult thing to feel pain for a choice we did not make. Thera could not be in the room with Rick as his body died. The agony she felt as his mother was too great to witness her son's death. While Rick was alive, Thera and Sterling did all they could to influence their son to make wise choices. Ultimately, Rick did not heed the council of his parents until the disease had done irreversible damage to his body, which eventually caused him to lose his life.

"I learned with Rick that I couldn't fix him. His life choices were his life choices, not mine. That was a really hard lesson for me to learn as a mother. I could influence those around me, but I could not make their

choices for them. When I lost my son, I felt completely helpless. Each tragic loss in my life has left me knowing that none of us have control over many of the things that happen in our life, and that I certainly have no control over this thing we call death. No, none of us do."

Rick fought an inward battle with himself every day. Sterling and Thera watched from the sidelines as their son lived in a self-destructive mode for so many years. One of the hardest things for a parent is to watch their children, no matter the age, make wrong choices that ultimately bring negative consequences and pain. The destroyer and his evil followers relentlessly torment all in this mortal life. They have only one objective, one goal, and that is to rob us of our peace and happiness.

Through Thera sharing her sacred experience with us when Rick appeared and spoke to her in the temple, this once devastated mother gained the peace she needed with regard to both her son and daughter who had died. Rick was no longer battling the addictions that took his life. He was there to take care of Trish, so that his sister was not alone when her life was tragically ended. Rick continues to move forward with his eternal progression, as will all of us.

Those who die do not cease to exist, for life is eternal. For any who have suffered the loss of someone, comfort can be found in knowing that your loved one is God's child. God is the Father of us all. He loves those of His children who have returned to Him. Heavenly Father loves you. His plan is grander than all of us! Part of the reason we are here is to learn to trust in Him and His Son. To trust that somehow, someway things will work out.

"My husband, children, great granddaughter, parents and loved ones who now abide in heaven are near me and each member of my family here. They watch over us. They joy over our happiness. They are with us through our difficult times. All of the girls in my family are beautiful and amazing daughters of God. All of the boys are valiant, strong sons of God. It is wonderful to have grandchildren who respect me as their grandmother. I love calls from my grandchildren. Each time I am able to visit with them my heart is filled with joy! Family is everything and family is forever. Just as our loved ones who have passed are with us, so too are your loved ones with you."

Thera trusts in those truths shared with you in this book. She carries them within her heart and lives them in her life. Her knowledge of God's plan is a sure knowledge that surpasses both faith and belief. Dear Thera knows that each one of us will return to the home where we once resided before we came here to earth. She trusts a loving Heavenly Father with those of her loved ones who have voyaged from this earth to heaven. Her trust brings peace to her soul.

Our lives here are but a fleeting moment for each one of us. Death is inevitable. Time is uninterrupted as it moves ever forward. With the passing of time, mortal life passes also. The Holy Bible and Book of Mormon give incredible testimonies from ancient prophetic accounts of God's plan for us as His children. Death is, and has always has been, a part of His flawless plan. One of the most touching accounts can be found in the Book of Mormon. After living a life of charity, the prophet Jacob is now old and is bidding farewell with the following words:

"The time passed away with us, and also our lives passed away like as it were unto us a dream..."

Jacob 7:26

"I know where my loved ones are. I know where I am on my eternal journey. I live each day with peace and comfort because of this knowledge. I have little time left here in mortality. When I have completed my mission here I will gladly reunite with my husband, children, great-granddaughter, parents and loved ones who await my return. I will be happy to go to the 'home' Father in Heaven and Jesus have prepared for our family. Our beautiful heavenly mansions, where we will all have an eternity of endless happy experiences to live as a forever family!

In quiet moments my thoughts often take me to the earthly life of Jesus Christ, my Elder brother. Jesus walked, taught and lived a perfect life of giving. Yet, the day came that God allowed even His only begotten son to die. I fully understand that the day will come when my loving Heavenly Father will also allow me to die. I have no fears of that day. I am ready to return to heaven whenever my time here is finished. My two sons remaining, along with every member of my family, understand that my love will be with them each day for the rest of their lives.

My family understands that those who have gone before, will indeed be there to welcome each of us when we return to our glorious heavenly home! When I close my eyes for the last time and take my final breath here on earth, I know with conviction that my eyes will immediately open to those for whom my heart cherishes and yearns for! My heavenly reunion will be the sweetest occurrence of my entire existence thus far."

What a gift! Such great comfort comes from the wisdom Thera has shared with each one of us. Death is something none of us need fear. With that being said, life is something we must respect, cherish, and appreciate. Walking through mortality knowing who we are as children of divinity blesses us with strength to never quit, even through the worst and darkest of times. Thera's poise and manner with which she speaks, even now in her weakened state from debilitating health challenges, exemplifies that quitting has never, nor will ever be an option. Thera knows that with our Father in

Heaven and our Elder Brother, Jesus Christ, she can get through anything and everything.

"I have a gold box and the words on the top read, 'Things For God To Handle'. I write down everything I know that I cannot handle, and then I kneel to pray. Through my prayer I turn those challenges over to the Lord asking for the wisdom to solve whatever it is I am facing. I then put the paper that I wrote into the box knowing that I am 'letting go and letting God'. Shortly after, solutions come."

Some of Thera's grandchildren asked their grandmother to put their problems in her box. She explained that by them writing their own challenges down, kneeling in prayer, and turning them over to God the answers they needed would come. Thera gave all of her grandchildren a special box. At times we can simply be too submerged in the situations that we find ourselves in, to think or see clearly. This can cause us to be trapped in the difficulty we are going through. When times such as these happen to Thera and her family, they write and pray giving their struggles to the Lord by putting their problems in their boxes. When they do this, they step back from dilemmas that seem to have no solutions. Doing this allows inspiration and solutions to come.

The Huish family turns their problems over to our Father in Heaven and Jesus Christ. Thera usually adds to her box in the evening before bed. This allows burdens to be lifted from off her shoulders so she can sleep. Her mind is then freed from being boggled down and trapped by stress.

We all need a box! Write down, pray about, and place your current problems in *your box*. Just like Thera and her family, you also can turn seemingly impossible difficulties over to God who will in turn inspire you. My friends, doing this is a small but great act of faith. Thera is an example of the power behind small acts of faith and the miracles that can come from them. She has been the recipient of obtaining strength and enlightenment from heaven many times over by praying, writing and using her box. Solutions have come to her. But, if not solutions, she has been blessed with the strength and peace needed to endure. The heavens are opened to those with the faith the size of a tiny mustard seed.

"I didn't get my little gold box until after enduring great anguish with the deaths of a few of my loved ones. I am grateful that I can turn my problems over to God. I am thankful we all can! My special box has helped me to learn that none of us are ever alone. Everyone has the ability to discover solutions to whatever it is they struggle with. All that is needed is a little box, a pen, paper, prayer, and a bit of faith."

Stepping back from a seemingly impossible circumstance, even for one night, allows us to wake up in the morning with eyes that see things in a new light. We awaken with a mind that is open to a fresh perspective. By turning our severest trials over to our Father and Elder Brother, we are able to be blessed with inspiration that will gently guide us in the right direction through the gift of the Holy Ghost. This can happen even with struggles that may seem trivial, but are none-the-less causing you stress in your life.

"I am human with many weaknesses. Instead of dwelling on all the things that are wrong with me I have chosen to accept me for who I am, flaws and all. I have chosen to fix me to the best of my ability. My imperfections have taught me invaluable lessons as I have endeavored to overcome them."

It is a fact that we are all human, and with humanity comes imperfections. At times we deprive ourselves of both peace and happiness by being our own most critical judge. Rather than allowing herself to be defeated during the times where she has stumbled, Thera's outlook has blessed her with the ability to have patience with herself through her weaknesses. This beautiful lady actually looks at her mistakes as opportunities for personal growth. We can each accept ourselves with the understanding that we are a work in progress. A few days ago, a friend wisely counseled me, "Larina, be your friend. Be *your* friend." Those simple words carry such profound counsel.

Since being required to endure one tragic experience after another, Thera has had little time to focus on being her own friend. Her personal wellbeing was placed on the back burner amidst each tragedy. Stress is one of the destroyer's strong tools for depleting one's health in our world of today. When a person has continual challenges without taking the time for relief or relaxation between those challenges, stress can contribute to serious health problems. It is no wonder Thera has suffered for many years with very serious health ailments.

Thera is the heroine of her own story. Her life undoubtedly exemplifies the phenomenal woman that she is. Through the closeness Thera and I share, I do know there are choices, which she has made that she would change if she could. Wouldn't we all? But again, our lives cannot be lived on *what if* and *if only*. Thera had Sterling by her side through so many devastating tribulations. Sterling wanted to help Thera. He wanted to provide strength and comfort for his wife in her times of most need. Men want to fix things, even those things that can't be fixed. Sterling was no different. This good man needed to console his wife, but Thera was determined she would get through every horrible hardship on her own.

God gives us each other for a reason. More often than not, a person's full healing after a traumatic event comes from both giving and receiving. I asked Thera if she felt that Sterling felt unneeded at times in their life together.

"I always knew that I didn't need anybody. I would say, 'Don't bother me. I can handle the situation.' Whatever I saw that I could do, I stepped

in and did. I controlled what I could. Doing that was not always the best thing for me, or for my wonderful husband."

At times while in survival mode, Thera's fortitude and resolve caused her to hold in emotions that would have been healthy for her to release to her loving husband. She has learned to accept love and help from her family, though still independent. Giving can be a true blessing for both the giver and the receiver. Please remember this before you put up a wall around yourself during times of crisis. Opening your heart, especially to those closest to you, can provide you with much needed comfort and strength. Keeping your heart open to those who desire to be there for you may just be the very solution God is providing you with.

Thera wishes for you to now open your heart to healing by accepting the love of those around you. Those who love you watch when you are hurting. Many times they feel helpless. Please remember this the next time someone close to you reaches out to help you.

"We would live in a very different world if we would all stop to consider how much our words, actions and attitudes influence and affect the lives of all those around us. Kindness and love go a long, long way. Learning from our personal shortcomings and improving who we are, because of our weaknesses, is a gift!"

By acknowledging personal weaknesses we can, with the Lord's help, turn them into strengths. Open your heart to the love of those who care for you so that they, as well as you, can heal. You have but one life and one physical body here in mortality. Place your personal wellbeing as the vital priority it must be. Learn to control the intake of stress, as well as the release of this potentially deadly condition. Last, but not least, live with a heart that overflows with love and gratitude.

"Each day I say thank you to Heavenly Father! I thank Him for my family, my home, that I can be home, that I can walk, and that I can get in my car and drive places. I thank Him for everything! I am so grateful to Him that I have family to love and a family who loves me, both here and in heaven. Life is truly wonderful!"

We are all delightfully unique as God's children. Yes, we are all flawed. And, yes, on occasions life itself can be an immense struggle. Never underestimate your resilience as a child of divinity. When it seems you are at your lowest point, the darkest place you have ever been, remember who you are. *YOU ARE A CHILD OF GOD.* Thera and I both promise you that regardless of what you are facing, or will face in the future, THE SUN WILL SHINE BRIGHTLY AGAIN IN YOUR LIFE! After the rain comes the rainbow. Learn from the experiences with which you are blessed to live, whether positive or negative. Be patient with yourself.

Be *your* friend.

"I continue daily to focus on doing my best to be Christ-like in the things that I do, say, and in the way I live. The times where my heart was shattered and broken within me made my ability to continue seem impossible. We are fragile beings of mortality while residing here on earth. Jesus Christ, our devoted Brother sacrificed His ALL for us. Through His love and healing, wonderful comfort and strength can always be ours."

What a gift! The Father and the Son's pure love for you, and for all of us, is the foundation of the perfect Plan of Redemption they have in place for us. Our Heavenly Father's work and glory is to bring to pass the immortality and eternal life of man. Through the miraculous resurrection of Jesus Christ, our Savior and Redeemer, death's grasp cannot hold any of us as God's children in eternal slumber.

I now quote from the book entitled *The Birth That We Call Death* by Paul H. Dunn and Richard M. Eyre:

"In a beautiful blue lagoon on a clear day, a fine sailing-ship spreads its brilliant white canvas in a fresh morning breeze and sails out to the open sea. We watch her glide away magnificently through the deep blue and gradually see her grow smaller and smaller as she nears the horizon. Finally, where the sea and sky meet, she slips silently from sight; and someone near me says, "There, she is gone!"

Gone where? Gone from sight, that is all. She is still as large in mast and hull and sail, still just as able to bear her load. And we can be sure that, just as we say, "There, she is gone!" Another says, "There, she comes!"

~Message from Our Dear Thera~

"As I come to the end of the day, my thoughts seem to all fade away. I find myself thinking of days gone by. I reflect on the many wonderful years that Sterling and I's home was filled with our children. Beautiful memories I will forever hold close to my heart of Sterling being our fearless leader, Val being the leader of our pack of children, then Trish, Rick, Bob and last but not least Nick. I find my thoughts turning to heaven to Sterling, Rick, Trish and Bob. I ask myself, "What could you have done differently?" I do not know, and as of today it does not matter. What matters is that families are forever, and that <u>family</u> is God's plan. I think of the things that I might have done, and I smile at the many things I did do. Birth and death are part of our eternal stories. I have thought of all

of this today.

I pray for all my children, grandchildren, great grandchildren and so on, that they will be protected from evils that exist here in mortality. Be aware of the darkness. Know that it is real, but remember that light will always, always overcome the dark. I pray for each member of my family to be blessed with the strength needed to withstand evil and to stay strong in their belief that we have a loving Heavenly Father and Savior, even Jesus Christ.

I am most grateful for all I have been blessed to experience. I am humble for all that I have. Of all that I have accomplished, the most important is that of being a good mother. Nothing was more important to me than following in my mother's footsteps and being a good wife and mother. I love my posterity! This book is what I leave for you, my cherished family, for I don't know how much longer I will remain here on earth.

I am blessed with wonderful, wonderful children! We are a family who loves each other. There are just three of us left now where there once were seven. We know the bonds that we share as family can NEVER be broken! There are no powers strong enough that can sever family relationships between us, for family is ordained of God. We believe it! We live it! And, we will continue having peace in that sure knowledge.

*Anyone wishing to live with the peace I am able to live with each day, can go to lds.org and request more information. It is well worth gaining the knowledge offered by doing this simple act.

When the appointed time arrives for every child of God to leave this temporal existence, each will once again meet with all of those of their loved ones who have gone before. Those loved ones joyously await our arrival. We will be received with open arms! That is why I can get up happy each morning. That is why I Get Up, Dress Up and Show Up."

The brightest crowns worn in heaven have been refined through furnaces of tribulation. We all experience dark days where we find ourselves thinking, "Nobody cares and nobody's coming." Be aware of who it is that sends negative thoughts. Be like our beautiful Thera. Continue ever forward remembering who you are as a child of divinity. And then, as Thera has done so many times before, simply straighten your crown.

CPSIA information can be obtained
at www.ICGtesting.com
Printed in the USA
BVHW051013280523
665003BV00020B/315